Little
GREEN
Dresses

Little
GREEN
Dresses

50
ORIGINAL PATTERNS
for Repurposed Dresses,
Tops, Skirts, and more

TINA SPARKLES
PHOTOGRAPHY BY ERICA BECKMAN

The Taunton Press

The Taunton Press
Inspiration for hands-on living®

The Taunton Press, Inc., 63 South Main Street, PO Box 5506, Newtown, CT 06470-5506
e-mail: tp@taunton.com

Editor: Erica Sanders-Foege
Copy editor: Anne Jones
Indexer: Lynne Lipkind
Cover design: Naomi Mizusaki/Supermarket
Interior design and layout: Naomi Mizusaki/Supermarket
Illustrator: Amy Sperber
Photographer: Erica Beckman
Stylist: Laura Allen
Hair stylist: Deirdre Novella
Makeup artist: Terese Bennett

The following names/manufacturers appearing in *Little Green Dresses* are trademarks:
Harley Davidson®, Ultrasuede™

Library of Congress Cataloging-in-Publication Data
Sparkles, Tina.
  Little green dresses : 50 original patterns for repurposed dresses, tops, skirts, and more / Tina
Sparkles ; photographer, Erica Beckman.
     p. cm.
  ISBN 978-1-60085-121-6
  1. Dressmaking–Patterns. 2. Clothing and dress–Remaking. I. Beckman, Erica. II. Title.

TT520.S74 2010
646.4'072–dc22

                          2010018012

Printed in the United States of America
10 9 8 7 6 5 4 3 2 1

To my mom, who used to sew dresses for me when I was a little girl and gave me my first sewing machine, and to my dad, who instilled in me the confidence that I can do anything.

ACKNOWLEDGMENTS

This book would not have been possible without the love and support of my man, Don Simpson. Thank you, sweetie! I am forever grateful to have my own version of Tim Gunn, Shauna Smith, the founder of the finest fashion sewing school Austin has ever known. Shauna taught me how to teach sewing and, in the process, made me a better designer and seamster. Her influence can be felt within many of these pages, and she was also the initial inspiration behind the "Genius Leggings" on page 239.

Since I'm a DIY gal, I received much of my fashion education by reading books, studying vintage patterns, practicing, and experimenting. I owe particular gratitude to *Reader's Digest Complete Guide to Sewing*, *The New Vogue Sewing Book*, *Patternmaking for Fashion Design* by Helen Joseph-Armstrong, *Make Your Own Dress Patterns* by Adele P. Margolis, as well as Simplicity, Butterick, and Kwik Sew Patterns.

Huge thanks and love go to Stephanie Trong, Claire James, Jen Delk, Antoinette Perez, Laura Allen, and Sandi Smith for testing, sewing, reading, and random feedback. Bundles of hugs and admiration go to Chia Guillory, Peggy Noland, Josephine Beckett, Jesse Kelly-Landes, Jennifer Perkins, Fredda Perkins, Amy Sperber, and Elizabeth Dye for designing projects for this book. Thanks also to Emily Christensen, Alyson Fox, Laura Dawson, Christine Haynes, Stephanie Verrieres, and Izzy Lane. A double dose of thanks goes to Amy Sperber for her beautiful illustrations and Jennifer Perkins for lending Naughty Secretary Club jewelry for the photo shoots.

I got lucky and had the best photographer and stylist, ever. I had so much fun working with you: Erica Beckman and Laura Allen! Thanks to the whole team: Katy Binder, Deirdre Novella, Terese Bennett, Jacqueline Bovaird, Marisa Manning, Kelly Kollar, Lupe Salinas, Sarah Cumming, Laurel St. Romain, Victoria Lee, Ayla Steadman, Chelsea Starr, Atim Birungi, Caterina Lopez, Valerie Brugueras, Angie Lee, Katelin Taylor, Nikita Kwong, and Lauren Udoh. Tara Tonini, I Love Factory, Lara Kazan, Keller, Irregular Choice, and Boosted provided lovely accessories for the shoots.

Thanks to Erica Sanders-Foege for giving me time and the right amount of nudging to develop my ideas. Thanks to Jenny Hart, Stacey Glick, the ACM, Matt Houser, Elizabeth Simon, Anna Conlan, Jill Lancaster, tech editor Linda Griepentrog, Talena Rasmussen, and my family.

CONTENTS

Introduction:
CONNECT THE DOTS

Attention girls of the future! If you love fashion and like to take DIY to the max, you are going to love this book where you will find 50 adorable DIY clothing patterns that any budding seamster can make for herself. The thing that makes these clothing projects exceptional is that they are all made with recycled and salvaged materials. You would never guess that the *Bell Jar Dress Coat* on page 167 was made from an old blanket, that the sultry *Cashmere Hoodie Dress* on page 181 was put together using discarded sweaters, or that the lovely *Wedding Cake Dress* on page 198 was once a couple of stained tablecloths.

Refashioned items like these are a breeze to make when you incorporate patterns into the mix, and you'll learn how to do this using your body measurements to draw the patterns from scratch. Since

many of the designs originate from simple shapes such as squares and rectangles, making your own patterns is not as complicated as you would think. Once you get the hang of it, you can even start to dream up and execute your own designs.

Aside from all the sewing fun, refashioning is linked to a couple of the most important issues and challenges of our lifetime—doing business in a humane way and protecting our environment—which means this book is also about being a DIY creative-activist. You might wonder how making a dress from an old blanket could actually help save the planet. Well, girls like you and me have the power to help change the world just by reinventing the way we dress. So, before we get into all the rad fashion, I would like to break down for you the new way to do it, starting with a little story about how this book came to be.

Back in 2005, I decided to conduct a wacky experiment. Instead of buying new clothes, I challenged myself to make my own clothes and shop only secondhand to add to my wardrobe stash. Originally, it all began with a sneaking suspicion that some of the stuff I was buying from large fashion retailers might have been made in sweatshops, and this crummy thought haunted me. It was mostly an abstract notion, though, since most clothing is made in China and Vietnam, and it was hard to check up on. So I eventually decided if there was even a chance that something I might buy was made in a sweat-shop, I'd rather skip the guilt and not buy it.

Besides, I was feeling pretty poor as far as cash to burn on clothes, so I jumped in headfirst and really started getting jazzed about the idea of making my own clothes—not that big of a deal for me since I was already a vintage and thrift shop junkie, had been sewing regularly for several years, and took a handful of extracurricular fashion and textile classes in college. In fact, I was thrilled at the prospect of taking my sewing and pattern-making skills to the next level. In one way, though, skipping the shopping habit actually was kind of a big deal. I was all of a sudden faced with the task of putting together a wardrobe for myself that was stylish and modern without buying the latest trends. Passing up the irresistible flings that were constantly coming down the fashion pike was really hard at first.

All of a sudden, clothes became simultaneously super cheap and on-pulse with the flirty and fast shifts of the world's greatest designers—talk about a fashion fantasyland! But I resisted the urge and instead started living in a fashion *sewing* fantasyland. In addition to sewing commercial patterns, I started experimenting with my own patterns and then started ripping up and remixing old clothes with cool patterns. Pretty soon, I didn't miss the trendy fashion flings at all. I realized I was able to satisfy my desire for "the new" by sewing fresh clothes for myself.

While ethical labor worries are one catalyst for my experiment, there's also the environment to consider. Apparently, clothing production and disposal have a significant impact on the environment. Greenhouse gases and other pollutants are released through the farming, manufacturing, and shipping of fiber, fabric, and garments all over the world. In addition, energy and valuable resources, such as water and oil, are used in great quantities to grow and manufacture textiles.[1] This is extremely wasteful considering billions of pounds of clothing and textiles end up in landfills each year.[2]

Luckily, a few fashion companies have become hip to these facts and some are already kicking into gear to find cleaner ways to do business. But the fashion industry is not alone in this problem. The whole situation is exponentially crazy due to the sheer volume of clothing produced, consumed, and discarded on a regular basis. Remember those fashion flings I was talking about earlier? In 2008, 19,507,834,000 new garments were consumed in the U.S.[3] This is about 64 garments per person and represents an increase of about 10 percent per person compared to 1998.[4] As the amount of clothing purchases increased, so too did the amount chucked in the trash. In 2008, 17,560,000,000 pounds of clothing and textiles were thrown away in the U.S.[5] This number has more than doubled

Little Green Dresses

- ⊕ **Any clothes in your closet on day 1**
- ⊕ **Clothes made, altered or refashioned by you**
- ⊕ **Reused clothing and textiles from places like thrift stores and clothes swaps**
- ⊕ **New eco and ethically friendly designer items**
- ⊕ **Small amounts of conventional new items**
- ⊕ **Perpetual reincarnations of all items in closet**

since 1995.[6] Don't get me wrong, I'm not trying to ruin the party by mentioning this stuff; I bring it up to stress the fact that we play a large role in the problem, which means we have incredible power when it comes to making positive changes. Essentially, what it all boils down to is everybody—the fashion industry as well as consumers—being more responsible.

What exactly does responsibility mean for a girl who just wants to dress extra cute? I have learned so much about how to live outside of traditional fashion and am pumped to share with you a super fun and practical three-part solution that most any lady can adopt. Don't worry, I'm not going to ask you to take it to the max and stop shopping altogether like I did. However, the first and most critical part of this solution does involve reducing the number of brand new clothing items you buy. Reduction, paired with the other aspects of this solution—thoughtful shopping and refashioning—conserves precious resources, keeps pollution out of our environment, saves new generations of clothes from going to the landfill, and leaves you with a truly unique wardrobe that makes a powerful statement.

STEP 1: REDUCE

Any rulebook on saving the planet will surely say the number-one solution to the world's environmental problems is to reduce. It's simple. If you reduce the amount of new items you consume, you save resources and keep new waste and pollution from entering our world. Realistically, reducing can be ultra tricky and it is tough to say how much each person should reduce. However, if we look at reduction in terms of carbon footprint, we can see how much reducing by even a tiny bit can help tons, literally. A low-ball carbon footprint estimate for one garment is 15 pounds.[7] If we multiply that by the total number of new garments consumed in 2008, it means at least 146 million tons of CO_2 was released into the air from our clothing purchases in just one year.[8] If each of us just reduced by one item per person, we could keep 2.2 million tons of CO_2 out of the atmosphere.

IN 2008, 17,560,000,000 POUNDS OF CLOTHING AND TEXTILES WERE THROWN AWAY IN THE U.S.[5]

This is the equivalent of taking more than 400,000 cars off the road.[9] Can you imagine what kind of difference we could make by dialing back even more? Looking to the future, scientists say we need to reduce our carbon levels by as much as 80 percent by 2050.[10] Faced with such a challenging target, it is clear that we must start now, even if it is just one item per year.

Now, I know many of us have already been shopping less. Try to think of how much good it is doing for the environment and take this opportunity to learn how to be happy and better off with less. When the economy is humming again, it will feel awesome to reduce on purpose and save loads of money.

STEP 2: RETHINK SHOPPING

Of course, I'm not requiring you never to shop retail again. It's important there be a balance between a healthy economy and a healthy environment, and this means making sure we don't put too many folks out of work (or business). It is crucial, though, that we start to evolve as fashion consumers who are more aware, selective, and savvy about our purchases. Each purchase is a vote or a signal to fashion companies that you support what they are doing and want them to do more of it. It keeps money flowing in the direction of progress.

Historically, since the introduction of mass production we have been nearly blind when it comes to what we know about our fashion choices and what our money is supporting. It seems as if beautiful dresses appear out of thin air, like magic, ready for us to buy, but the truth is our clothes have already had a long and heavy journey before arriving in our shopping baskets. Contemplating this story is the first step in becoming a new fashion consumer. I must warn you, though, the supply chain that takes a piece of clothing from start to finish is complicated beyond belief and can be overwhelming for the average person to sort through.

Since there are so many elements to consider, "the right" decisions can be fuzzy and varied, which means being an informed consumer can sometimes seem like a crazy and confusing mess. The good news is that there are ways to shop smart without all the complex sorting and huge headaches. Following the guidelines below will help you feel good about shopping and proud of the items that you purchase.

SCIENTISTS SAY WE NEED TO REDUCE OUR CARBON LEVELS BY AS MUCH AS 80% BY 2050.[10]

BUY FROM PROGRESSIVE BRANDS

Check up on your favorite clothing brands to make sure they are taking positive steps to make their products more responsible toward the environment and people. Some examples include improving working conditions at factories, offering sustainable products, or developing cleaner and more efficient operations. Besides a product's hangtag, this type of information can typically be found on a company's Web site in the form of a Corporate Social Responsibility (CSR) report. These reports vary in length, frequency, and detail, but essentially are an opportunity for brands to tell us about all the great things they are doing and promise to do to make the world a better place.

Check up every once in a while and stick only with the brands that *continue* to impress you. Beware of "green washing," or the making of misleading claims on eco-friendliness. Double-check to see if the company has outside verification or endorsements on these reports. If you cannot find info on your favorite brand, write them and ask them to provide it!

When it comes to fashion and shopping, I believe the future belongs to companies who are transparent about their manufacturing processes and product impact. In this optical fashion future, companies will provide accurate and accessible information regarding the history of each of their products so that consumers can see the impacts of their clothing choices to make more informed decisions. Some companies are ahead of the curve and have already begun to label their garments with exact carbon and energy footprints as well as digital tracking. To find background info on most major U.S. retailers, go to http://en.wikipedia.org/wiki/Category:Clothing_retailers_of_the_United_States.

BUY FROM LOCAL DESIGNERS AND MANUFACTURERS

In 2008, 97 percent of the clothing purchased in the U.S. was imported from other countries.[11] This number has been increasing over the years, while at the same time, over one million jobs have been lost in the U.S. textile and manufacturing industry.[12] Buying a garment that was designed and made in the good ol' USA gives an American a job, boosts our economy, and helps to create some balance within the global market.

Many sustainability experts stress the importance of

strengthening local economies to prepare us for the new energy future—meaning, when we run out of natural resources, like fossil fuels, that now allow us to ship goods long distances. Buying a dress made in your hometown is not only cool, but smart, since it helps to build a stable local economy.

BUY FAIR TRADE AND ETHICAL FROM INTERNATIONAL SOURCES

A large portion of clothing purchased in the U.S. is made in developing countries, which means it is made by the world's poorest and most vulnerable people. On one hand, this is a good thing since it provides them with a livelihood and means to feed their families, but, if left unchecked, free trade can also lead to exploitation of these people and their resources. Part of our social purpose and obligation should be to make sure everyone in the human family is being treated fairly. Fair Trade certified products ensure that certain standards are met when dealing with farmers, artisans, and hired workers in developing countries. A Fair Trade certification program for garments is currently being developed for the U.S.[13] If your favorite brand manufacturer does not sell Fair Trade certified products yet, check their CSR or Web site to see what they are doing to make sure workers along their supply chains get a fair shake.

BUY QUALITY CLOTHING

Most clothing made these days falls into the categories of cheap and poorly made. While these items are affordable, they end up costing you more because they tend to fall apart quickly. What's worse is that since many of these throw-away items are made with synthetic materials, they will likely clog up landfills for generations. The smarter alternative is to develop a "for keeps" attitude, which means buying quality-made clothing that you are deeply and madly in love with. Sure, well-made clothes cost more, but you know you will want to wear them over and over again.

BUY FROM INDIE DESIGNERS: THE NEW ORIGINALS

I don't know about you, but I hate looking like everyone else. In addition to lack of quality, mass production of clothing has led to the democratization of fashion, which means that everyone from 4-year-olds to grandmas have access to the latest design ideas. On one hand, this sounds great, but it also means that we all end up looking the same. Making your own clothes is a surefire way to avoid this, but we'll talk more about that later.

Another way to maintain your individuality is to buy from small, independent designers. These designers are typically not associated with, or supported by, large, commercial

IN 2008, 97% OF THE CLOTHING PURCHASED IN THE U.S. WAS IMPORTED FROM OTHER COUNTRIES.[11]

organizations and have more control over the production and distribution of their designs. In addition to having optical fashion qualities due to a closer connection to the maker, indie designs are made in small quantities, which make them inherently more exclusive. Micro brands have the freedom to take fashion risks that set off new and exciting ideas.

BUY CLOTHING MADE WITH ECO-DIVERSE FIBERS

There is not a single fiber out there without some unfavorable impact on the environment. Right now, polyester and conventionally grown cotton make up about 80 percent of textile production worldwide and both have pretty bad environmental reputations.[14] The chemical pesticides and synthetic fertilizers used on crops like conventional cotton have devastating effects on soil, air, water, and people; and polyester fiber production requires large quantities of petroleum and creates hazardous emissions.[15] Some sustainable textile experts suggest we need a more diverse distribution between all types of textiles,[16] so look for items made with organic or low-chemical fibers or alternative fibers like lyocell, peace silk, linen, hemp, or bamboo. Avoid buying new synthetic fibers unless they are recycled or recyclable.

STEP 3:
REWEAR, REFRESH, AND REFASHION

In the U.S., billions of pounds of clothes and textiles are thrown out each year and the latest statistics show only about 17 percent of them are recycled.[17] That means roughly 14 billion pounds of textiles are thrown into landfills or incinerated each year. Reducing and rethinking our shopping habits will certainly help to reduce these numbers over time, but we can keep even more clothing out of the waste stream by giving them new lives.

REWEAR AND REFRESH

Whether a clothing item is from the back of your closet, purchased from a thrift store, or scored from a clothes swap, keeping it out of the dump is as easy as wearing it! I bet you can find a dusty gem with potential hiding somewhere. Make it feel exciting again by trying it on with the newer items in your closet. Jeans that were once banished for having too short of a hem can all of a sudden become your new favorites when tucked into the knee-high boots you recently found at the thrift store.

Many times, clothes get pushed to the back of the closet or are discarded due to minor flaws or fit issues. Take items like these to an alterations shop. They can usually be mended quickly and cheaply. Clothing can also be refreshed in creative ways. If you don't like the color, dye it! If it is too plain, spice it up with some embellishing.

Thrift stores, vintage and resale shops, garage sales, and online clothing exchanges are also super options for reviving used clothing. Most thrift stores are busting at the seams with barely worn items in perfect condition and you can often find many name brand items at surprisingly affordable prices.

Clothes swaps are simply the most fun way to get cool used clothes because you get to hang with your friends and have a big outfit party together. To host a clothes swap, invite all your best girlfriends to clean out their closets and bring all their unwanted items to the swap. Make your own rules for the swap, such as each girl can take home a certain number of items or just have a free-for-all where anyone can take home anything they want. To find out more about organizing a clothes swap, do a simple search on the Internet.

REFASHION

Finally, we arrive at the best part of the solution, and what this book is all about: refashioning. To me, this part of the solution is what glues the whole approach together. Paying attention and being active can be hard, but it's easier when you have something to keep you excited and motivated.

There are two ways to go about refashioning. First, there is the random approach, where the process is inspired by a particular garment or object. You start by trying it on and then proceed to pin, tuck, trim, twist, tie, or stitch it in whatever way feels natural to you. I love this type of refashioning because each item has its own story and set of possibilities. There are a handful of random refashioning projects in this book but most of the projects are made using my favorite method: refashioning with patterns.

This type of refashioning can be done by anyone who knows how to sew and use a pattern. Used clothing and textile items are stripped of their fabric and components and then patterns are placed on the fabric just like they would be placed on purchased yardage. There are a few tricks to figuring out pattern placement, but it is nothing you can't handle. The beauty is that you can use any pattern, whether they are DIY patterns or commercial patterns, and the results are always neatly unique. Refashioning clothes gives you the ability to personalize and customize your wardrobe like no other and is the ultimate in eco- and ethical-friendly fashion.

CONCLUSION OF MY EXPERIMENT

The biggest thing I've learned five years into my experiment is that people like you and me really can help save the world because the thinking automatically goes beyond just fashion. When you adopt a lifestyle like this, you can't help but start to see other things in your life that you can creatively reinvent or do differently. You begin to connect the dots between your individual life and the bigger picture, one at a time. The electronics, shoes, toys, packaging, gadgets, and other products that surround our daily lives all have a history and impact that should be considered.

This next year, I challenge you to reduce your brand new clothing purchases by a minimum of one item. Instead of buying a new dress, refashion a dress for yourself, buy a vintage or secondhand dress, or attend a clothing swap to get a free dress. Or, buy one better quality dress rather than two cheap dresses. To keep the momentum going, increase your reduction each year according to your own lifestyle. As more and more of us get in on the action, a positive and creative revolution will be born!

If you are like me, I bet you are all hyped up and in the ready position to jump and make things happen right now. To get you started, Chapter 1 covers the basic sewing techniques required to make the projects in this book, and Chapter 2 gets you up to speed on using and creating patterns. Feel free to drop in at whatever point feels appropriate for you. The rest of the book is projects, classified under skill levels 1, 2, 3, and 4, with the easier projects toward the beginning of each chapter. Every project has instructions that walk you through the process of drawing the pattern and sewing the pattern. Many of the projects will require the use of a building pattern. These patterns either come from previous projects in the book or commercial pattern companies. What's killer is, after practicing the techniques and projects here, you'll start to imagine your own ideas and will see refashion potential in just about anything. Now go on, it's time to tackle this wild, wild world in a responsible yet foxy fashion.

xo,
Tina Sparkles

FOOTNOTES

1 Kate Fletcher, *Sustainable Fashion & Textiles* (London; Sterling, VA: Earthscan, 2008), chapter 1; *Environmental Health Perspectives*, Volume 115.

2 Environmental Protection Agency 2008 Trash and Recycling Facts Report. www.epa.gov/osw/nonhaz/municipal/pubs/msw2008rpt.pdf

3 American Apparel and Footwear Association Annual Trends Report 2007, figure 4. www.apparelandfootwear.org/UserFiles/File/Statistics/trends2007Annual.pdf

4 Calculation is the percent change from 1998 to 2008 of the American Apparel and Footwear Association's U.S. apparel consumption numbers divided by U.S. population according to the Census Bureau for each year. www.apparelandfootwear.org/Statistics.asp

5 Environmental Protection Agency 2008 Trash and Recycling Facts Report, includes footwear. www.epa.gov/osw/nonhaz/pubs/msw2008rpt.pdf

6 Environmental Protection Agency 1995 Trash and Recycling Facts Report, includes footwear. www.epa.gov/osw/nonhaz/municipal/pubs/msw95.pdf

7 Calculation is an average of available carbon footprint estimates from clothing manufacturers currently disclosing this information. This specific sample size has 17 garments.

8 American Apparel and Footwear Association Annual Trends Report 2007, figure 4. Calculation is U.S. consumption of apparel multiplied by 15 pounds of CO_2. www.apparelandfootwear.org/UserFiles/File/Statistics/trends2007Annual.pdf

9 Calculation based on statistics cited in the Clean Energy Jobs and American Power Act, which states that 25,000 tons of annual carbon pollution is equivalent to the output of 4,600 cars. http://kerry.senate.gov/cleanenergyjobsandamericanpower/pdf/PRI.pdf

10 Intergovernmental Panel on Climate Change. www.ipcc.ch/publications_and_data/publications_and_data_reports.htm#1

11 American Apparel and Footwear Association Annual Trends Report 2007, figure 5. www.apparelandfootwear.org/UserFiles/File/Statistics/trends2007Annual.pdf

12 American Apparel and Footwear Association Annual Trends Report 2007, figure 12. www.apparelandfootwear.org/UserFiles/File/Statistics/trends2007Annual.pdf

13 www.transfairusa.org/FT%20Garnet%20Standards%20Feasibility%20Study.pdf

14 Kate Fletcher, *Sustainable Fashion & Textiles* (London; Sterling, VA: Earthscan, 2008), chapter 1.

15 Ibid. Also *Environmental Health Perspectives*, Volume 115; The World Health Organization estimates 20,000 people die each year from pesticide poisoning.

16 Kate Fletcher, *Sustainable Fashion & Textiles* (London; Sterling, VA: Earthscan, 2008), chapter 1.

17 Environmental Protection Agency 2008 Trash and Recycling Facts Report. www.epa.gov/osw/nonhaz/municipal/pubs/msw2008rpt.pdf

Chapter 1
SEW UP
TECHNIQUES

You know that star feeling you get when you're wearing a really cute new outfit? Well, that same high is quadrupled when it's an outfit you made for yourself. Sewing your own clothes has many advantages above and beyond merely shopping for ready-made clothes. In fact, the whole process is so creative and exciting, it can become even more addictive than shopping.

Whenever I start a new project, I'm flooded with dreamy thoughts of where I might debut my new outfit or what I'll pair it with in my closet. Seeing a project develop from a twinkle in my eye to something I can actually wear is the most rewarding part of it all. Of course, getting the skills to pull this off can take a little time, but don't be scared! Sewing is actually simple and anyone can learn.

Essentially, sewing is attaching one shaped piece of fabric to another using stitches created with a sewing machine or a hand needle and thread. After you learn to use a sewing machine, get some experience handling fabric, and practice a few essential techniques, it's smooth sailing. I admit, you'll probably have an occasional setback (even seasoned seamsters mess up), but the minor frustrations that come with sewing are worth it and most anything you stitch can be undone. So relax; sewing is a blast!

Equip Yourself: Sewing Tools

- Sewing machine with standard attachments
- Extra machine needles in common sizes: 70/10, 80/12, 90/14
- Assorted threads
- Extra bobbins
- Pins and pincushion
- Sharp scissors and pinking shears
- Thread nippers
- Tape measure
- Seam gauge
- Seam ripper
- Blunt-point tracing wheel
- Tracing paper
- Chalk or removable fabric pencil
- Steam iron and ironing board
- Tailor's ham
- Tube turner
- Hand sewing needles
- Safety pins

Refashioning Your Sewing Room Stash

In addition to your regular tools and supplies, it's handy to have a stash of recycled buttons, zippers, notions, findings, and remnants on hand in case of on-the-spot inspiration. If you have room, it's nice to have a garment rack filled with items that you might like to cut up and repurpose. Shop thrift stores for treasures in colors and textures that inspire you. The rack is also a good place to keep items from your own wardrobe that need mending or freshening up.

This chapter is about the sewing techniques essential for completing the patterns and projects in this book. Trying to read and understand all the techniques at once might make your head spin, but don't worry, you don't need to memorize or know how to do everything just to get started.

The techniques are grouped into four levels and each of the projects is categorized into one of the levels, so start by skimming through the chapter to familiarize yourself with some of the ideas and concepts and figure out which level is appropriate for you. Flip back here to find the techniques required for each project or when you're ready to learn more and take on more challenging projects. For those who are already familiar with basic sewing techniques, feel free to use this chapter as a reference.

Regardless of how many sewing techniques you know, one of the most critical skills in the world of sewing is how to use and choose fabric, so this is where the chapter will begin. For those of us who like to recycle already existing materials, there are pointers throughout the chapter on how to use fabric from old clothes and how to refresh and refashion the old into the new.

It's important to note that this chapter doesn't cover how to use a sewing machine. Some people are fine figuring this out with the help of their owner's manual, while others prefer a little more guidance from a teacher or friend. Either way, make sure you have spent a little time bonding with your sewing machine.

If you are a beginning seamster, I recommend you read a few basic sewing reference books, then try out a few beginner projects before attempting the ones in the chapters that follow. Also, check out classes or sewing groups in your area. In the Resources and References section (see page 248), you'll find book and class information listed.

Everyone has their own sewing style. At one extreme, you have the patient perfectionists. They typically work slowly and steadily, and will redo things over and over again until things are just right. At the other end of the spectrum, you have the rock 'n' roll seamsters. They break all the rules and embrace flaws as unique aspects of their creations. I personally like to be right in the middle. My best advice is to have fun and try not to get worked up over minor imperfections. Whatever your style of sewing, it's time to get started because you have lots of wonderful clothes waiting to be made!

FABRIC

One of the most important decisions you make when sewing something for yourself is the choice of fabric and materials, in terms of creating a fashionable garment and impacting the environment. Getting your materials for sewing projects from already existing garments or other resources is an easy way to make sure that your new creations are easy on the planet. If you do buy new fabric, it's important to consider the same fiber issues as you would when buying new clothes (see page 7).

Whatever the fiber or source, you need to understand two main fabric-making processes—weaving and knitting—and how to match these with the right projects so things turn out as beautifully as you had imagined they would.

Harvesting Fabric and Materials from Old Clothes

Old clothes are like junkyard cars waiting to be used for their parts. Fabric, zippers, buttons, hooks and eyes, snaps, elastic, boning, hook-and-loop fasteners, and much more can all be pulled from old garments and reused in future fashion projects. There are many ways to approach deconstructing a garment, and the differences depend on the amount of time you have to invest in the process. The most time-intensive method includes using a seam ripper to remove all the seams in the garment. This method requires patience but maximizes the amount of usable material. It also allows you to separate yourself from what the item was in a past life.

It's not always necessary or possible to disassemble a garment completely. A faster approach to harvesting involves free-form cutting directly into an assembled garment to remove specific sections without regard to the seams or detailing. Whenever I choose this method, I try to cut right next to the seams to get as much

usable fabric space as possible. In all cases, the amount of care you take to cut depends on how much of the original garment detailing you want to reuse and how much fabric is needed for the new project.

When harvesting fabric to reuse with patterns, the trick is finding enough areas of the original garment large enough to place the new pattern pieces on the fabric in the correct grainline orientation. Sometimes you can just place pattern pieces directly on top of a garment as is, but in many cases details that give shape such as darts, side seams, waistbands, and necklines keep the fabric from lying flat. These design elements need to be removed to get a flat working area, or you can simply try to work around them.

If there isn't enough fabric in one repurposed garment to complete your new project, consider using fabric from two separate garments to create a patchwork or color-block look.

Refashioning is like a puzzle, and the fun of it is figuring out what parts of the original garment you want to keep, what parts you want to change, and how to incorporate new pattern pieces into the mix for the reconstruction.

WOVEN FABRICS

Weaving yarns to create fabric for clothing and textiles is an art that dates back centuries. It can be done by hand or by machine, but in both cases it's almost always done on a loom. Simple weaving combines two sets of yarns—the lengthwise warp and the crosswise weft—that intersect at right angles to create a gridlike pattern. When designing and sewing with woven fabrics, it's important to identify these directions within the fabric so that you can properly align your pattern pieces on the fabric. Some examples of woven fabrics are broadcloth, canvas, corduroy, denim, flannel, muslin, satin, taffeta, tweed, and twill.

WOVEN STRUCTURE

LENGTHWISE DIRECTION

The lengthwise direction is typically the stronger direction on woven fabric, and there are several methods for identifying it. If you have yardage, look for the selvage, which runs parallel to the lengthwise yarns. The selvage is sometimes a different color than the rest of the fabric; it might have brand or color information printed on it or it may have little holes in it where it was attached to the machinery during the finishing process.

When working with fabric from recycled garments, you won't have a selvage to guide you, so locating the lengthwise direction is a little bit trickier. Since the lengthwise direction is stronger, you can try gently tugging at the fabric in both directions to determine which one is most resistant.

Look closely at the fabric and find the weave. Hold the fabric with both hands and tug along one direction of the fabric, and then turn the fabric in the other direction and do the same thing. Whichever direction feels or sounds stronger is probably the lengthwise direction. If both directions feel strong or similar, then align your project grainline in either direction.

Another hint for determining the lengthwise direction on recycled garments is to look at how the fabric was oriented on the original garment. Garments are usually designed with the lengthwise direction running vertically, meaning the crosswise direction of the fabric follows the horizontal lines on the body, which tends to require more give when worn.

CROSSWISE DIRECTION

Yarns in the crosswise direction are woven perpendicular to the lengthwise yarns and go over and under them in various patterns depending on the fabric. This is the creative direction of most fabrics. In addition to the variation in weaves, novelty yarns are sometimes used in this direction to create different types of fabrics. The crosswise direction can be used as the alternative grainline when necessary for designing. An example of creative grain changing would be when using striped fabric —cut it on the lengthwise or crosswise grain, depending on the desired look. When using recycled garments, it's not

Bolt of fabric

Selvage edge

Folded edge

Lengthwise

Crosswise

Lengthwise

Crosswise

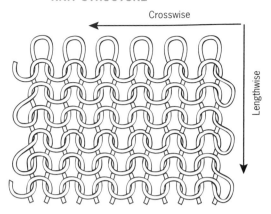

Crosswise

Lengthwise

always possible to utilize the lengthwise grain, so substitute the crosswise grain if needed. When you buy fabric yardage, be sure to check the width; the most common widths are 45 in., 54 in., and 60 in.

BIAS DIRECTION

There is a third direction on woven fabrics called the bias. It's a 45° angle to the lengthwise threads. The bias direction has stretch and is used on fitted garments that require a bit of give.

Fabric cut on the bias can be fussy and delicate, but it is the only option to build in stretch in woven fabrics, unless the yarns in your fabric contain a stretchable fiber such as spandex. The bias direction is also used to make trims and bindings because it allows you to go around curves without puckering.

Cutting pattern pieces on the bias requires more fabric than traditional lengthwise or crosswise placements, and often leaves odd-shaped remnants for your scrap bag.

KNIT FABRICS

Knit fabrics are everywhere. These are our T-shirts, sweaters, socks, hoodies, tights, bathing suits, and leggings. What these items have in common is stretch. You can make a knit fabric out of the same fibers as woven fabric but the construction process is different. Some examples of knit fabrics are double knit, interlock, jersey, ribbing, sweatering, and tricot.

Sewing with Knits

Here are a few tips to keep in mind when sewing with knit fabrics.

- Use a ballpoint needle. Some knits have a tendency to run. A ballpoint needle pushes the fabric's knit loops to the side as it forms stitches, so the yarns don't break and create holes.

- Slightly stretch the fabric as you sew if you are using a straight stitch, or use a narrow zigzag stitch. These techniques allow the seam to flex as the fabric stretches.

LOOPS

Knit yarns are connected in flexible loops that are free to change form as we move or stretch our bodies. Like woven fabric, knits have lengthwise and crosswise directions but the amount of stretch in each direction can vary. Choosing a knit is influenced by how much stretch you need for a particular project.

To test the knit stretch, use the stretch test ruler shown on page 16. Cut a 4-in. fabric square, fold it in half along the crosswise direction, anchor one end of the fabric to the left side of the ruler, and stretch it to see how far it goes along the test ruler. There are three categories: light stretch, average stretch, and super stretch. Let go of the fabric and make sure it bounces back to its original size. Unfold the fabric and fold it in half the other way to test stretch in the other direction.

Place pattern pieces on the fabric with the most stretch going around the body. Knits that stretch greatly in both directions are ideal for bathing suits, leotards, and leggings. Ready-made patterns intended for knits will list stretch recommendations and will likely have a similar stretch ruler printed on the pattern envelope for testing.

CHOOSING THE RIGHT TYPE OF FABRIC

All fabrics are not interchangeable. One type of fabric might be perfect for one project but unsuitable for another. Knowing about fabric structures will help you match fabrics and projects, but there are other factors to consider as well.

WEIGHT AND DRAPE

Some fabrics are heavy and stiff while others are lightweight and fluid. Choose a fabric with the appropriate weight for the type of garment you're making. For instance, light- to medium-weight fabrics are suitable for items like blouses, skirts, and dresses. Medium- to heavyweight fabrics work great for skirts, pants, and coats. Choose more fluid fabrics when making garments with fullness or gathers, and stiffer fabrics for designs with more structure.

TEXTURE AND FEEL

One of the key techniques for choosing fabric is quite simple: just touch it! How does the fabric feel? Is it soft and smooth or is it itchy and uncomfortable? It's very important to choose a fabric that feels good against your skin; otherwise, you might end up with a pretty garment that you'll never want to wear.

DESIGN AND COLOR

Choose fabrics with colors and prints that complement you and what's currently in your closet. It's important to like the fabric design, but more important is whether you'll like wearing it. You might not love wearing what looked like a groovy paisley print once it becomes a garment. If in doubt, find a mirror and drape it on yourself. Does it bring out your best features or your worst?

Colors and prints can also be used to determine if a fabric is right for a particular pattern. Loud and intricate prints work well on simple garment patterns, while more muted fabric designs or solids can play up clothing styles with complicated lines.

FABRIC ILLUSTRATION KEY

Refer to the following legend to interpret the sewing illustrations for all the patterns in this book.

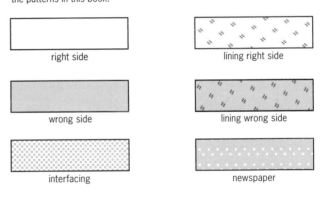

right side

lining right side

wrong side

lining wrong side

interfacing

newspaper

KNIT STRETCH TEST RULER

Anchor folded fabric edge here

Light

Average

Super

Refreshing

Piles of great clothes end up in thrift stores and wonderful garments often get pushed to the back of the closet due to minor problems. Small repairs like missing buttons, popped seams, stains, or slight size alterations are ultra-quick fixes for anyone with Level 1 sewing experience.

- Embellish a garment with jewels, embroidery, trims, appliqués, patches, paint, or screen printed images to cover up stains or flaws.

- Swap out the buttons or dye the garment a new color for an easy update with big impact.

- Adjust hems to meet your needs. Change the length of your pants, skirt, sleeve, or blouse by removing the old hem and stitching a new one. For tapered hems, create a facing to match the edge shape instead of doing a traditional hem.

- Don't fret if your favorite dress comes apart at the seams. Turn the garment inside out, pin the seams back together, and use either a hand backstitch or a machine straight stitch to close the seam.

- Suture rips, tears or moth holes in a garment with a hand needle and thread. Depending on the size of the hole, you may need to back it up with a patch or scrap of fabric. Fusible interfacing in a matching color can also work to repair tiny holes.

- Loosen a tight item without much fuss by releasing some of the seam allowances. Turn the garment inside out, use your seam ripper to remove the stitches along the area in question (temporarily detach other parts of the garment if necessary), pin the seam together, and draw a new seamline closer to the seam allowance edge. Taper the new stitching line to the original one and restitch. If you let out both side seams on a skirt by ¼ in., you'll get an extra 1 in. of width. Use a steam iron to press out any needle holes from the original stitching line. If you don't have extra space in the seam allowance to let out, another slightly trickier and less conventional option is to do a fabric graft from another area of the garment or use fabric from a separate matching garment. For example, split open a blouse along the centers or side seams and sew extra fabric in panels or triangles to add extra space. Make sure to pay attention to the grainlines for best success. You can also graft fabric from another garment.

- Make a garment slightly smaller widthwise by sewing deeper side seams. Turn the garment inside out, temporarily remove other parts if they're in the way, and draw new seamlines with a fabric pencil. Stitch new seams, remove the old stitches with a seam ripper, and trim the excess seam allowance. Try not to go any deeper than about ½ in. on each seam or you may distort the garment shape. To take out more width, turn the garment inside out and sew folded fabric tucks parallel to the lengthwise grainline to taper the fit. To take out 1 in. of width, make the tuck fold ½ in. deep. These new stitches will create visible style lines on the outside of the garment. For a twist, stitch the folds on the outside of the garment to add design interest.

- Experiment to make a garment fit just right on your body. Put the garment on inside out, and manipulate the fabric in whatever way feels natural until you get something that fits and creates a look you like. Use pins and chalk to mark your work. During this process, you can create new design details or it might simply end up a big mess. It's a risk you have to take sometimes to achieve creative results!

SEWING LEVEL 1

These are the basic requirements for making the patterns in this book.

SEWING A SEAM

A seam is a line of stitching that holds together two (sometimes more) fabric edges. Seams can be straight or curved, and are normally the same distance from the raw edge of the fabric throughout the entire length. Seams are typically sewn with the right sides of the fabric facing each other, but there are exceptions. Backstitch at the beginning and end of the seam to secure.

CREATING AND FINISHING A SEAM

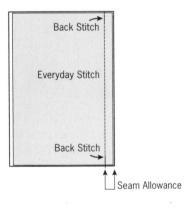

Back Stitch

Everyday Stitch

Back Stitch

Seam Allowance

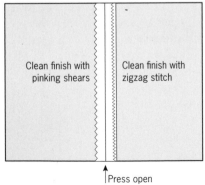

Clean finish with pinking shears

Clean finish with zigzag stitch

Press open

PINNING

Seams are usually pinned together before they're stitched. Some experienced or carefree sewers like to skip this step, but I recommend it for the newly initiated. Place pins perpendicular to the seamline for neatness and easy removal. Remove pins as you approach them, as sewing over pins might bend or break the machine needle. If you're working with a particularly pesky seam, keep the pins in place and use your handwheel to sew past the pins manually.

SEAM ALLOWANCE

This is the distance from the edge of the fabric to the stitching line. Most commercial patterns give you ⅝-in. seam allowance, but ½-in. seams are also common. To sew a seam with a consistent seam allowance, position your fabric under the presser foot with the raw edges against the appropriate seam guideline and make sure it glides along this line the entire time you're sewing.

PRESSING SEAMS

Pressing seams with an iron is an integral part of the sewing process and can make or break a project. Seams should be pressed as they are sewn. The best method is to press the seam flat and then separate the two seam allowances and press them open like wings. Some situations might require the seam just to be pressed flat.

CLEAN-FINISHING SEAMS

Woven fabric raw edges typically fray and unravel if left unfinished. There are many ways to finish raw edges but one of the easiest is to trim the raw edges with pinking shears. Another method is to use a zigzag stitch with a normal length and medium width near the raw edge of the fabric, and trim any rough edges.

Alternatively, a serger can be used to clean-finish edges. Sometimes, the best method for clean-finishing will depend on your fabric. Experiment with scrap fabric to figure out the best method for yours. Press and clean-finish seams as you sew them. For straight seams, stitch and press open the seam allowances before clean-finishing. For curved seams, clean-finish the edges after sewing but before clipping and pressing open the seams.

Stitches, Stitches, and More Stitches

While some sewing machines boast hundreds of decorative stitch options, when it comes down to sewing up a garment, a few stitch variations are all you need.

BASIC STITCHES

EVERYDAY STITCH

This is the most common type of stitch used to sew together two pieces of fabric in a seam. It's a straight stitch with a length near the middle of your length selector dial, typically at about 2.5. Your sewing machine manual should let you know the ideal setting for everyday sewing, but if not, set your machine to sew 10 to 12 stitches per in.

BASTING STITCH

A basting stitch is a long straight stitch and used for temporary stitching (the long stitch length makes it easy to remove), gathering, easing, and topstitching. To create a basting stitch, adjust the length selector to a long stitch length. For many machines, the longest stitch length available is the perfect length for basting.

STAY STITCH

A stay stitch is an everyday straight stitch most commonly used to stabilize and keep curved edges of fabric from distorting and can also be used to keep things in place when working with multiple layers.

BACKSTITCH

The reverse function on your machine is used to secure the beginning and end of seams by going in reverse briefly at each point. Always backstitch seams.

ZIGZAG STITCH

A zigzag stitch can be used to sew knits or clean-finish raw edges of fabric, and can also be used as a decorative topstitch. To create a zigzag stitch, select the zigzag function on your stitch selector and adjust the length and the width of the stitch to get various results.

TOPSTITCH

This is a functional or decorative stitch sewn on the outside of a garment and is commonly used to reinforce seams or keep seam allowances flat. It can have various looks and lengths depending on your project or preference.

HAND HEM STITCH

Love it or hate it, hand stitching is sometimes necessary when sewing together a garment. I used to avoid hand stitching because it takes more time, but all of a sudden I realized how relaxing and meditative it can be to put on some music, pop in a movie, or chat with friends while hand sewing a project. I also found that finishing off hems with hand stitching instead of machine stitching can really take a project to the next level as far as looking neat.

The hand hem stitch is an easy and quick way to hand stitch hems, facings, or bindings, and does not show much, if any, on the outside of a garment. Bring your needle up through the back side of the hem/facing edge so that the knot is hidden underneath. Pass the needle through the tiniest bit of fabric on the garment (one or two threads) and then up through the hem/facing edge again. Repeat at intervals of about ¼ in. to 1 in. depending on how secure you want your stitch to be.

HAND HEM STITCH

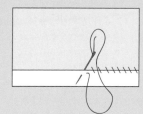

NOTCHING, CLIPPING, AND TRIMMING SEAMS

When working with curved seams, clip or notch within the curved seam allowance to help release some of the tension and allow the seam to lie flat. Outward or convex curves are notched with little triangular wedges and inward or concave curves are simply clipped. Important: Don't clip or notch closer than ⅛ in. to the seamline. Sometimes you can skip the notching and clipping and just trim the seam allowances to ¼ in.

NOTCHING, CLIPPING, AND TRIMMING SEAMS

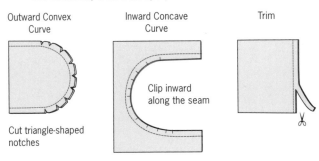

Outward Convex Curve

Cut triangle-shaped notches

Inward Concave Curve

Clip inward along the seam

Trim

PIVOTING

Occasionally, you will need to turn a sharp corner or pivot slightly while you are stitching. To do so, stitch to the turning point and make sure your needle is piercing the fabric. If the needle is not in the fabric, turn the handwheel toward you to sink the needle into the fabric. Lift up the presser foot, pivot your fabric, put the presser foot back down, and continue sewing. Often, you end up with a weird-looking stitch at your pivot point if the needle is not in the fabric.

HEMMING

A hem is typically the last step in sewing a garment. Hems are sewn on the lower edges of skirts, dresses, blouses, pants, and sleeves to finish them. Essentially, the raw edge is folded under and sewn to the inside of the garment either by machine or hand depending on the type of hem and the look desired.

STRAIGHT HEM

For garments with a straight lower edge, there are lots of hemming options. Make the hem deep or shallow, use a sewing machine, or sew it by hand if you don't want the

stitching to show on the outside. Fold and press the raw edge under ½ in., then again fold the edge under the desired hem depth and pin it to the garment inside. Stitch the hem in place along the upper folded edge.

NARROW ROLLED HEM

This hem works well on lightweight and sheer fabrics and is quick to sew. Fold and press the garment edge under ¼ in. twice and stitch in place along the upper folded edge. An easy trick to sewing ¼ in. from the edge is to align the folded outside edge with the right edge of the presser foot. This works on most machines but measure to be sure.

CURVED HEM

For garments with a curved edge, a hand-stitched hem is recommended so the edge doesn't pucker; however, a very shallow machine-stitched hem can sometimes work. To hem a curved edge, fold and press the raw edge under ¼ in. to ½ in., then again fold under the desired hem depth. The upper folded edge won't lie smoothly on curved hems because it's wider than the area where you want to attach it. The deeper the hem, the more problematic it will be. To solve this, the

STRAIGHT HEM

Fold again and stitch

Fold and press

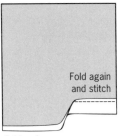

NARROW ROLLED HEM

Fold again and stitch

Fold and press

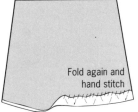

CURVED HEM

Fold again and hand stitch

Fold and press ¼ in.

wider edge needs to be eased in to match. Pin in wide regular intervals along the folded edge, placing the pins perpendicular to the fold. If you have ripples along the hem edge, pull up the excess space using a basting stitch until it matches the garment width, and then hand-stitch in place. If the edge is only slightly wider, skip the basting and hand-stitch the edge in place, distributing the minor ease evenly around the hem edge.

CASING

A casing is a folded garment edge or separate fabric strip that encloses a drawstring or elastic.

FOLDED-EDGE CASING

A folded-edge casing is commonly used for waistbands on skirts and pants. Simply fold the finished fabric edge under and edgestitch it in place to make a tunnel. Make sure the casing is wide enough to enclose the elastic/drawstring plus ¼ in. for ease. If you're using elastic, leave a small opening in the casing stitching so you can thread the elastic through, stitch the ends of elastic together (making sure they're not twisted), and then stitch the opening closed. If you're using a drawstring, create a buttonhole before folding down the casing and then stitch the entire lower edge of the casing closed. Thread the drawstring through the buttonhole.

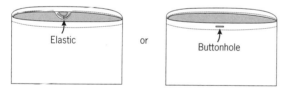

FOLDED-EDGE CASING

Elastic   or   Buttonhole

SEPARATE CASING

A separate casing can be sewn to the inside or outside of a garment anywhere you want to create fullness. It's made from a bias fabric strip cut to the length desired plus ½ in. The width should be equal to the elastic/drawstring size, plus ¾ in. Press under and stitch the short ends ¼ in., and then press under the long edges ¼ in. Pin the casing to the garment facedown and stitch it in place along the long edges. Leave the short ends free to thread the drawstring through.

SEPARATE CASING

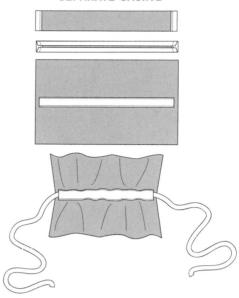

TUBES

Tubes can be used in many ways—as drawstrings, handles, belts, and spaghetti straps. To make a tube, cut a long strip of fabric the desired length and double the desired width plus ½ in. Fold the strip of fabric in half lengthwise, right sides together, and stitch the long raw edges together using a ¼-in.-wide seam. Turn the tube right-side out with a tube turner and press it flat with the seam to one side or centered down the back. Depending on how you will use it, you may or may not need to finish the short ends. For drawstrings, simply tie a knot at the end of the drawstring and trim the raw edge. For belts, tuck the edges inside the tube and topstitch.

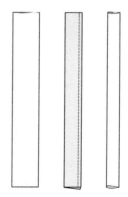

SEWING LEVEL 2

Level 2 techniques are a little more challenging than Level 1 and include more essential sewing skills.

INTERFACING

Interfacing is a separate piece of fabric stitched or fused to the wrong side of areas that need extra stability or stiffness, such as a collar, placket, waistband, facing, or cuffs. The easiest and most common type of interfacing is fusible. It has adhesive on one side and is applied with an iron.

There are various weights and types available. The weight you choose depends on how stiff you want the garment area to be. A good rule of thumb is to choose a weight close to the original fabric weight. Sew-in interfacing is also available—simply cut the required pattern piece and sew it to the matching garment piece wrong side within the seamline.

FACING

A facing typically extends just a few inches from the edge of the garment and is an exact duplicate of the garment edge shape to which it's sewn. After stitching, the facing is turned to the inside to finish areas like necklines or armholes. To attach a neckline facing, stitch together the front and back bodice pieces and the facings at the shoulder and press the seams open. Finish the outer facing edges by turning under ¼ in. or zigzagging. With the right sides together, pin the facing to the garment neckline, matching the shoulder seams and raw edges. Stitch the facing to the garment along the neckline raw edge and understitch (see drawings at right).

UNDERSTITCHING

Understitching is a line of stitching used to keep seam allowances and facings on the inside of a garment. Once a facing is sewn to an edge, the seam allowances are trimmed and pressed toward the facing. From the facing right side, stitch the seam allowances in place close to the seamline on the facing side. The facing is then turned to the inside of the garment, pressed, and may be hand-stitched in place along the outer edges of the facing.

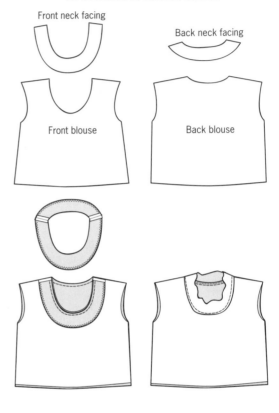

ATTACHING A NECK FACING

Front neck facing

Back neck facing

Front blouse

Back blouse

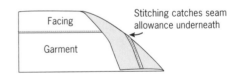

UNDERSTITCHING

Facing

Garment

Stitching catches seam allowance underneath

BINDING

Binding is another method for finishing the outside edges of a garment. It's done using strips of bias fabric so they can stretch and conform to curved edges easily. The strips are sewn to places like neckline or armhole edges and can then be folded inside like a facing.

There are many methods for applying binding to an edge. One of the easiest ways is to fold and press one long edge under ½ in., then pin and stitch the unfolded edge of the bias strip to the garment edge with right sides and raw edges together. After sewing, trim the seam allowances to ¼ in. Fold and press the bias strip to the garment's wrong side, encasing the raw edges, then stitch it in place along the fold by hand or machine. The entire binding width can be folded under, or it may be folded only halfway so it shows on the garment outside.

Many times, the ends of a binding are sewn together to create a loop before they are attached to a circular garment edge, such as on a sleeve or hem edge. To create a circular bias strip, trim the short edges on the straight grain, and pin the diagonal edges together with right sides facing so that the strips form an upside down V. Stitch in place along the raw edges, press open the seam, and trim the extensions.

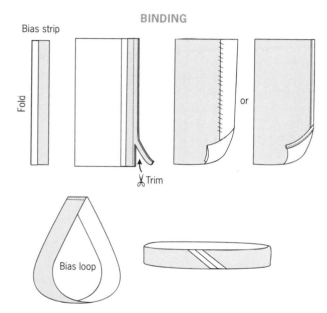

BINDING

Bias strip

Fold

or

Trim

Bias loop

BANDING

Banding is similar to binding; however, the strips don't have to be cut on the bias and they stay on the outside of the garment as a design element. Bands can be used to finish raw edges on sleeves, hems, or other openings.

To make a continuous band, stitch the short ends' right sides together and press the seam allowances open, then fold the band in half lengthwise with the wrong sides and raw edges together. Pin the band to the garment edge right side, matching all the raw edges. Stitch in place through the three layers,

press the seam allowances toward the band, clean-finish the raw edges, and topstitch close to the seam catching the seam allowance underneath. If you don't want visible stitching, catch the seam allowances by hand, or skip this step entirely.

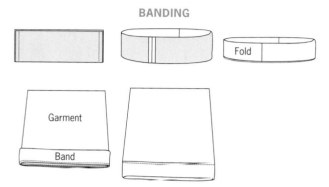

BANDING

Fold

Garment

Band

GATHERING/EASING

Easing or gathering a fabric piece is a common sewing technique and it's easy. To gather a fabric edge, stitch two parallel rows of basting stitches ¼ in. apart within the seam allowance with one row of stitches right next to the seamline. Leave long thread ends and don't backstitch. Pull the bobbin threads to gather the fabric along the stitching line. The difference between gathering and easing is that gathering is a design element meant to show on the outside of the garment; easing is more subtle and doesn't show any fullness on the outside of the garment. Easing is used when you need to sew two edges together that aren't exactly the same length, such as on sleeve caps, curved hems, and princess seams.

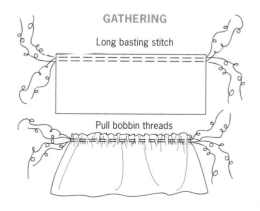

GATHERING

Long basting stitch

Pull bobbin threads

GATHERED RUFFLE

To make a gathered ruffle, cut a length of fabric two to three times the finished length. Clean-finish the lower long and side edges with a narrow hem and gather the upper edge using two rows of basting stitches (see gathering on page 23). Pull the bobbin threads until the ruffle is the desired ruffle length.

CREATING A GATHERED RUFFLE

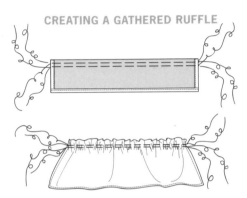

BUTTONHOLES

Making a buttonhole is not as intimidating as it might first seem. It's essentially two rows of narrow zigzag stitches closed at each end with reinforcement stitches. Most sewing machines have buttonhole mechanisms, so check your manual for instructions. If you don't have a buttonhole maker, stitch them manually. Either way, the area where buttonholes are placed needs to be interfaced for stability.

BUTTONHOLE LENGTH

Determine how long your buttonhole needs to be by measuring your button length and height. Add these two numbers together and add in another $\frac{1}{8}$ in. If you're making a buttonhole for a drawstring, the folded drawstring needs to be able to enter and exit the hole easily.

MANUAL BUTTONHOLES

On the fabric right side, draw a line with a fabric pencil the length of the buttonhole. If available, use a buttonhole or satin stitch foot on the machine. Use a narrow, close zigzag to stitch on both sides of the line. Change the settings to a medium-width zigzag and very short length (this is your reinforcement stitch) and stitch across the ends of the zigzag lines, closing the gap between the side zigzag rows. Place a pin at one end

of the buttonhole stitching to use as a stopper and use a seam ripper to cut carefully between the stitching lines to open the buttonhole. It's a good idea to practice on a comparable fabric scrap before stitching on your garment.

CREATING A MANUAL BUTTONHOLE

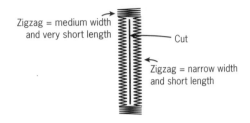

Zigzag = medium width and very short length — Cut

Zigzag = narrow width and short length

SEWING ON A BUTTON

There are two types of button attachments: shank and flat. For both types, thread a needle with a doubled thread length and start by bringing the needle through the fabric on the garment right side just underneath where the button will be placed. Secure the thread by backstitching in place twice.

SHANK BUTTONS

Shank buttons are sewn to a garment through the extension loop on the button underside. Bring the needle through the shank and then through to the garment wrong side. Bring the needle back through to the front, continue sewing through the loop until the button is secure; stitch in place several times to secure the thread.

FLAT BUTTONS

To sew on a flat button, create a thread shank so the overlapping fabric around the buttonhole will have room to rest without puckering. Sew the button in place with a toothpick or a large pin between the holes to create some slack in the attachment thread. After the button is secure, remove the toothpick and move the button to the top of the thread creating a bit of space below the button. Wrap the thread around the space tightly to form a shank. Stitch in place several times to secure.

MAKING YOUR OWN BUTTONS

The type of button you use on a garment can make or break it. A perfectly charming way to make sure your buttons match your garment is to use remnants to make your own buttons.

COVERED BUTTONS

It's easy to recycle dirty or ugly buttons by covering them with a small circular piece of fabric. Cut out a circle approximately 1½ times the size of the original button. Use a hand sewing needle and a double thread to sew a running stitch around the circle edge. Place the button facedown on the wrong side of the fabric and hold it in place with your finger as you draw up the stitches to enclose the button. Backstitch several times to secure the edges. Back the button with a small circle of fabric glued in place to hide the raw edges. If the original button doesn't have a shank, use bunched fabric-to create one. Another option is to get a button-covering kit or button rings from your local fabric store.

COVERING A BUTTON

CHINESE KNOT BUTTONS

Use strips of fabric to make a long tube (see instructions on page 21) and then loop it together as shown. Keep the loops loose until after the third step, and then slowly and evenly draw the loops closer together until you get a nicely shaped ball. The wider the tube, the bigger the button. This takes a little practice to get it right. Once the knot is shaped, trim off the tube ends and hand-stitch them down to finish the button.

CHINESE KNOT BUTTONS

Start

SEWING LEVEL 3

To sew up a Level 3 project, you'll need to know how to sew a dart and install a zipper.

DARTS

Darts give shape to flat pieces of fabric so they can contour around our curvy bodies. They're used in places such as the bust, hips, and waist; anywhere on our body that has shape. Essentially, darts are triangular folds sewn into the fabric, with the points heading toward the fuller parts of the body. Darts are not required to create a garment, but are needed if you want a garment that fits nice and snug.

SEWING A BASIC DART

Use a blunt tracing wheel and tracing paper to transfer the dart markings to the fabric wrong side. Fold the fabric right sides together along the dart center, matching the dart legs to one another; pin the fold in place. Start stitching along the dart legs at the widest part of the dart, positioning your fabric with the point of the dart in line with the needle, and make sure to backstitch. Approach the point of the dart slowly, and taper the stitching off the folded edge. Don't backstitch at the dart point; instead, tie a knot with the thread ends. Press darts toward the garment center if they're vertical, and press them down if they're horizontal. Use a tailor's ham or other appropriate curved surface to press darts without flattening their tips.

SEWING A BASIC DART

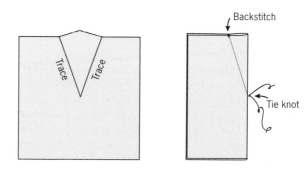

Trace   Trace

Backstitch

Tie knot

ZIPPERS

There are different types of zippers and ways to sew them into a garment. Below you will find the two most common types of zipper applications. The first step for installing any zipper is to figure out how long it needs to be. On skirts, pants, and dresses, the zipper needs to open to the hip level. To determine the zipper length, measure the seam from the garment upper edge down to hip level (the pattern will likely have a notch at hip level).

INVISIBLE ZIPPER

My favorite type of zipper is the invisible zipper. It seems to work for just about anything, has a clean finished look, and is no harder to install than conventional zippers. You'll need an invisible zipper foot as well as a regular zipper foot for the sewing machine. Unlike traditional zippers, an invisible zipper is sewn into an open seam.

With the garment right-side out and the zipper in the open position, pin the invisible zipper facedown on one edge of the garment with the zipper teeth along the seamline and the zipper tape toward the seam allowance edge. If the upper edge of the garment is already finished, position the zipper stop a hair below the finished edge. If the upper garment edge isn't finished, align the upper zipper stop with the garment seamline.

With a regular zipper foot on the machine, baste the zipper in place along the tape edge as far down the zipper as you can. Change to the invisible zipper foot and adjust the machine to a regular stitch length. Stitch the zipper in place by placing the zipper coil underneath the foot groove and stitch as close to the coil as possible without catching it. Stitch as far as the machine will allow and make sure to backstitch. Pin the other side of the zipper to the opposite side opening, making sure the zipper isn't twisted.

Baste and stitch the zipper in place just like the other side. Zip up the zipper and stitch the remainder of the seam together below the zipper using a regular zipper foot. Start as close to the zipper as possible and just above the end of the side stitching lines. There may be a slight gap. If the upper garment edge was already finished, turn down the upper zipper tape, fold the facing or zipper seam allowance inward so that it encloses the tape, and hand-stitch it in place.

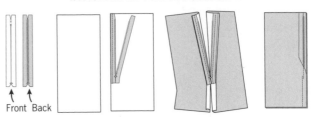

Front Back

CENTERED ZIPPER

A common zipper application is the centered zipper. Unlike an invisible zipper, a centered zipper is sewn into a closed seam. Stitch the seam below the zipper notch using an everyday stitch and making sure to backstitch. Stitch the seam together above the notch with a basting stitch. Press the entire seam open.

With the zipper closed, pin it to the garment with the right side of the zipper facedown on the open seam and the zipper stop at the end of the basted area. The pressed fabric edge should be centered over the zipper teeth. Open the zipper an inch or two to slide the pull tab out of the way. Using the zipper foot, start stitching along the right side of the zipper tape, getting as close to the zipper coil as the foot will allow.

When you reach the zipper pull, stop, make sure the needle is piercing the zipper tape, lift the presser foot, and close the zipper to get it out of the way. Put the presser foot back down and continue sewing to the end of the zipper. Once you pass the bottom zipper stop, pivot to stitch across the zipper and pivot again to stitch the other side in place. Move the zipper pull as necessary. Once the zipper is sewn in place, remove the basting stitches to reveal the zipper on the outside of the garment.

Keep in mind that your stitching will show on the outside of the garment so it's important to keep it straight. If it helps, baste the zipper in place first, then stitch from the outside of the garment.

CENTERED ZIPPER APPLICATION

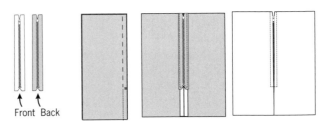

Front Back

SEWING LEVEL 4

Projects listed with Sewing Level 4 do not actually require additional knowledge of any special techniques; however, these projects will require a few extra things. For one, you'll need more experience at the machine, and more sewing and preparation time. On the mental side, you'll need to bring your rock 'n' roll attitude, independent thinking, and extra patience for experimenting.

Random Refashioning: Developing Your Eye

Shopping secondhand for refashioning purposes is a bit different than shopping for new clothes off the rack. When you buy new items, you expect to be able to wear clothing immediately as is, so you never really think of garments outside of their current look. When you buy to repurpose, you must use your imagination to think about what the garment can become. At first glance, you might pass over an item because it doesn't appear to be something you'd ever wear, but learning to see potential will open your world to countless sewing adventures. Here are some tips for repurpose shopping:

- Think outside the garment; turn it upside down, inside out, or twist it up. Sometimes making something fresh is as easy as wearing it in a different way.

- Imagine elements like sleeves and plackets moved or removed, a neckline reshaped, or a waistline in an alternate location.

- Envision dramatic improvements by simply altering the length of the hem or shortening the sleeves.

- Use a repurposed garment you like as a pattern for a new one sewn in different fabric.

- Look for large-size garments with interesting fabrics—they give you more to work with for refashioning.

- Experiment with fabric manipulation techniques like fringing, braiding, stuffing, gathering, or crinkling to add interest to an existing garment.

- Combine one or more garments by swapping out parts. Take a collar from one garment and put it on another one. Cut off the skirt portion of a dress and attach it to a blouse to create a new dress.

- Use fabric from several different garments to create one new one by patch-working or color-blocking them together. Take swatches of fabric with you to the thrift store to match potential items. In addition to color matching, you'll want to make sure to look for compatible texture, weight, and fabric care.

- Choose an item based on individual elements you like about it and remove the rest. Design something new around the details you love.

- Sometimes the best solution for a big and gaudy garment is to cut it down and just use small amounts of the original. For example, a loud print might be too much for an entire dress, but perfect for a trim or small detail.

- Grab your scissors and be brave. Experiment and just see what happens!

Chapter 2
USING & CREATING PATTERNS

Patterns are flat paper representations of the fabric pieces sewn together to create a garment. Patterns can range from simple geometric shapes such as rectangles and circles to other, more obscure shapes that can really boggle the mind. They're placed on top of fabric as a guide for cutting out the shapes that make up a design. To me, patterns are the star of the party when it comes to refashioning. They allow you to go beyond random reconstruction to get a clean-finished look. Patterns can be easily paired with harvested fabric to recycle items without the haphazard feel common to many refashioned projects.

To get your hands on clothing patterns, you can draw your own (my favorite method), purchase commercial ones from a store, find vintage patterns at thrift stores, or go online to buy and download them.

USING PATTERNS

After you get to know the anatomy of a typical pattern, figuring out how to place a pattern on fabric is a matter of comparing the markings and information on the pattern pieces and in the accompanying guide sheet (for commercial versions) with the fabric grainlines. Each pattern will have information printed on the pieces, including the pattern name, how many of each piece you need to cut, grainlines to help with proper placement on the fabric, and various construction markings such as notches, darts, buttonhole placements, and zipper position.

EXAMPLE PATTERN

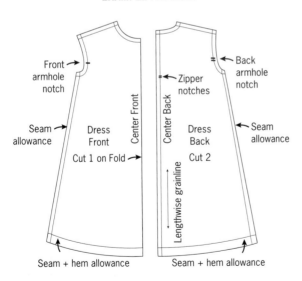

Front armhole notch

Back armhole notch

Zipper notches

Center Front

Center Back

Seam allowance

Dress Front
Cut 1 on Fold

Dress Back
Cut 2

Seam allowance

Lengthwise grainline

Seam + hem allowance

Seam + hem allowance

DETERMINING YARDAGE

The amount of fabric required for a pattern varies depending on the pattern pieces and the fabric width. To determine the yardage needed for patterns that you make yourself, first measure and multiply the length and width of each pattern piece, then multiply that by how many of each piece you need to cut (for pieces that are cut on the fold, multiply by two). Add up the calculations for all your pattern pieces to determine the total number of sq. in. needed.

If your fabric is 45 in. wide, divide your total number by 1,620 to determine how many yards you will need. For 54 in.-wide fabric, divide by 1,944 and for 60 in.-wide fabric, divide by 2,160.

Napped and directional fabrics may require more material than normal. When refashioning, it is hard to know if a garment has enough yardage until you take it apart, but you can always estimate by measuring sections of the fabric.

CUTTING OUT THE PATTERN

Many patterns are made of thin pinnable tissue. I recycle newspapers and paper grocery bags to make my patterns and they pin pretty easily as well.

When pinning the pattern down, keep everything flat on the table and make sure to place the pins inside and close to the cutting lines. If a heavier paper is used, secure the pattern in place using fabric weights (rocks, figurines, and snow globes work great!) instead of pins, and then trace around the pattern piece with fabric chalk, and cut following the chalk marks.

If you have a large cutting mat and a steady hand, you can use a rotary cutter instead of scissors. In either case, keep all the layers flat on the table while you cut.

CUTTING ON THE FOLD

Since our bodies are somewhat symmetrical, pattern pieces typically represent just one side of the body. These half patterns simplify the patternmaking process as well as the cutting process. To get a whole piece of fabric from a half pattern, the center of the pattern piece is placed on a folded fabric edge. To determine when to place a pattern on a fabric fold, look for the words "Cut on Fold," typically found along the center front or center back edges.

Fold your fabric so the fold is parallel to the lengthwise grain and the double-layer fabric is wide enough to cut the

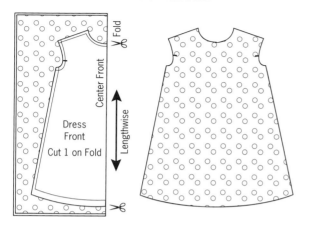

Center Front · Fold

Lengthwise

Dress
Front
Cut 1 on Fold

pattern piece. The selvages can either be on top of each other or simply parallel to each other.

Place the pattern piece on the fabric with the center edge *exactly* on the fold. Pin it in place and cut around all the edges except the one on the fold. The fabric opens to reveal a whole piece.

Pattern pieces are sometimes cut on a bias fold, so watch for the grainline at a 45° angle to the center.

CUTTING SEPARATELY

Not all pattern pieces will be cut on the fold. Half patterns can be cut in twos and then sewn together along the center edges to create the whole. This center seam creates openings for zippers and other closures. For pieces cut separately, look for the grainline marked on the pattern. When you place the

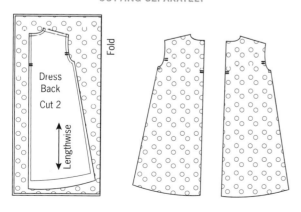

Fold

Dress
Back
Cut 2

Lengthwise

pattern on the fabric, this line must be parallel to the lengthwise grain of the fabric. When you need to cut two of a pattern piece, cut two at one time by cutting through a double layer of fabric. If you need to cut through a single fabric layer but need two pieces, cut one piece with the pattern facing up and one piece with the pattern facing down, keeping the fabric in a consistent orientation—this creates a right and left half.

CUTTING DIRECTIONAL FABRICS

Some napped fabrics such as velvet and corduroy have a different look to them depending on the direction of the nap. A napped fabric can look dark and dull or light and shiny in one lengthwise direction as opposed to the other. Other fabrics might have a singular direction because of a printed design, such as a flower, tree, animal, or words. When cutting directional fabrics like these, make sure the upper edges of *all* pieces are placed in the same direction and the direction makes sense for the design. To test the look of each direction, hold the fabric up against your body in front of a mirror.

MARKING

Once you have your pattern pieces cut out, transfer any markings, such as darts and notches, from the paper pattern to the fabric before you remove the pattern.

TRACING

Construction details are transferred from the pattern to the fabric using washable tracing paper and a blunt-point tracing wheel. Tracing paper comes in many different colors, so choose one that will show up well on your fabric and is removable. With the pattern still pinned to the fabric, position the tracing paper underneath or between the layers of your fabric so that the colored side is facing the fabric wrong side. Fold the tracing paper to trace two opposing surfaces at once. Use the tracing wheel to transfer the markings. Occasionally, you'll need to trace a detail to the fabric right side.

MARKING NOTCHES

Notches help you line up adjacent garment pieces when sewing them together. Single and double notches are the most common. The easiest way to mark notches is to clip inward along the fabric edge, no longer than ¼ in. Alternatively, you can clip small outward triangle notches while you cut out the pattern.

DIY PATTERNS

Commercial and ready-made patterns are convenient, but DIY patterns are great for those of us with body measurements that vary from the standard chart, because you draw them using your very own measurements. While there are entire textbooks dedicated to patternmaking and alteration, getting started doesn't have to be scary or complicated. You can draw lots of smart designs for yourself after learning just a handful of key techniques and ideas, organized here in three levels.

Level 1 is for the total beginner and covers the tools and practices you'll use regularly. After reading through Level 1, hop on over to the projects section and try out an easy project like the **Ultra Miniskirt** (page 75)! When you're ready, Levels 2 and 3 will take you further. Keep in mind, these sections will get you started in the right direction, but the real lessons will be learned as you work through the projects.

To me, DIY patternmaking is all about having fun with shapes in an artistic yet mathematical way, and experimenting until you get it right. And as with any creative art, once you get familiar with some of the rules, you can go and break them.

LEVEL 1 PATTERN DRAWING
The first step to becoming a DIY patternmaker is learning how to use the various rulers and the sharp tracing wheel. This section will also cover how to finish a pattern with labels and seam allowance and how to measure the body.

SQUARE A LINE
As its name suggests, the L-square ruler is shaped like an "L" and is used to create square corners and perpendicular lines when drafting a pattern. The triangle ruler can be used to square lines and angles as well, but also comes in handy when drawing bias grainlines. When drawing squares and rectangles, the length is typically drawn vertically and the width horizontally, keeping the directions consistent with the fabric grain.

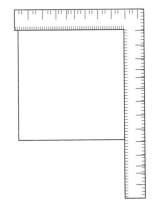

Equip Yourself

- Newspaper or newsprint, paper grocery bags or recycled craft paper
- Tape (clear, low-tack, removable is best)
- Scissors
- Pencils
- Markers (several different colors)
- Measuring tape
- Yardstick
- See-through flexible ruler
- L-square ruler
- Curved hip ruler
- French curve ruler
- Triangle ruler (to draw bias grainlines)
- Sharp tracing wheel (Different from the blunt one for marking fabric, this has points to mark paper.)
- Test fabric (old sheets, linens, or muslin)

USING L-SQUARE AND TRIANGLE RULERS

USING CURVED RULERS

The French curve ruler is used to create necklines, armholes, sleeve caps, and waistlines. Curved hip rulers are used to create hems, waistlines, and hip curves as well as other random pattern curves. Use the inner and outer edges of the rulers to create both outward and inward curves. Work with two rulers at once to create an opposing curve. Each curved ruler tapers to a straight edge; use this straight edge when you need to taper a curve so that it intersects with another line at a square angle. Center front and center back edges are typically met with a square angle to avoid a peak.

USING CURVED RULERS

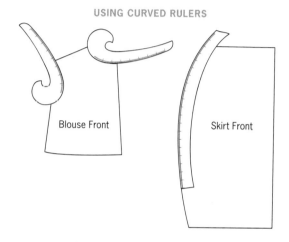

Blouse Front

Skirt Front

FIX-UPS

Many times an alteration will result in an awkward or broken line in a pattern. These blips need to be cleaned up before you can cut and sew the pattern. Grab your curved and straight rulers to smooth out any sharp angles, fill in inconsistencies, and blend lines.

FINISHING A PATTERN

Finish your patterns by labeling each piece with the name of the garment and the specific pattern piece. Also label each piece with cutting information, such as how many to cut and whether or not to cut it on the fold. If a pattern is not cut on the fold, it should have a grainline. Mark notches along adjoining edges for sewing convenience.

Finished patterns need seam allowances along all edges that will be sewn to another pattern piece. Center front and

back edges cut on the fold don't need seam allowances. All the projects in this book will use ½-in. seam allowances unless otherwise indicated; however, seam allowances can be any depth you choose. To add a ½-in. seam allowance to your pattern, use a clear ruler to make spaced, tiny dots ½ in. from the seamline, then connect the dots using the rulers.

Seam allowances along sharp angles, curves, and points will sometimes result in corner overhangs. To clean up these seam allowances, fold the seam allowance to the inside and trim along the opposing seams. Alternatively, you can trim any seam allowance overhang after you've sewn up the garment.

Hem allowances are needed at garment edges that will be turned and finished and are added in the same way as seam allowances. To make things less confusing, remove seam allowances before altering an existing pattern.

TRACING

You can make a new pattern by altering a template or already existing pattern. To copy a pattern, place it on top of a blank piece of paper, tape it in place, and trace it with a sharp tracing wheel. The tracing wheel will leave tiny puncture marks on the paper. Next, remove the original pattern and use your rulers and a pencil to connect the trace marks.

TESTING A PATTERN

It's always a good idea to sew a test garment after drawing or altering a pattern, just to be sure everything works. Test garments are typically made with muslin fabric in a weight close to the final fabric, but you can also use thrift store sheets and linens. Occasionally, things may not turn out like you imagine, so you'll want to continue to tweak the pattern. Sometimes the test is different from your intention but better than you could have imagined!

Measure Up!

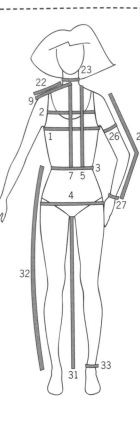

Knowing your unique body dimensions is essential when you're sewing your own clothes. In most cases, a few main measurements are all you need, but occasionally more in-depth measuring is necessary.

When measuring yourself, wear snug-fitting clothes with no extra bulk, and put on the type of undergarments you wear most often. For the in-depth measurements, it's important to wear fitted, *woven* garments with side seams to distinguish between the front and back of the body. Also, make sure your woven garment has an armhole that feels comfortable. Stand up straight, yet natural, and make sure the measuring tape is not too tight and not too loose as you measure. A few of the in-depth measurements are more accurate when someone else takes them—you really need to be standing still.

QUICK MEASUREMENTS

1 **Full Bust:** Measure around the fullest part of the bust and back, making sure the tape is parallel to the ground all the way around.

2 **Full High Bust:** Measure around the body just above the full bust.

3 **Full Waist:** Measure around the waist at its smallest point. Find this spot and keep it as a reference for other measurements by tying a piece of narrow elastic around your waist and letting it settle.

4 **Full Hip:** Measure around the fullest part of your hipline, typically 7 in. to 10 in. below the waist.

5 **Full Front Length:** Measure from the high shoulder at the neck to the waist.

6 **Full Back Length:** Measure from the high shoulder at the neck to the waist.

7 **Center Front Length:** Measure from the front neck base to the waist.

8 **Center Back Length:** Measure from the back neck bending point to the waist.

9 **Center Front Width:** Measure from the front neck base to the shoulder tip.

10 **Center Back Width:** Measure from the back neck bone to the shoulder tip.

IN-DEPTH MEASUREMENTS

11 **Front Bust:** Measure from side seam to side seam across the fullest part of the bust.

12 **Wide Back:** Measure from side seam to side seam across the fullest part of the back.

13 **Across Chest:** Measure from mid armhole to mid armhole across the front.

14 **Across Upper Back:** Measure from mid armhole to mid armhole across the back.

15 **Front Waist Width:** Measure from side seam to side seam across the front waist.

16 **Back Waist Width:** Measure from side seam to side seam across the back waist.

17 **Front Hip:** Measure from side seam to side seam across the front hip.

18 **Back Hip:** Measure from side seam to side seam across the back hip.

19 **Bust Level:** Measure from the shoulder tip to bust point.

20 **Bust Bridge:** Measure from bust point to bust point.

21 **Halter:** Measure from the high shoulder at neck to underarm at the side seam (sometimes called the strap measurement).

22 **Shoulder Length:** Measure from the high shoulder at neck to shoulder tip.

23 **Neck:** Measure around the widest part of the neck.

24 **Arm Length:** Measure from the tip of the shoulder to the wrist with arm bent.

25 **Arm Span:** Measure from wrist to wrist with arms outstretched and the measuring tape behind your head.

26 **Bicep:** Measure around the fullest part of the upper arm.

27 **Wrist:** Measure around the wrist.

28 **Side:** Measure from the underarm to the waist along the garment side seam.

29 **Side Hip Length:** Measure from the waist to hip level along side seam.

30 **Crotch Depth:** Sit on a chair and measure from the waist to the top of the chair seat along the side hip.

31 **Inseam:** Measure along the inside of the leg from the crotch down to just below the ankle.

32 **Outseam:** Measure from the waist to just below the ankle along the side seam.

33 **Ankle:** Measure around the ankle.

DART MEASUREMENTS

A pattern with darts requires special measurement. The Dart Start measurement will help you place your dart in the correct position. Front Dart and Back Dart measurements are used to determine the width of your darts. The project instructions will tell you specifically how to use these measurements.

- **Dart Start:** if full waist = 24 in., dart start = 3 in. Add ⅛ in. for every in. over 24 in.
- **Back Dart:** 2 in.
- **Front Dart:** 1 in.

Note: If the difference between your Full Waist and your Full Hip is 10 in., then your Front and Back Darts are as listed. For each in. less than 10 in., subtract roughly ⅛ in. For each in. more than 10 in., add roughly ⅛ in.

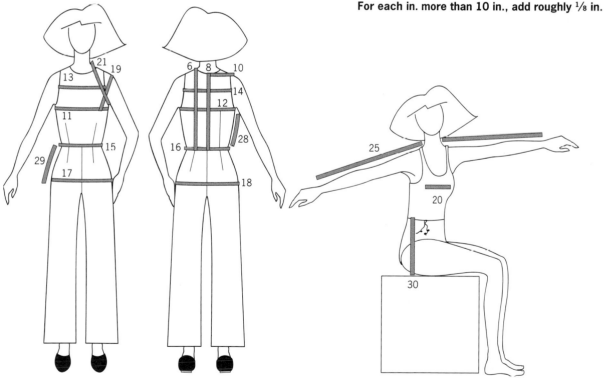

LEVEL 2 PATTERN DRAWING

Once you are comfortable creating a basic finished pattern, you are ready for Level 2. Here you will learn how to create facings, how to add style lines, and how to make simple alterations to a pattern's length and width, among other techniques.

FACINGS

The neckline edge is sometimes sewn to a separate pattern piece called a facing. The facing is then tucked inside the garment after it's sewn to leave a clean-finished edge. Facings can also be used on the armholes of sleeveless garments and on shaped hems.

Facing patterns are created after the main pattern piece is finalized but before adding seam allowances. When altering an already existing pattern, if you make any changes to faced garment edges, such as the neckline or armhole, you'll need to make the same changes to the facing pattern. Sometimes it's easier to make a new facing pattern to match the new design instead of trying to replicate the alterations.

Neckline facing To make a neckline facing, place the front and back patterns on a piece of paper and trace the outer edges along the neck opening, shoulder, and centers. Extend the shape out 2 in. from the traced neckline shape.

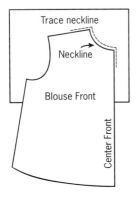

Armhole facing To make an armhole facing, place the front and back pattern pieces on a piece of paper; then trace the outer edge of the armhole curve as well as the side and shoulder edges of the pattern. Extend the shape out 2 in. following the armhole curve shape.

SEPARATE ARMHOLE FACING

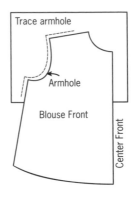
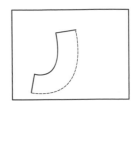

STYLE LINES

Style lines are any visible lines or curves on a garment including necklines, hemlines, and seamlines. You can change the look of these lines or add new ones. Adding new style lines to a pattern is useful when working with recycled clothing and remnants, since many times you have limited amounts of fabric; you can color-block or patchwork fabric pieces together to fill out the pattern. To avoid confusion, work from a pattern without seam allowance. To add new style lines, draw lines where desired from one edge to another, mark

ADDING STYLE LINES

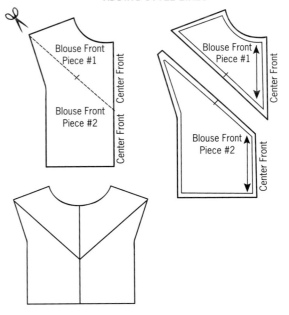
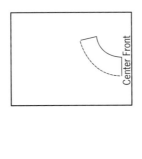

distinct notches along the lines, and label each piece. Cut along the lines to separate the pattern pieces and add seam allowances to all the edges.

ALTERING LENGTH

On garments with a straight hem, adding or subtracting pattern length is as easy as changing the hem location. If the hem is not straight, or if there are darts or other design elements, you need to add or subtract length within the pattern.

Shortening Draw a line across the pattern perpendicular to center front/center back in an area away from darts or style lines; label it "A." Decide how much length you want to remove and draw another line this distance above line A and label it "B." Cut along line A and tape it to line B, matching the center lines. Blend and correct the outer pattern edges as needed.

Lengthening Draw a line across the pattern perpendicular to center front/center back in an area away from darts or style lines; mark a notch along the line and then cut along the line to separate the two pattern sections. Decide how much length to add, and on a separate piece of paper, draw two parallel lines this distance apart. Tape the cut pattern edges to these lines, making sure the center edges and notches are aligned. Blend and correct the outer pattern edges as needed, being mindful of fit.

VOLUMIZE

Extra volume, or ease, can be added to patterns to give extra comfort, or it can be added as a design element, for example, in a billowy blouse.

Adding fullness To add fullness, draw lines on the pattern from one edge to another in whatever direction you like, cut through the lines, spread them open, and tape the edges to a piece of newsprint underneath your pattern. Remember that adding additional fullness may impact adjacent garment pieces. Experiment with the location, direction, and amount of fullness added, and always sew a test before committing to a final pattern.

Decreasing fullness To decrease fullness, draw and cut lines across your pattern but overlap them instead of spreading them. This will affect the garment fit, so make a test sample.

SHORTENING

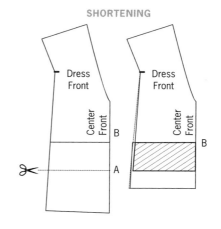

LENGTHENING

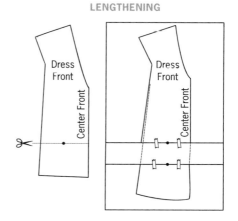

ADDING FULLNESS

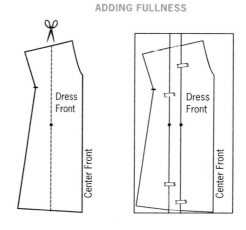

LEVEL 3 PATTERN DRAWING

THE "YOU" DRESS

Many times, new patterns are formed using a basic fitted dress pattern as a template. The template includes the bodice front, bodice back, sleeve, skirt front, and skirt back. When sewn together, these pieces create a dress that conforms to your curves through the use of darts and shaping.

This basic dress template can be used over and over to design new looks; once you have a pattern that fits, you can alter it in infinite ways to create new designs. I recommend picking up a commercial pattern (see Resources and References, page 248, for full list) for a basic dress.

For a special challenge, draw a set of basic patterns using your unique body measurements by following the instructions below. This method can take time, patience, and a knack for problem solving. If you choose this method, work with a friend.

BODICE FRONT

1 Draw a rectangle with the width equal to your **Front Bust** measurement divided by two plus 1½ in. and the length equal to your **Front Full Length** measurement plus ¼ in. Label the right edge "Center Front."

2 Draw a parallel line 1¼ in. from the left side. Along the upper edge, measure over from center front your **Center Front Width** measurement and mark with a dot. Mark another dot 1½ in. below the first dot and label it "A." Using your **Center Front Length** measurement plus ¼ in., measure this distance from the lower edge. Mark a dot and label it "C."

3 Draw a line the length of your **Shoulder Length** measurement, connecting dot A to the top rectangle line. Mark a dot where the lines meet and label it "B." With your French curve ruler, connect B to C, making sure the curved line meets C at a square angle.

4 Draw a temporary line from dot B to the inner left line the length of your **Halter** measurement. Mark a dot where the lines meet and label it "D."

5 Divide your **Center Front Length** measurement by five, measure down this distance from dot C along the center front, mark with a dot, and label it "E." Divide your **Across Chest** measurement by two and add ¼ in. Square a temporary line this length from dot E, mark a dot, and label it "F." Use a French curve ruler to connect dots A, F, and D to create your armhole.

6 Draw a line the length of your **Side** measurement, connecting dot D to the outer left edge. Mark a dot where the lines meet and label it "G."

7 Mark dot "H" along the lower edge, measuring out from center front your **Dart Start** measurement. Mark dot "I" along the center front, ¼ in. up from the lower edge. Connect dots G, H, and I to create the waistline.

8 Divide your **Front Waist** measurement in half and add ¼ in. Subtract your **Dart Start** measurement from that calculation. Measure this distance from dot G along the waistline, mark a dot and label it "J."

9 Place your ruler on the pattern, connecting dot A and dot I. Draw a temporary diagonal line from dot A the length of your **Bust Level** measurement. Mark with a dot and label it "K."

10 Divide your **Bust Bridge** measurement in half. With this calculation, draw a temporary line from the center front that goes through dot K. Mark the end of this line with a dot and label it with a star. This is your bust point.

11 Connect the bust point to dot H to create a dart leg. Measure the dart leg and draw another one this length, connecting the bust point and dot J. Redraw the waist with slightly curved lines connecting dots I and G with the dart legs.

12 To sew up the bodice, create a dart point ½ in. below the bust point, draw new dart legs, true the dart, and add seam allowances to all edges except for the center front. When tracing the bodice to create new designs, keep the dart point at the bust point.

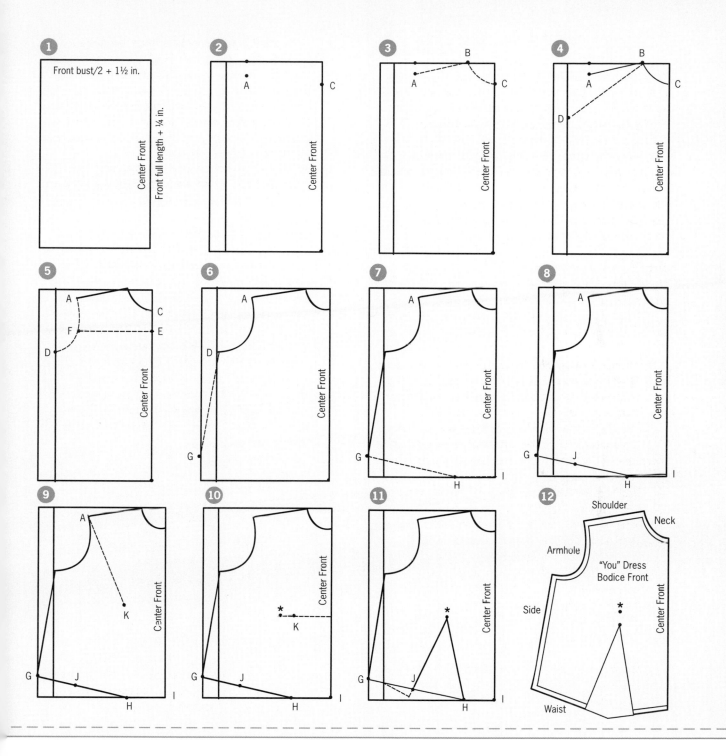

1
Front bust/2 + 1½ in.

Center Front
Front full length + ¼ in.

2
A
C
Center Front

3
B
A
C
Center Front

4
B
A
C
D
Center Front

5
A
C
F
E
D
Center Front

6
A
D
G
Center Front

7
A
G
H
I
Center Front

8
A
G
J
H
I
Center Front

9
A
K
G
J
H
I
Center Front

10
*
K
G
J
H
I
Center Front

11
*
G
J
H
I
Center Front

12
Shoulder
Neck
Armhole
"You" Dress
Bodice Front
Side
*
Center Front
Waist

BODICE BACK

1   Draw a rectangle with the width equal to your **Wide Back** measurement divided by two plus ¼ in. and the length equal to your **Back Full Length** measurement plus ¼ in. Label the left edge "Center Back."

2   Along the upper edge, measure over from center back your **Center Back Width** measurement and mark with a dot. Mark another dot 2 in. below the first dot and label it "A." Along the center back edge, measure up from the lower edge your **Center Back Length** measurement plus ¼ in., mark a dot and label it "C."

3   Draw a line the length of your **Shoulder Length** measurement, connecting dot A to the upper line. Mark a dot where the lines meet and label it "B." With your French curve ruler, connect dot B to dot C, making sure the curved line meets dot C at a square angle.

4   Divide your **Back Waist** measurement in half and add 1¾ in. Using this calculation, mark dot D along the lower edge, measuring over from the center back.

5   Draw a line the length of your **Side** measurement, connecting dot D to the right edge. Mark a dot where the lines meet and label it "E." Measure up ¼ in. from the lower edge along center back and mark with dot "F." Connect dot F to dot D.

6   Measure from dot C to dot F and divide this number by four. Mark a dot this distance down from dot C along the center front and label it "G."

7   Divide your **Across Upper Back** measurement in half and add ¼ in. Draw a perpendicular line from dot G this distance. This is the horizontal balance line (HBL). Label the end of the line with dot "H." Use a French curve ruler to connect dots A, H, and E. The upper majority of the curve should be near straight.

8   Mark dot "I" along the lower edge, measuring out the distance of your **Dart Start** measurement from center back. Measure out another 1½ in. from dot I and mark dot "J." Mark the midpoint between dots I and J.

9   Draw a temporary perpendicular line from the center back to the underarm point, and then draw another temporary line connecting the midpoint between dots I and J to the temporary line.

10 Measure down 1 in. from the top of the midpoint line and mark with dot "K." Connect dot K and dot J to create a dart leg. Measure the dart leg and draw another dart leg this same length, connecting dot K and dot I. The dart leg might pass through I. Redraw the waist with slightly curved lines connecting dots F and D with the dart legs.

11 To sew up the bodice, make the dart true and add seam allowances to edges.

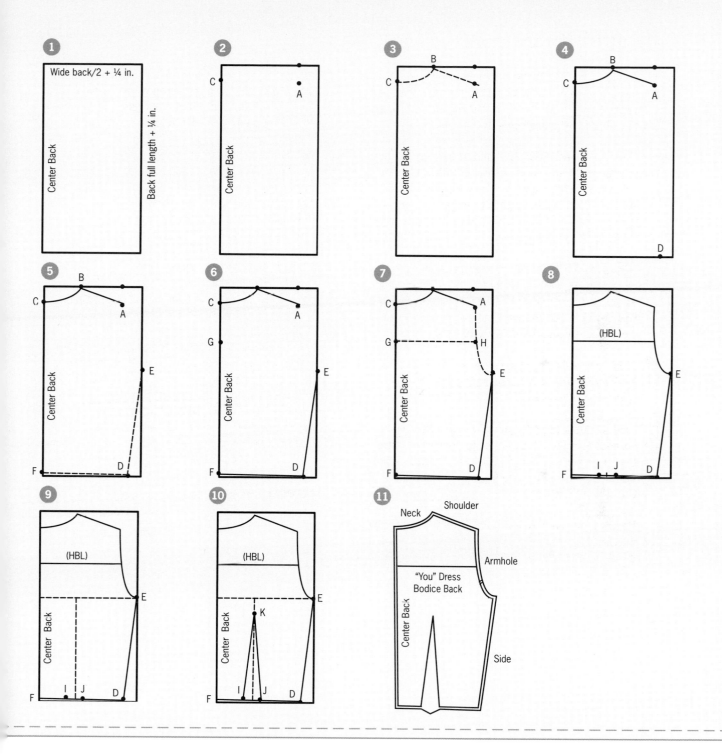

1 Wide back/2 + ¼ in.

Center Back

Back full length + ¼ in.

2 C A
Center Back

3 B C A
Center Back

4 B C A
Center Back D

5 B C A E
Center Back F D

6 B C A G E
Center Back F D

7 C A G H E
Center Back F D

8 (HBL) E
Center Back F I J D

9 (HBL) E
Center Back F I J D

10 (HBL) E K
Center Back F I J D

11 Neck Shoulder Armhole
"You" Dress Bodice Back
Center Back Side

SLEEVE

1 Draw a rectangle with the width equal to your **Bicep** measurement divided by two plus ¼ in. and the length equal to your **Arm Length** measurement. Label the right edge "Center."

2 Measure the curves on your front and back bodice armholes, add the measurements together and divide by three. Round up the calculation to the closest ¼ in. Measure down this distance from the top of the rectangle and draw a line indicating your bicep level.

3 Draw a diagonal line connecting the upper right corner of the rectangle with the lower left corner of the bicep line. Measure the diagonal line and divide it by four. Mark two dots on the diagonal this distance from each end. Label the dots "A" and "B" as shown.

4 Use a French curve ruler to draw the sleeve cap as shown flipping the ruler to create the opposing curves. The curve should be about ⅜ in. inward from dot A and ⅝ in. outward from dot B.

5 Mark a double notch where the curve crosses the diagonal and cut out the sleeve.

6 So far, we've been working with the back of the sleeve. Since the front half of the sleeve cap is slightly different from the back, trace a full pattern and make some slight tweaks. Fold a large piece of paper and tape the back pattern to the paper with the center line on the fold. Trace around the entire pattern with a sharp tracing wheel.

7 Unfold the paper and use your rulers to draw the full pattern, following along the tracing marks. Draw a new sleeve cap on the front side of the pattern. Recall the general location of points A and B in step **3**; the front curve differs from the back curve at these areas by ¼ in. Curve outward ¼ in. at area B and inward ¼ in. at area A. Mark a single notch along the front curve.

8 Mark the elbow level halfway between the bicep and the hem.

9 To sew the sleeve, add seam allowances to all edges. Measure the distances from the bicep line to the notches along the curves and use these measurements to add corresponding notches along the armholes on the front and back bodices. Add an additional notch to the sleeve cap center.

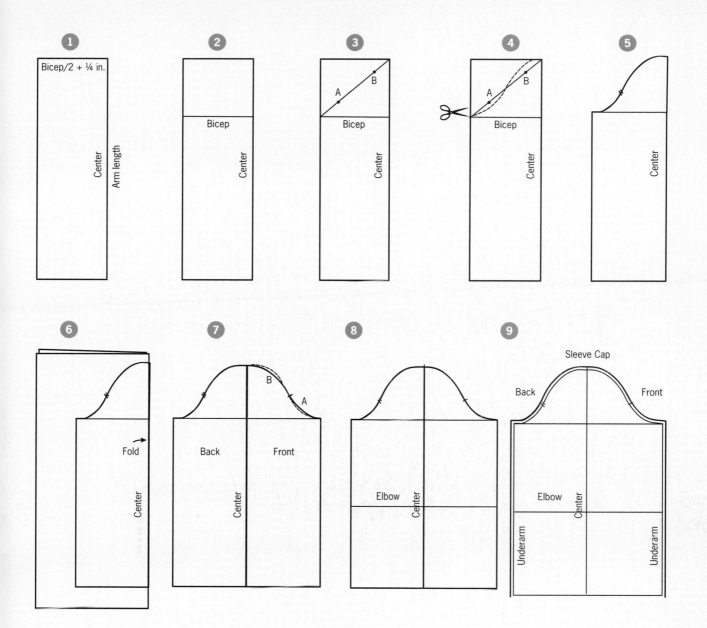

1. Bicep/2 + ¼ in.

Center
Arm length

2. Bicep

Center

3. A B

Bicep

Center

4. A B

Bicep

Center

5. Center

6. Fold

Center

7. B

A

Back | Front

Center

8. Elbow

Center

9. Sleeve Cap

Back | Front

Elbow

Center

Underarm | Underarm

SKIRT

1 Divide your **Full Hip** measurement in half and add 1 in. Draw a rectangle with this calculation as the width and the length equal to the measurement of your **Side Hip Length**. Label the left side "Center Back," the right side "Center Front," and the lower edge "hip."

2 Divide your **Back Hip** in half and add ½ in. Measure over this distance from the center back along the upper and lower edges and mark with dots. Connect the dots and label line "S."

3 Divide your **Back Waist** measurement in half, add it to your **Back Dart** measurement and add ¼ in. From the center back, measure over this distance along the upper edge, and mark with a dot. Divide your **Front Waist** measurement in half, add to it your **Front Dart** measurement and add ¼ in. From the center front, measure over this distance along the upper edge and mark with a dot. From the top, measure down ¼ in. along the center front and ½ in. along the center back, and mark with dots. Use a curved ruler to connect the dots and draw very shallow waist curves, as shown. Make sure the waist curves meet the center front and center back at square angles.

4 Use a curved hip ruler to draw sides, connecting the dots along the top edge to line S. Move your ruler along the pattern until it touches both the dot and line S, making sure the straight portion of the ruler is on top of line S at the hipline.

5 Measuring over from the center back, mark a dot along the waistline the distance of your **Dart Start** measurement. Label it dot "A." Divide your **Back Dart** measurement in half, measure over this distance from dot A, and mark dot "B." Measure 1¼ in. from dot B and mark dot "C." Divide your **Back Dart** measurement in half, measure over this distance from dot C, and mark dot "D."

6 Mark the midpoints between A and B, and C and D. Draw 5 in. perpendicular lines from the upper rectangle edge that go through the midpoints. Connect the dots to the bottom of their midpoint lines to create darts. Adjust the dart legs as necessary to make sure that they are all the same length. Redraw the waistline as necessary.

7 Measuring from the center front and using your **Front Dart** measurement, repeat steps **5** and **6** to create the front darts. The midpoint lines are 3 in. long instead of 5 in. These are general dart lengths. For larger sizes, increase the dart length; for smaller sizes, decrease it. You may need to experiment to achieve the desired shaping.

8 Extend downward equally from the center front, center back, and line S to your desired skirt length and mark the finished length.

9 To sew the skirt, separate the front and back patterns, true the darts, and add seam allowance to all edges except center front. Add a hem allowance to the skirt's lower edge. Mark a double notch along center back at hip level. Mark single notches along the sides at hip level.

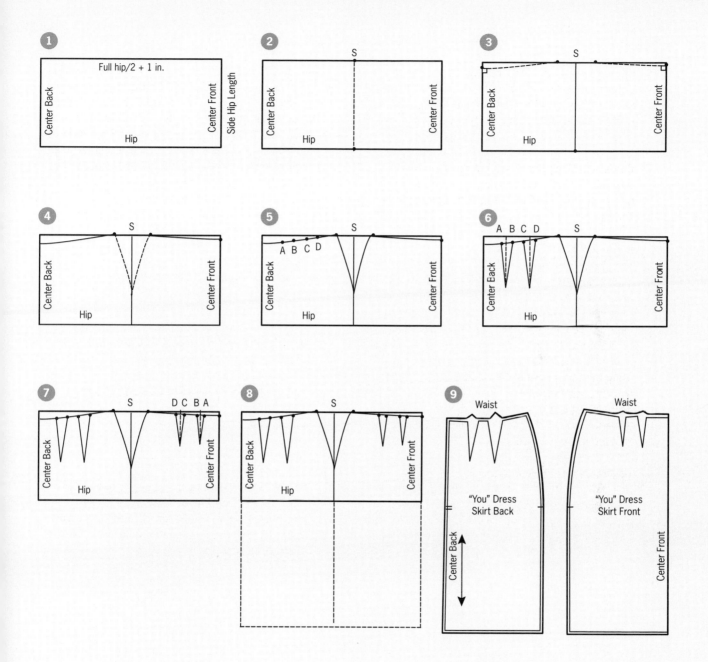

CUT UP, SEW UP

Make a test from muslin or a repurposed sheet to test for fit and comfort. Sew up the main pieces and don't worry about finishing.

1 Cut one each of the bodice front and skirt front, both on the fold. Cut two each of the bodice back, skirt back, and sleeve. Clip notches and trace the darts.

2 Sew all darts and press them toward the center.

3 Right sides together, pin and stitch the front bodice to the back bodice along the shoulders and the sides. Press open the seam allowances.

4 Right sides together, pin and stitch the underarm seam together on one of the sleeves. Press open the seam allowances. Stitch two rows of basting stitches within the sleeve cap seam allowance between the notches.

5 Pin the bodice and sleeve right sides together. Match the sleeve underarm seam to the bodice side seam, match the bodice shoulder seam to the top notch on the sleeve, and match the front and back sleeve notches (single to single and double to double) to the armhole. Pull up the basting stitches to ease the sleeve cap and stitch it in place sleeve side up.

6 Repeat steps **4** and **5** for the other sleeve.

7 With the right sides together, pin and stitch the skirt front piece to the skirt back pieces along the sides, matching notches. Press open the seam allowances.

8 With right sides together, pin and stitch the bodice to the skirt, matching side seams. Press the seam allowances toward the skirt.

9 Install a zipper at the center back seam. Press open the seam allowances below it.

10 Trim the seam allowance from the neck edge for an accurate visual of the neckline.

11 Try on the dress and make adjustments as needed before using the patterns to create new designs.

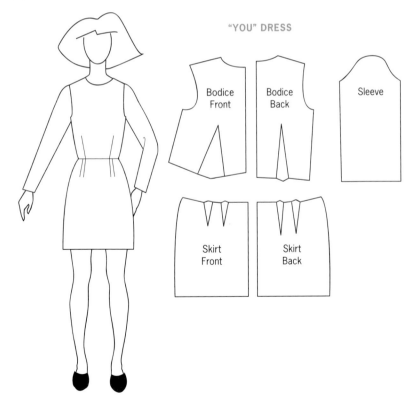

"YOU" DRESS

Bodice Front

Bodice Back

Sleeve

Skirt Front

Skirt Back

MOVING DARTS

Darts can be moved and manipulated in many neat ways. On a basic bodice front, darts can be moved to locations all around the perimeter with the dart always pointing toward the bust. On a basic skirt, darts are typically found near the waistline pointing toward the hips and bottom. Remember, the purpose of a dart is to create a rounded section of fabric to cover a rounded body area, so unless you're going for something avant-garde, make sure all your darts point toward those round body parts.

To move a dart, mark a point along the perimeter of the pattern to indicate the new dart location, draw a cutting line from the new point to the old dart point, cut out the old dart, cut along the line from the outside edge to just short of the dart point, close the original dart, and voilà, a new dart appears in the new spot.

This same process can be used to move a dart on any pattern. When moving darts on a bodice front, make sure the dart point is on top of the bust point before moving the dart. If it isn't, move the dart point to the bust point and redraw the dart legs from the bust point. Once you finish moving the dart to a new location, move the dart point off the bust point by at least ½ in. and redraw the dart legs along the slashed edges, tapering to the point.

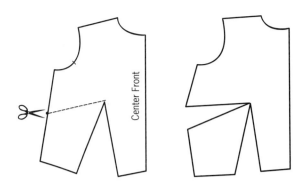

TRUE DARTS

When darts are created, moved, or manipulated, a new seamline shape along the dart end must be established; this is called "truing the dart." To true a new dart, tape paper behind the dart and along the wide dart end, and then fold and tape the dart as it would be when sewn. Use your ruler to draw the seamline, cut along the seamline, and then open up the dart to reveal the new edge. It's handy to add seam allowances while the dart is folded to save some time.

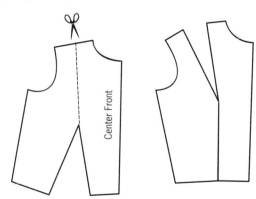

SPLIT AND COMBINE DARTS

In addition to moving darts around, you can also combine and split darts to change the pattern look. Combine two or more darts to create one big dart, or split a big dart into multiple little darts by using the same process for moving darts. In this case, though, you'll work with multiple cutting lines to the bust point, and close and open darts in varied amounts.

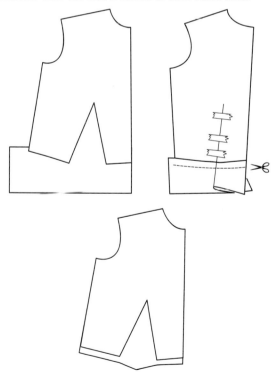

MIXING AND MATCHING

Once you learn basic patternmaking techniques, use them to alter *any* pattern, including ready-made patterns. You can also mix and match various pattern pieces with each other to come up with new designs, a practice commonly referred to as "Frankenstein patterning."

In general, things typically work out better if you mix and match pattern pieces from the same brand because the same basic templates were likely used to create each of their designs, making the various parts somewhat interchangeable. This is particularly important when you want to mix in something like sleeves, which are made to fit specific armholes.

However, you don't always have to stick with the same company and you can even design your own pieces to match ready-made patterns. For instance, you might design a bodice from your basic fitted pattern and match it with a skirt from a ready-made pattern to create a dress. The trick is to make sure the adjoining edges match up. In this case, be sure the bodice waistline edge matches the skirt waistline edge.

CREATING A COPYCAT

One of the most amazing things about learning to draw patterns is that after you start to understand the process, you can see any garment and figure out how to make your own version. There are many methods for creating an exact copy of a garment and countless other ways to be inspired by an existing garment or design idea.

USING THE ORIGINAL

If you don't mind taking it apart, remove all the seams from a repurposing garment and use the pieces to create a paper pattern. Then duplicate the design exactly or alter one or more of the pattern pieces to create something fresh.

A TRACING

If you want to keep the original garment intact, trace it with a sharp tracing wheel to create a pattern. The trick is learning to see the individual pattern pieces within a finished garment.

Pin or tape a piece of newsprint to a corkboard and then use pushpins to fasten the garment on top of the paper. Pin one pattern piece at a time, making sure everything is flat, and use the tracing wheel to trace around each piece. Once you have all the parts of the garment traced, use your rulers to connect the dots, true up the pattern pieces, and add seam allowances. It gets tricky when you want to trace garments with darts, complicated detailing, or fullness, so start with a simple design.

A READY-MADE

Another option for exploring an inspiring idea is to search for a similar shape and feel in a ready-made pattern. Flip through the catalogs at your local sewing store or browse online to find one close to the original and figure out what you need to do to alter it toward your inspiration.

A TRUE ORIGINAL

If you want an added patternmaking challenge, analyze the lines of a garment and try to reproduce it from a basic fitted pattern. After you get into the patternmaking groove, you will realize how rewarding it is to look at or dream up any design and puzzle it together for yourself.

Deep V Mini Dress, page 129

Chapter 3
TOPS

Let's start with several blouses and tops you will love making and mixing into your wardrobe. The **Rectangle Tie Shrug** on page 53 has a simple shape that will get you some no-sweat experience using rulers, adding seam allowance, and labeling patterns. **Such a Square Blouse** on page 61 is one of my favorite go-to tops due to its versatile style and quick sew up. It can also be easily altered and enhanced to create designs like the **Cha Cha Blouse** on page 69. To round things out, indie-darling, Peggy Noland, designed an avant-garde piece for this chapter. Her **Oversized Caged Hoodie** on page 57 has a complex and intriguing aesthetic, yet it is actually easy enough for any seamster to make! Sew it up, y'all.

RECTANGLE TIE SHRUG

Pattern Level 1 Sewing Level 1

Pump up the volume and add a pop of interest to any outfit with this tie-front shrug. It's almost like a scarf with sleeves, so you can layer it atop most anything! As the name suggests, it's three rectangles sewn together, which means a lightning fast sew-up.

Use a lightweight woven fabric that looks good on both sides, since the right *and* wrong side show at the tied area. Look for approximately 1 yd. or less of fabric from salvaged skirts, dresses, or curtains, and practice the narrow roll hem technique before trying this project. Since the design calls for a lightweight fabric, use a small-size needle.

DIY PATTERN

1 Add 2 in. to your **Arm Span** measurement and jot it down as "width." (Your **Arm Span** measurement is from wrist to wrist, so if you want shorter sleeves, like the ones shown, measure from elbow to elbow instead.) Place your measuring tape on your shoulder near your neck and measure down to just below your bust. Add 2 in. to this number and jot it down as "length." Draw a rectangle on a piece of paper using the length and width measurements.

2 Find the exact center on both long edges of the rectangle and mark with dots. Connect the dots and cut along the line to separate the two sides of the rectangle. Label one side "Shrug Back" and the other "Shrug Front."

3 On the back piece, label the right side "Center Back." Measure from the back of your neck to the middle of your shoulder. On the upper edge of the pattern, measure over this distance from center back and mark a notch to indicate the neckline opening. Divide your **Full Bust** measurement by four and add 1½ in. On the lower rectangle edge, measure over from center back this distance and mark with a double notch to indicate the lower opening.

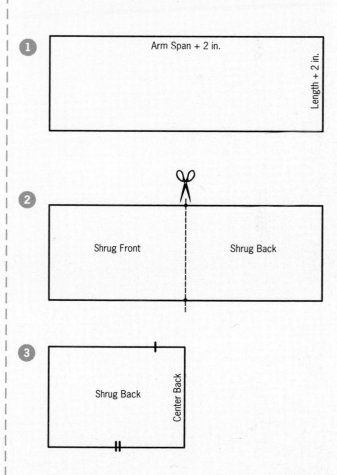

4 Repeat step **3** for the front piece, except label one edge "Center Front." Extend the front pattern piece from center front to make the tie extension. I doubled the size of the front piece, but you can make your tie extension as long as you want. The center front line now acts as a grainline indicator.

5 Add ½-in. seam allowance to all edges except center back. On the back piece, write "Cut 1 on Fold." On the front piece, write "Cut 2" and draw a grainline at center front.

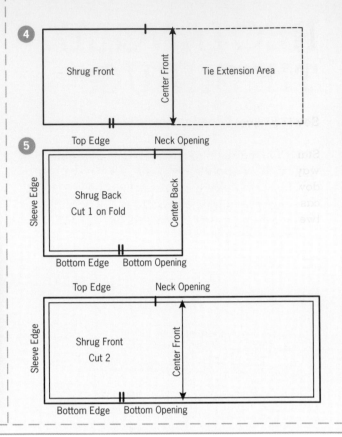

Mix It Up

⊕ Increase the length of the back piece to your waist and instead of using the front piece, cut two back pieces to create a modern boxy blouse with extra-wide armholes.

⊕ Change the width of the rectangle to create various arm lengths or gather and cuff the sleeve.

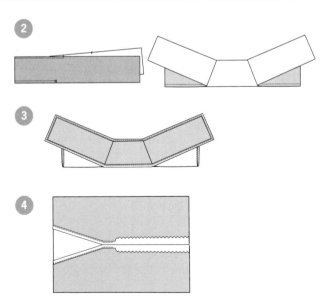

CUT UP, SEW UP

1 Cut one back on the fold and two full front pieces. Clip notches.

2 Right sides together, match one front piece to the back at the notches. Starting from the sleeve edge, pin and stitch the front to the back along the upper and lower edges, stopping at the notches. Press open the seam allowances. Repeat to stitch the other front piece to the back piece.

3 At the raw edges, create a narrow rolled hem. This should include the neckline, front extensions, and sleeve edges. Where the rolled hem meets a seam, roll slightly into the seam allowance.

4 Clean-finish the raw edges on the inside seams with pinking shears or a serger.

UPSIDE-DOWN TUNIC

Sewing Level 1

Measure Up!

Halter 21
(Check out page 34 for specific measuring instructions.)

Start thinking about garments in out-of-the-ordinary ways to come up with something new. Turned upside down, a dowdy elastic-waist skirt can become a casually chic tunic after making just a few minor tweaks. Look for a skirt that has a button-front placket and an elastic waist, preferably with side seam pockets. The skirt should fit you or be a little too big. A knee-length skirt will give you a tunic, but if you get a longer skirt, you can make an upside-down dress instead.

CUT UP, SEW UP

1 Measure from the lower skirt edge along the side seams, your **Halter** measurement. Mark with pins.

2 Use a seam ripper to undo the hem near the side seams. Unpick a few inches of the hem on both sides of each side seam and then unpick the side seams until you reach the pin marks.

3 Secure the stitching on the side seams at the pin marks.

4 Clean-finish any raw edges on the opened side seams. Fold each of the edges under and stitch them in place using the original seam allowance.

5 Fold and stitch the original hem back in place. You should now have a skirt with two clean-finished slits at the side seams.

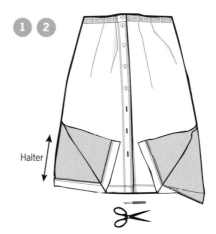

6 With the skirt right-side out, pin the front skirt hem to the back skirt hem wrong sides facing. Starting at one of the sides, continue pinning the hem together until you are 6 in. from the placket, and then stitch the hems together with a 1½-in. seam allowance (or the original hem depth). Repeat for the other side of the skirt. The seam allowances for the seams you just created will be on the outside of the garment.

7 Fold the seam toward the back of the skirt. Starting from the side, pin and edgestitch it down, stopping 7 in. from the placket. Repeat for the other side of the skirt.

8 Turn the skirt upside down and behold your new tunic! Wear it with the first few buttons undone so that the placket opens out like a collar. The original pockets are upside down but can be used as is.

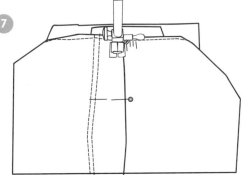

Mix It Up

⊕ Start out with a super-long skirt. Trim 10 to 12 in. from the lower edge of the skirt. Follow the directions to create your tunic. You'll have to create a new hem. Use the trimmed yardage to embellish the tunic with extra pockets or other fun details.

⊕ If your original skirt has a large amount of volume at the hem, try gathering it with a drawstring to create a draped look at the shoulder.

OVERSIZED CAGED HOODIE

By Peggy Noland

Sewing Level 2

This unisex felt hoodie is an artistically unique garment large enough to go over your coat in the winter, yet it can also be worn in warmer temperatures; talk about a superb layering element! Peggy made hers from an easy-sew, eco-friendly felt made from recycled plastic bottles. Choose this same felt in an array of colors, or recycle any type of medium- to heavyweight no-fray fabric (like faux-suede) to make your hoodie. One size will fit most, but you can always make the hoodie bigger by starting out with wider sections of fabric.

CUT UP, SEW UP

1 Cut two 20 in. x 5 in. rectangles from stretch knit to use for the waistband and four 10 in. x 5 in. rectangles to use for sleeve bands. For wider bands, cut wider rectangles.

2 With the longer rectangle edges representing the upper and lower portions of the body, cut 10 in. x 20 in. vertical rectangles from the lower sides of the 60 in. x 30 in. sections of no-fray fabric to make an oversized T-shirt shape.

3 Using a see-through ruler and fabric pencil, mark a 1-in. border around the edges of each body and neck section, then mark 3 in. squares all over each section, keeping a 1-in. border between each square. Use a cutting knife or small scissors to cut out each square, being careful not to cut into the 1-in. border.

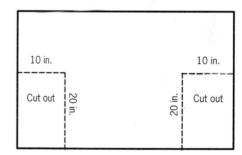

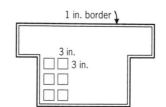

4   Right sides together, pin and stitch the front body to the back body along the underarm and side seams, then pin and stitch along the sleeve/shoulder edges, leaving a 14-in. gap at the center for a neck opening.

5   Right sides together, pin and stitch the two neck pieces together along the long edges.

6   Right sides together, pin and stitch the neck piece to the body around the neck opening, matching raw edges and seamlines.

7   Right sides together, pin and stitch the two waistband rectangles together along the short ends to create a circle. Fold the circle in half along the long edge, with wrong sides facing.

8   Use a basting stitch to gather the lower body edge to more closely match the width of the waistband. Right sides together, slip the folded waistband over the body waist, matching raw edges and side seams. Pin and stitch the waistband to the body, stitching through all three layers, stretching the band as necessary to fit (see page 23 for more on banding).

9   Repeat the banding process for each of the sleeve cuffs.

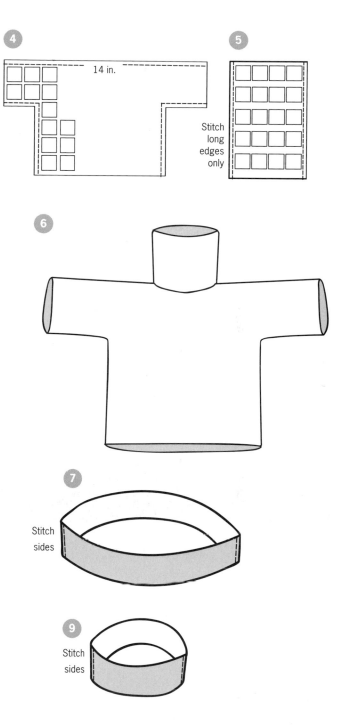

4   14 in.

5   Stitch long edges only

6

7   Stitch sides

9   Stitch sides

SUCH A SQUARE BLOUSE

Pattern Level 2   Sewing Level 2

Far from boring, this square blouse will be part of the code with your gal-pal gang in no time. It plays well with fitted minis as well as many other types of bottoms and sews up like a dream. The basic shape means oodles of possibilities when it comes to fabric selection. Make it stiff like a robot with a medium- to heavyweight woven fabric or loosen it up with something a little lighter. Look to recycle one big garment with about 1 to 1½ yd. of usable space, or use two separate garments: one for the front of the blouse and one for the back! Once you have the finished pattern in hand, you'll get a feel for how much space to look for in a recycled garment.

Special Gear

⊕ ½ yd. interfacing in a weight appropriate for your fabric.

DIY PATTERN

1 Divide your **Full Bust** measurement by two and add 2 in. Draw a square with this number as the width and length. Find the exact center of the upper edge, draw a perpendicular line connecting the upper and lower sides of the square; cut along this line to separate the pieces. Label one piece "Front" and one piece "Back." Label the edges along the cut lines "Center Front" and "Center Back." The opposite long edges are the side seams.

2 Divide your **Neck** measurement by four and measure inward this distance from centers along the pattern upper edges and mark with dots. Label the dots "N."

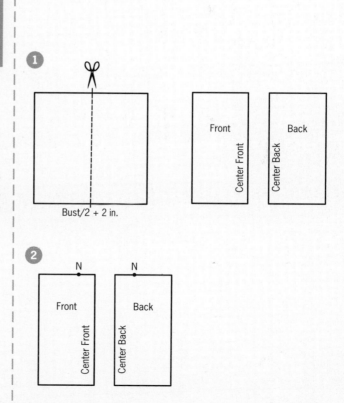

3 On both pattern pieces, draw a diagonal cutting line the length of your **Halter** measurement plus 1 in. connecting dot N to the side. Hint: Place the start of your ruler on dot N and move the ruler around until it hits the side at the correct measurement. Mark the points with a dot and label them "S." Cut along the diagonal lines starting at dot N, but do not cut all the way through to the side. Stop just short of dot S so that the pieces stay together. Set the patterns aside for a few moments.

4 Use a large piece of paper and draw two horizontal, parallel lines 1 in. apart near the paper upper edge. Place the back bodice pattern piece on top of the paper and tape it in place so that the center back neck edge is on the lower line and the tip of the triangle (dot N) is hitting the upper line. Use your sharp tracing wheel to trace around the perimeter of the pattern and use a curved ruler to draw a neckline connecting the tip of the triangle (dot N) with the neck edge at center back. Remove the original pattern piece and use your rulers to connect the tracing marks.

5 Repeat step **4** to complete the front bodice pattern, with one exception. The curved neckline on the front pattern will dip lower than the back, so before drawing the neckline, measure down 1 in. or more along the center front and connect the tip of the triangle (dot N) to this new point with your curved ruler.

6 To have a nice finished edge along the neckline, create a facing. For each of the pattern pieces, place a piece of paper underneath and trace the neckline shape including 2 in. of the center front and back lines and 2 in. of the shoulder lines. Finish the facing patterns by drawing a curved line consistently 2 in. from the neckline curve, closing up the pattern.

7 Add ½-in. seam allowances to all pattern pieces, except along the center front and center back edges. Label the patterns "Such a Square Blouse Front" and "Such a Square Blouse Back." Along center front and center back on all pattern pieces, write "Cut 1 on Fold." Mark notches at the underarms.

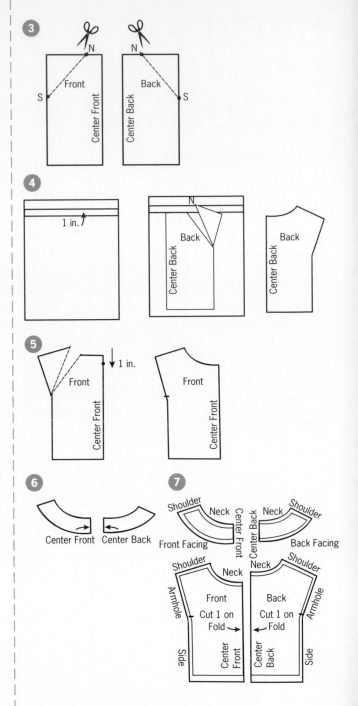

CUT UP, SEW UP

1   Cut one each of the following pieces on the fold: blouse front, blouse back, front neck facing, and back neck facing. Clip the armhole notches. Cut the facing patterns from interfacing, trim off the seam allowances, and apply to the wrong side of the facing pieces according to the manufacturer's instructions.

2   Right sides together, place the front and back blouse pieces on top of each other. Pin and stitch the shoulder edges together. Press open the seam allowances and clean-finish the seams.

3   Repeat step **2** for the facing pieces. Clean-finish the long outer edge of the fabric.

4   Open out the blouse on a table right-side up. Place the facing right-side down on top of the blouse. Pin and stitch the facing to the blouse neck edge, matching shoulder seams and raw edges. Trim the seam allowance to ¼ in. and press all layers toward the facing. From the right side of the facing, understitch close to the seam, catching the seam allowances underneath. Turn the facing toward the inside of the blouse and press along the neck edge. Hand stitch to the inside of the blouse at the shoulder seams.

5   Narrowly roll hem the armhole edges just past the notches.

6   Right sides together, pin and stitch the side seams, starting at the armhole notches. Press open the seam allowances and clean-finish.

7   Hem the lower blouse edge. Fold and press the raw edge to the inside ½ in. Fold again another ½ in. to hide the raw edge and pin in place. Stitch around the edge close to the first fold.

Mix It Up

⊕ For a longer sleeve, extend parallel shoulder and underarm lines and curve at the underarm point.

⊕ Make your original square smaller by skipping the 2 in. at DIY Pattern step 1 and use an average stretch knit instead of a woven fabric.

⊕ Alter the pattern at the hem to adjust the length; to make a dress from this blouse, check out page 123.

⊕ Create a new style line diagonally across the front pattern piece and stitch it using two different fabrics.

⊕ Change the neckline shape to resemble a V.

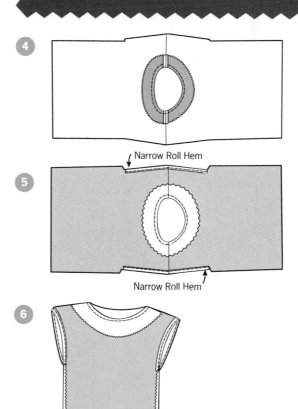

4

5   Narrow Roll Hem

Narrow Roll Hem

6

SLOUCHY VEST

Pattern Level 2 Sewing Level 2

Nothing sharpens an outfit like a smart vest. I especially love that you can mix this versatile element with both frilly skirts or layer it over jeans and a T-shirt. The loose fit, big buttons, and double-breasted closure on this vest add a soft twist to this classic wardrobe staple. Drawing the pattern is a time investment that will pay off later when you make the **Poster Art Dress** (page 153) or the **Vest Dress** (page 165). Check your stash for medium- to heavyweight woven fabrics to use on your vest. Use the same fabric for both the outside and lining or choose contrasting fabrics for the occasional peek at the inside that slouchy vests allow. Depending on your size, a yd. or two of fabric ought to be plenty.

Measure Up!

Full Front Length	5	Wide Back	12
Full Back Length	6	Across Chest	13
Center Front Length	7	Across Upper Back	14
Center Back Length	8	Back Waist Width	16
Center Front Width	9	Halter	21
Center Back Width	10	Shoulder Length	22
Front Bust	11	Side	28

(Check out page 34 for specific measuring instructions.)

Special Gear

⊕ Extra recycled fabric for lining

⊕ ¼ yd. light- to medium-weight interfacing

⊕ Four 1-in. buttons or buttons to cover

DIY PATTERN

1 Follow steps **1** through **6** from the directions on page 38 for the **"YOU" DRESS BODICE Front**.

2 Mark a dot 4 in. above the waistline at center front. Extend outward from center front 2½ in. starting at this dot.

3 Mark a dot 3 in. from the neck along the shoulder line. Mark a dot 5 in. below the underarm point along the side seam. Use a curved ruler to connect the dots and create a new armhole shape, and then connect the shoulder at the neck point with the extended center front to create the front neckline shape.

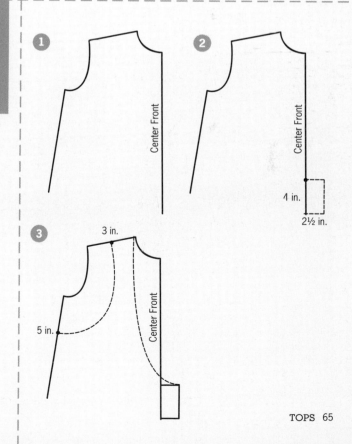

4 Measure 3 in. down and to the left from center front waistline and mark with a dot. Use a curved ruler to make connecting lines to this dot from the side seam and the extended center front, as shown.

5 Follow steps **1** through **7** of the directions on page 40 for the **"YOU" DRESS BODICE Back**.

6 Mark a dot 3 in. from the neck along the shoulder line. Mark a dot 5 in. below the underarm point along the side seam. Use a curved ruler to connect the dots and create a deep racer-back armhole shape.

7 Add ½-in. seam allowances to both the front and back patterns, except along the center back. On the front pattern, write "Cut 2" and "Cut 2 in Lining." The center front line acts as a grainline. On the back pattern, write "Cut 1 on Fold" and "Cut 1 Lining on Fold."

8 Draw a rectangle 5 in. wide and 4 in. long. Label "Interfacing" and write "Cut 2."

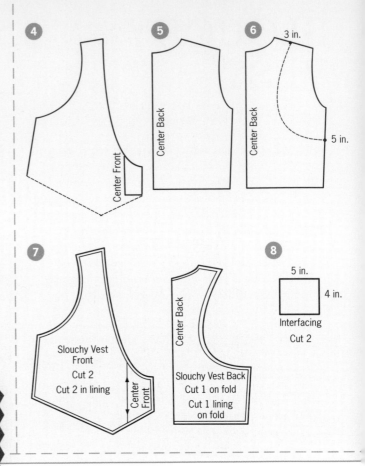

Mix It Up

⊕ Add piping and faux pockets in a contrasting fabric.

⊕ Experiment with the shape of the neckline, armholes, and waistline to change the look altogether.

⊕ Make the vest reversible by using snaps instead of buttons and creating a faux button look on each side.

⊕ Complete DIY Pattern step 1, connect the side to center front with a curved line, squaring at the intersections. Complete DIY Pattern step 5. You now have a basic front and back blouse pattern. Use this pattern to create any type of blouse you can imagine.

CUT UP, SEW UP

1 Cut four vest fronts: two from fashion fabric and two from lining. Cut two vest backs on the fold: one from fashion fabric and one from lining. Cut two of the interfacing pattern.

2 Apply the interfacing to the wrong side of the front vest pieces along the center extension according to the manufacturer's instructions, making sure the interfacing does not extend into the seam allowance.

3 Right sides together, pin and stitch the vest front pieces to the vest back at the shoulders. Press open the seam allowances. Repeat for the lining pieces.

4 Right sides together, pin and stitch the lining to the vest along all edges except for the sides. Trim the seams to ¼ in. and turn the vest right-side out, gently pulling the front sections through the shoulders and out the back sides. Press the vest along all the sewn edges to neaten.

5 Right sides together, pin and stitch the vest sides together (not the lining). Once the vest fabric is sewn together, start to pin the lining right sides together where the vest and lining intersect. Pin and stitch as much of the lining as you can. Flip what remains of the lining to the inside and hand stitch it in place.

6 Use a ruler and fabric pencil to mark 1¼ in. buttonholes on the right front extension, as shown. Stitch the buttonholes, overlap the placket, and sew the buttons in place underneath.

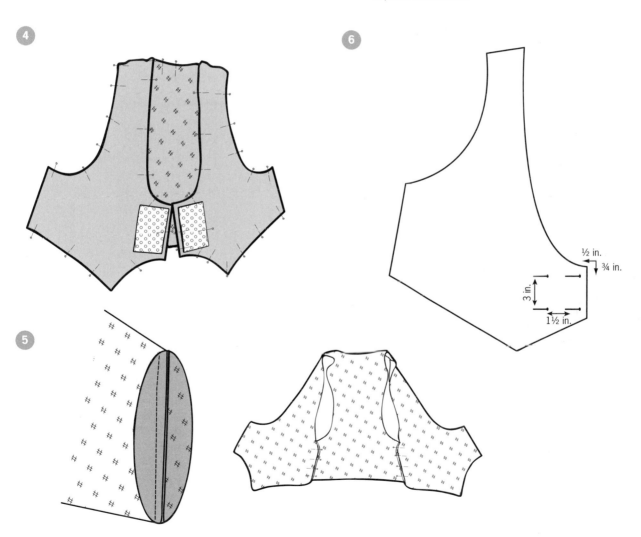

½ in.
¾ in.
3 in.
1½ in.

CHA CHA BLOUSE

Pattern Level 2 Sewing Level 2

Twirl, twist, and bop to the beat in this flirty and feminine blouse. It's got a single ruffle along the neckline that will float and bounce as you do, and since the neckline is wide, it can either perch at the tips of your shoulders or drop down on one side for a little asymmetrical action. The blouse cinches up at the waist with elastic and easily matches up with a pencil skirt, knit tube skirt, high-waist shorts, or leggings. The ruffle and binding will require a bit of fabric, so stick to recycling large lightweight woven garments on this one.

Measure Up!

Center Front Width **9**
Center Back Width **10**
(Check out page 34 for specific measuring instructions.)

Special Gear

⊕ SUCH A SQUARE BLOUSE pattern from page 61 (no seam allowance)

⊕ 3/8-in.-wide elastic the length of your waist measurement

DIY PATTERN

1 Trace the **SUCH A SQUARE BLOUSE Front** and **Back** patterns onto paper. Include notches.

2 On the front pattern, measure down 2 in. from the neck along the center front and mark with a dot. Measure 2 in. from the neck along the shoulder line and mark with a dot. Connect the dots with a smooth curve consistently 2 in. from the edge. Cut along the line to create the new neckline. Repeat for the back pattern. If you prefer a wider or deeper neckline, alter these dimensions to the size you prefer, but keep in mind your **Center Front** and **Center Back Width** measurements so the neckline doesn't completely fall off your shoulders.

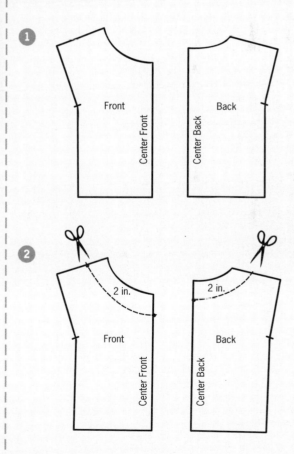

3 Measure and record the new front and back pattern necklines. Add the two measurements together and multiply by two. Draw a rectangle with this calculation as the width and 1 in. as the length. Label the pattern with "Neckline Binding" and "Cut 1." Draw a bias grainline at a 45° angle from the short side of the rectangle.

4 Multiply your front neckline measurement by four. Draw a rectangle with this calculation as the width and 4 in. as the length. Label the pattern with "Front Ruffle" and "Cut 1." Draw a grainline arrow parallel to the short side of the rectangle. Find the midpoint along the upper long edge and mark with a notch. Use the back neckline measurement to repeat the process and create a back ruffle pattern.

5 Add ½-in. seam allowances to all pattern pieces, except along the center front and center back edges of the blouse.

Mix It Up

- ⊕ Create additional ruffles and stitch them around the blouse perimeter.

- ⊕ Instead of the narrow elastic casing, create a wide casing with a big tube drawstring tied in a bow at the waist. You'll need to create a buttonhole for the drawstring to tie.

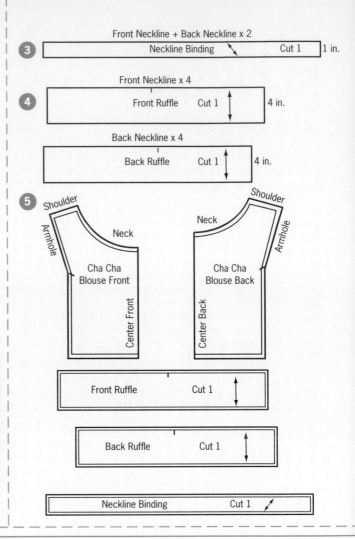

CUT UP, SEW UP

1 Cut one blouse front and one blouse back each on the fold. Cut one front ruffle and one back ruffle. Cut one neckline binding on the bias. Clip notches. Clip additional notches along the neckline of the blouses at center front and center back.

2 Right sides together, place the front and back blouse pieces on top of each other. Pin and stitch the shoulder edges together. Press open the seam allowances and clean-finish the edges.

3 Right sides together, pin and stitch the front ruffle to the back ruffle along the short edges to create one big circle. Press open the seam allowances and clean-finish the edges.

4 Narrow roll hem the lower edge of the ruffle.

5 Gather the upper ruffle edge using two rows of basting stitches, and adjust the gathers to fit the blouse neckline.

6 Pin and stitch the gathered edge of the ruffle to the neckline with the wrong side of the ruffle facing the right side of blouse, matching seams and notches.

7 Right sides together, stitch the short ends of the neckline binding together to create a circle (see page 22). Fold and press the binding in half **widthwise** with wrong sides facing and raw edges together, then unfold and press one of the long edges under ½ in.

8 Right sides together, pin the unfolded edge of the binding to the neckline edge of the blouse with the ruffle sandwiched between the two; stitch using a ½-in. seam allowance. Trim the seam to ¼ in., press all seam allowances toward the binding, and either hand stitch or topstitch the folded edge of the binding to the inside of the blouse concealing the seam.

9 Narrow roll hem the armhole edges just past the notches (see illustrations for **SUCH A SQUARE BLOUSE** on page 63).

10 Right sides together, pin and stitch the side seams together, starting at the armhole notches. Press open and clean-finish the seam allowances.

11 To create a casing, fold and press under ½ in. along the lower blouse edge. Fold under again ½ in. and pin in place. Stitch the casing in place along the first folded edge, leaving 1 in. unstitched to insert elastic into the casing.

12 Cut a piece of elastic equal to your waist measurement. Secure a safety pin to each end of the elastic and thread it through the casing. Once it is pulled all the way through the casing, overlap the ends ½ in. and stitch together, making sure the elastic is not twisted. Stitch the casing opening closed.

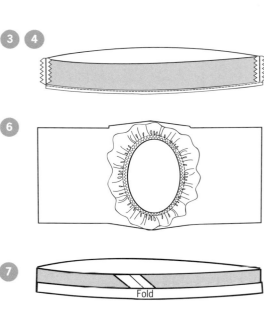

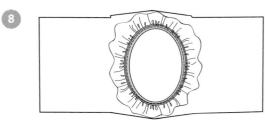

Fold

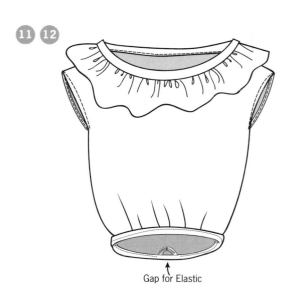

Gap for Elastic

Chapter 4
SKIRTS

Things don't have to be hard to be perfectly cute! Take the **Ultra Miniskirt** on page 75 for example; it has two seams, a hem, and an elastic casing and can be made in an afternoon. The **Suit Skirt** on page 81 is also a swift little number designed by one of the UK's most clever restyle designers, Josie Beckett.

An essential in any lady's closet is the **Trusty Pencil Skirt** on page 85. This sleek skirt will get tons of play in your everyday wardrobe and is your introduction to the world of darts. Add some volume to the pencil skirt and get the energetic **Bubble Skirt** on page 101 or move around the darts and add multiple new style lines to create the color-blocked **Swoosh Skirt** on page 109.

The most adored skirt in my closet is the flirty **Tiered Skirt** on page 95. Surely you will fall in love with the design, too, once you see how the ruffled tiers can be adjusted wildly so they gather and twinkle to your exact liking.

ULTRA MINISKIRT

Pattern Level 1   Sewing Level 1

I must admit, I'm obsessed with short skirts and love the idea of spotlighting lovely legs. This nervy elastic-waist skirt can be scene-stealing in oh-so-many different ways. Try it over bare legs, knee-length or mini bike shorts, arty leggings or straight-up panty hose. Wear it dressed up with a blouse, belt, and heels, or down with a T-shirt and puffy socks. The nature of this design makes it ideal for refashioning because it requires a small amount of yardage. Hunt around for light- to medium-weight woven or knit fabrics and effortlessly fill your wardrobe with miniskirts in all sorts of colors and prints.

Measure Up!

Full Waist 3
Full Hip 4
(Check out page 34 for specific measuring instructions.)

Special Gear

⊕ ⅝-in.-wide elastic, the length of your full waist measurement

DIY PATTERN

1. Add 6 in. to your **Full Hip** measurement and divide it by two. Jot this calculation down as "Width." Measure from your waist down to the finished skirt length and jot this down as "Length." Draw a rectangle with these measurements.

2. Find the midpoint along the upper and lower rectangle edges and mark with dots. Draw a line connecting the dots. Cut along this line to separate the rectangle into two pattern pieces. Label one side "Ultra Miniskirt Front" and the other side "Ultra Miniskirt Back."

3. On the front skirt, label the right edge "Center Front." On the back skirt, label the left edge "Center Back." The opposite edges are the skirt sides. Measure down 4 in. on each side and mark a notch.

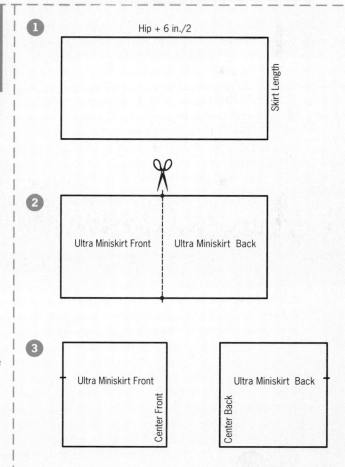

4 On both the front and back pieces, create a folded edge casing by extending the skirt upward 1¼ in.

5 Add ½-in. seam allowances to both pattern pieces on all edges except the centers. Add an additional 1 in. to the lower edges for a hem. On both patterns, write "Cut 1 on Fold."

Ultra Miniskirt Front — Center Front

Ultra Miniskirt Back — Center Back

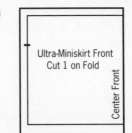

Ultra-Miniskirt Front Cut 1 on Fold — Center Front

Ultra-Miniskirt Back Cut 1 on Fold — Center Back

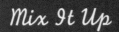

Mix It Up

⊕ Increase the length of your original rectangle to make the skirt longer or increase the width to add more fullness.

⊕ Create a skirt from a trapezoid instead of a rectangle for fun shaping.

CUT UP, SEW UP

1 Cut one front skirt and one back skirt, each on the fold. Clip the notches.

2 Right sides together, pin and stitch the skirt front and back side seams together, matching the notches. Press open and clean-finish the seam allowances.

3 To create a casing, use your seam gauge to measure, fold, and press the upper skirt edge under ½ in. Fold the edge under another ¾ in. and pin it in place. Stitch the casing in place along the first folded edge, leaving 1 in. unstitched to insert the elastic into the casing.

4 Cut a piece of ⅝-in.-wide elastic equal to your **Full Waist** measurement. Attach a safety pin to both ends of the elastic and thread it through the casing. Once it's pulled all the way through the casing, overlap the ends of the elastic ½ in. and stitch them together, making sure the elastic isn't twisted. Stitch the casing opening closed.

5 Hem the lower skirt edge. Fold and press the edge under ½ in. Fold the edge under another 1 in. and pin it in place. Stitch the hem in place along the first folded edge. You might have noticed by now that folded-edge casings and hems are almost exactly alike!

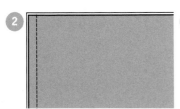

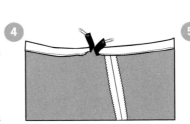

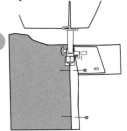

PREPPY RECTANGLE SKIRT

Pattern Level 2 Sewing Level 2

Pop your collar and grab your boat shoes, it's time to go sailing! This classic skirt with front pockets and drawstring waist has instant prepster flair when paired with a bright fitted polo. I recycled a paintbrush print dress from the 1980s to make my skirt, but you can achieve all sorts of looks depending on the print or color you choose. Stick with medium-weight woven fabrics for this project and look for at least a yard or two of usable material.

Measure Up!

Full Hip ④

(Check out page 34 for specific measuring instructions.)

Special Gear

⊕ Scrap of interfacing.

DIY PATTERN

1 Add 4 in. to your **Full Hip** measurement and divide that sum by two. Measure from your waist down to the finished skirt length (above knee or higher). Draw a rectangle with your hip calculation as the width and your skirt length as the length. Find the midpoint along the upper and lower edges of the rectangle and mark with dots. Draw a line connecting the dots. Cut along this line to separate the rectangle into two pattern pieces. Label one side "Preppy Rectangle Skirt Front" and the other "Preppy Rectangle Skirt Back."

2 On the skirt back, designate the left side as "Center Back." On the opposite side, use a curved ruler to draw a slight hip curve toward the upper edge of the skirt. Curve inward by an inch as you approach the upper edge and extend the side upward by ½ in. Connect the raised side to the top waist with a smooth curve. Write "Cut 1 on Fold."

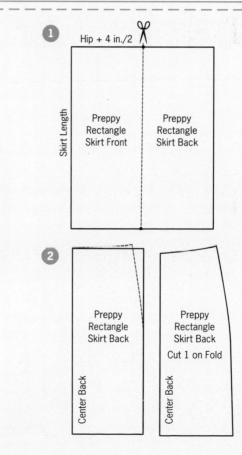

3 Repeat step **2** for the front skirt, except designate the right side as "Center Front."

4 Measure the waistline on the skirt front pattern. Use this measurement to draw a 2-in.-tall rectangle. Designate the right side as "Center." Label with "Waist Casing" and "Cut 2 on Fold."

5 On the skirt front pattern, draw your desired front pocket outer shape. Label this line "A."

6 Measure over at least 1 in. from line A along the waistline toward the center front and mark with a dot. Decide how deep you want the inside of the pocket to extend below line A at the side seam and mark with a dot. Connect the dots to draw your inner pocket shape. Label this line "B."

7 Place a piece of paper under the skirt front pattern and with your sharp tracing wheel, trace the waistline starting at the side seam and ending at line B. Trace line B and then trace the side seam from line B to the waistline. Mark notches where line A meets the waistline and the side seam. Draw a grainline parallel to center front. Label this new pattern piece with "Pocket" and "Cut 2."

8 Place a piece of paper under the skirt front pattern and with your sharp tracing wheel, trace line A and line B. Trace the waistline and the side seam connecting line A and line B. Draw a grainline parallel to center front. Label this new pattern piece with "Pocket Facing" and "Cut 2."

9 On the front skirt pattern, cut along line A and discard the resulting section. Erase line B.

10 Add ½-in. seam allowances to all edges, except along the centers. Add an additional 1 in. to the lower skirt edges for the hem.

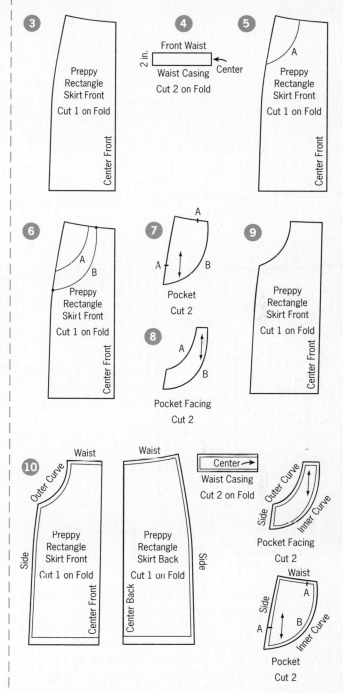

CUT UP, SEW UP

1 Cut one skirt front, one skirt back, and two waistline casings on the fold. Cut two pockets and two pocket facings. Clip notches. Cut a rectangle of fabric big enough to create a drawstring tube at least double your full waist measurement and ¾ in. wide (see page 21).

2 Right sides together, pin and stitch the pocket facings to the skirt front along the outer curved lines. Trim the seam allowances to ¼ in. and press them toward the facing. Understitch then turn the pocket facing toward the inside of the skirt and press.

3 Right sides together, pin and stitch the pocket pieces to the pocket facings along the inner curved edges. Clean-finish the curved edges.

4 Pin and baste the pockets to the skirt along the waist and side edges, matching the skirt edges to the notches on the pocket.

5 Right sides together, pin and stitch the skirt front to the skirt back along the sides. Press open and clean-finish the seam allowances.

6 Right sides together, pin and stitch the two waistline casings along the short ends to create a circle. Press open the seam allowances.

7 Fold the casing in half with wrong sides and raw edges together. Press flat. Decide which side of the casing will be the front. Open out the casing, apply the interfacing scrap to the inside center front and then stitch two ¾ in. vertical buttonholes next to each other. Refold the casing.

8 Pin and stitch the casing to the skirt, matching raw edges and side seams, making sure the side with the button-holes faces the skirt front. Stitch through all three layers. Clean-finish the seam allowances and press them toward the skirt. Topstitch close to the seam on the skirt side, catching the seam allowances underneath.

9 Create a long tube drawstring to thread through the waistline casing. Tie knots and trim the ends of the drawstring for a clean-finish.

10 Hem the skirt's lower edge. Fold and press the edge under ½ in. Fold the edge under another 1 in. and pin the hem in place. Stitch in place along the first folded edge.

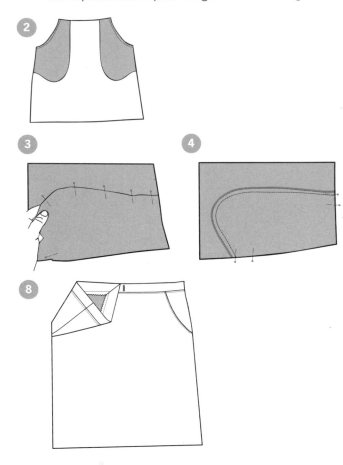

SUIT SKIRT

By Josephine Beckett

Sewing Level 2

Sport coats and suit jackets are not just for wearing to work anymore. With Josie's special treatment, they now make girls happy in the form of a mini suit skirt.

Choose a man or woman's suit jacket and make sure that, buttoned up, the bottom section fits over your hips. Whether you go for elegant black wool, like Josie, or opt for a loud plaid, try to look for a double-breasted suit jacket with interesting buttons.

A belt tie from an old coat, a man's tie, or a heavy ribbon can all be used for your waistband, or grab a bit of matching fabric to sew your own.

This skirt is quick to sew up—in a flash of scissors and stitches you'll turn an unremarkable jacket into a smart mini.

Measure Up!

Full Waist 3
(Check out page 34 for specific measuring instructions.)

Josephine Beckett

Josie is a fashion girl who didn't study fashion and a designer who doesn't follow trends. Quite simply, she makes clothes she loves. Her garments are lovingly made from vintage or hard-to-find materials, many from all over the world. Josie's line of refashioned clothing, Whereareyounow?, currently stocks a concession in three of TopShop's flagship stores in London, as well as a range of independent boutiques. For more information, visit www.whereisjosienow.com.

Mix It Up

⊕ For added fun, change the buttons or add lace trim.

⊕ Wear it backward for a different look altogether.

⊕ Cut off the sleeves from the jacket top section and shape the armholes to create a baggy mini-vest.

CUT UP, SEW UP

1 Fold the lapels of the buttoned jacket under so they lie flat on top of each other.

2 Decide how long you want your skirt to be. Measure from your waist down to where you want the finished skirt length. The recommended length for a size 6/8 is approximately 14 in. Adjust as needed for your size. On the jacket, measure up from the hemline this distance and add ½ in. for seam allowances. Use a fabric pencil to mark a cutting line all the way around the jacket and then cut the skirt from the jacket through single layers.

3 Unbutton the skirt and open it out so you are looking at one long strip of fabric. Clean-finish the upper raw edge.

4 If you are recycling a tie or ribbon for your waistband, skip to step **5**. To make a waistband from scratch, measure the upper edge of the skirt and cut a 4-in.-wide rectangle of fabric this length plus about 30 in. Right sides together, fold the rectangle in half lengthwise with right sides facing. Pin and stitch 15 in. of each side of the long raw edges together with a ½-in. seam allowance, leaving the middle unstitched. Pin and stitch the short ends. Trim the stitched seam allowances to ¼ in., but don't trim the unstitched middle section. Turn the waistband ties right-side out and press them flat.

5 Right sides together, pin and stitch the waistband to the upper edge of the skirt. Allow enough extra length at both ends to tie it in front. If the skirt overlaps by a significant amount, make sure the tie end of the underlay side starts at the overlap. Because the upper edge of the skirt was clean-finished in step **3**, the underlap will be fine left as is. If you made your own waistband, center the unstitched middle section on the upper skirt edge, and pin, stitch, and clean-finish the raw edges.

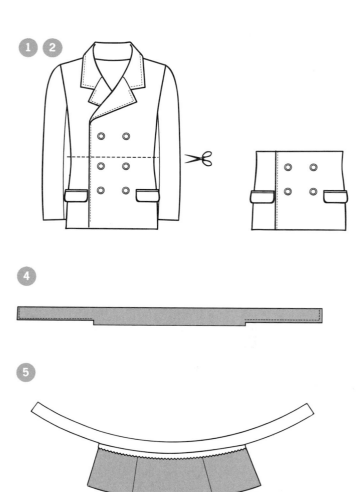

TRUSTY PENCIL SKIRT

Pattern Level 2 Sewing Level 3

Every girl needs a trusty black pencil skirt in her closet. From a normal day at the office to a white-hot Friday night, you can style a pencil skirt to work in almost any situation. Lately, my favorite options include tucking in a sweet blouse and wrapping the waist with an eye-catching wide belt or layering a ridiculously large sweater over the slim shape.

Measure Up!

Full Waist ③
(Check out page 34 for specific measuring instructions.)

Since the skirt hugs the body, the best fabrics to use are medium-weight woven ones with a bit of stretch, or light-stretch stable knit fabrics. I recycled a long boring black dress to make my trusty pencil skirt. Try to find something similar for yours since you'll need at least a yard of fabric to put it together.

Special Gear

⊕ **"YOU" DRESS SKIRT Front and Back patterns from page 44** or a ready-made basic skirt pattern (no seam or hem allowance)

⊕ Invisible zipper (see page 26 in Chapter 1 for more about determining length)

⊕ ½ in. button

⊕ ⅛ yd. light- to medium-weight interfacing

DIY PATTERN

1 Trace the **"YOU" DRESS SKIRT Front** and **Back** patterns. Measure in 1 to 2 in. along the hemline from the side seams and mark with dots. Use a curved ruler to draw new tapered side seams starting from the hip. On the back pattern, draw a 2-in. x 7-in. rectangle extension along the center back to create a kick pleat.

2 Draw a rectangle the width equal to your **Full Waist** measurement plus 2 in. and 3 in. long. Label as "Waistband" and "Cut 1."

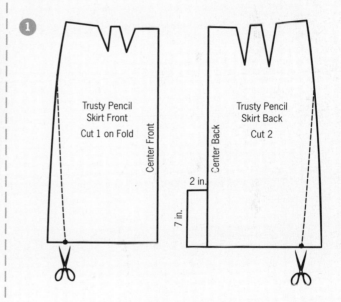

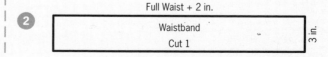

3 True the darts and add ½-in. seam allowances to all pattern edges, except along the center front. Add an additional 1 in. to the lower edge of each skirt pattern for the hem. Since the skirt is tapered inward, the hem area should taper outward slightly. Draw a grainline on the skirt back parallel to center back and on the waistband parallel to the short sides. Mark a double notch at hip level along the center back seam.

Mix It Up

⊕ Instead of creating a skirt with a waistband and a folded hem, create facings to match the waistline and the hem.

⊕ Shorten the skirt and skip the kick pleat, such as the one shown on page 60.

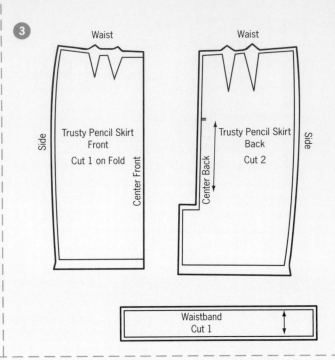

CUT UP, SEW UP

1 Cut one skirt front on the fold. Cut two skirt backs and one waistband. Clip notches. Trace the darts on the wrong side of the skirt pieces with tracing paper and a tracing wheel.

2 Stitch all the darts and press them toward the center.

3 Right sides together, pin and stitch the back skirt pieces to the front skirt along the side seams. Press open and clean-finish the seam allowances.

4 Install the invisible zipper along the center back seam and close up the remainder of the seam stopping ½ in. below the start of the kick pleat.

5 Right sides together, pin and stitch the long outer edge of the kick pleat together. Use a basting stitch to temporarily close the kick pleat along the center back. Press open the center back seam and the kick pleat, matching the center back seam with the center seam of the kick pleat. Stitch the kick pleat in place along the upper end and remove the basting stitches.

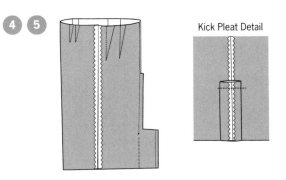

Kick Pleat Detail

6 Wrong sides together, fold and press the waistband in half with the fold parallel to the long edges. Unfold the waistband and apply a 1½-in.-wide strip of interfacing to the wrong side of the waistband piece along one side of the foldline, making sure the interfacing does not cross over into the seam allowances.

7 Clean-finish the long edge of the interfaced half of the waistband. Fold and press 1 in. of the finished edge under ½ in. on both ends.

8 Rights sides together, fold the waistband in half long edges together. Keep the interfaced edges folded under and stitch the short ends closed. Trim the seams to ¼ in. Turn the waistband right-side out and press flat.

9 Starting on the center back right side, pin and stitch the skirt edge to the non-interfaced side of the waistband right sides together. One side of the back waistband should extend from the skirt by 1 in. Once stitched, turn the waistband up and press the seams toward the waistband inside.

10 From the right side of the skirt, topstitch right on top of the seam that connects the skirt to the waistband, catching the long clean-finished edge of the waistband underneath.

11 Sew a button on the extended back waistband tab and a buttonhole on the other side.

12 Hem the lower skirt edge. Fold and press the edge under ½ in. Fold the edge under another 1 in. and pin the hem in place. Stitch in place along the first folded edge.

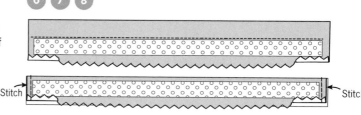

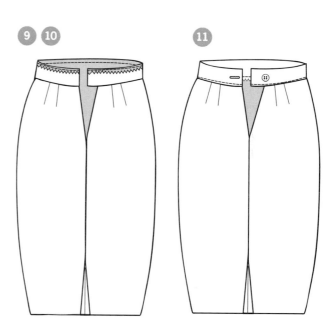

A-LINE SKIRT

Pattern Level 3 Sewing Level 3

Another timeless skirt silhouette is the A-line skirt;
so named because its "A" shape is narrow at the top
and wide at the bottom. This simple design is quite
versatile since it hangs and fits differently depending on what fabric you use and how you orient the
paper pattern on the fabric. Choose something in a
medium- to heavyweight fabric and cut the skirt on
the lengthwise direction to get a more tailored skirt,
or choose a lightweight fabric and place the pattern

on the bias to get a soft, drapey skirt that hangs closer
to the body. Woven fabrics are recommended, but
confident seamsters should feel free to experiment
with light-stretch firm knits cut on lengthwise grain.

Measure Up!

Full Hip ④		Side Hip Length ㉙
Front Waist Width ⑮		Back Dart
Back Waist Width ⑯		Front Dart
Back Hip ⑱		Dart Start

(Check out page 34 for specific measuring instructions.)

Special Gear

⊕ Invisible zipper (see page 26 in Chapter 1 for more
   about determining length)

⊕ ¼ yd. light- to medium-weight interfacing

DIY PATTERN

1 Follow the **"YOU" DRESS SKIRT** steps **1** to **4** on
   page 44.

2 Divide your **Back Dart** measurement in half and then
   add to this calculation your **Dart Start** measurement
   plus ⅝ in. Mark a dot along the waistline this distance
   from center back. Divide your **Front Dart** measurement
   in half and then add to this calculation your **Dart Start**
   measurement plus ⅝ in. Mark a dot along the waistline
   this distance from center front.

3 Draw a 4½-in. line parallel to center front/center back
   from each of the dots along the waistline.

4 Add your **Back Dart** and **Front Dart** measurements
   together, and then divide that calculation by four. Measure
   out this distance from both sides of each waistline dot
   and mark with dots. Connect each of the new dots to the
   bottom points of the lines to create darts. Extend the
   lower pattern edges to your desired skirt length.

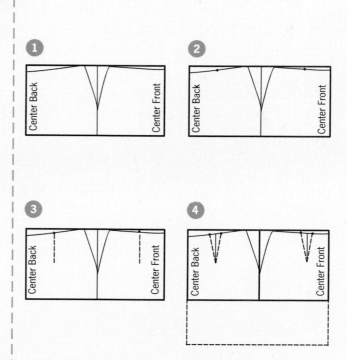

5 Cut and separate the front and back patterns. Draw a line from the dart point to the hem, parallel to center front/center back on each pattern.

6 Starting at the hem, cut along the lines, stopping just short of the dart points. Close the darts and tape them closed to shift the fullness from the darts to the hem. Measure the width of the gap in the hem and jot it down for future use as "flare."

7 Secure each of the patterns to a fresh piece of paper. Trace around the pattern with a sharp tracing wheel. Remove the cut up pattern and use rulers and a pencil to follow the tracing marks and clean up the pattern, creating smooth waistlines and hems.

8 If you want more flare, divide the "flare" measurement in half and extend outward along the hem this distance. Taper the new side seam to meet the hip, making sure the side seam length stays the same and that the intersection of the side seam and the hem is square. Smooth the hem as necessary.

9 To create a waistline facing, place a piece of paper under each of the patterns and trace the waistline shape, 2 in. of the center front/center back lines, and 2 in. of the side seams. Finish the facing patterns by drawing a curved line consistently 2 in. from the waistline curve, closing up the pattern. Label with "Front Waist Facing" and "Back Waist Facing."

10 Add ½-in. seam allowances to all pattern edges except along center fronts and center backs. Add an additional 1 in. to the lower edges for the hem. Draw an alternative bias grainline on each skirt pattern 45° from the center front and center back and write "Cut 1 on Fold."

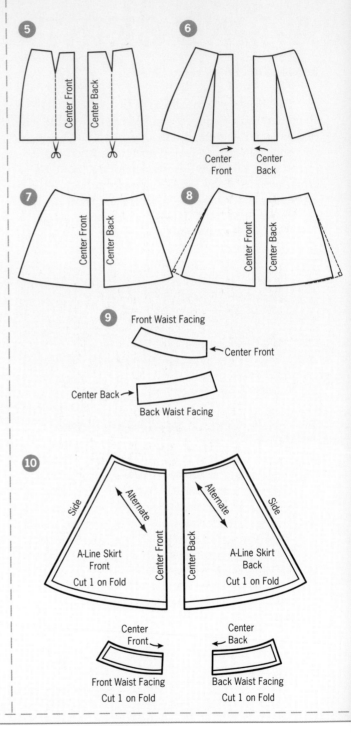

CUT UP, SEW UP

1 Cut one skirt front, one skirt back, one front facing, and one back facing, each on the fold. You can either fold woven fabric along the lengthwise grain or bias; knit skirts should only be cut on the lengthwise grain. Cut each of the facing patterns from interfacing and apply to the facing wrong sides. Open up each of the pieces face-up on the table. Clip a notch 3 in. from the waistline on the right edge of the front skirt and the left edge of the back skirt. Clip a notch on the left edge of the front facing and the right edge of the back facing.

2 Right sides together, pin and stitch the front skirt to the back skirt along the notched side. Press open and clean-finish the seam allowances.

3 Right sides together, pin and stitch the front facing to the back facing along the notched side. Press open and clean-finish the seam allowances. Clean-finish the lower facing edge.

4 Install an invisible zipper along the open skirt side seam and close up the remainder of the seam below the zipper.

5 Right sides together, pin and stitch the facing to the skirt waist, matching side seams. Trim the seam to ¼ in., press it toward the facing, and understitch. Turn the short raw edges of the facing under and hand stitch them to the zipper. Hand stitch the lower edge of the facing to the inside of the skirt.

6 If you cut the skirt on the bias, let it hang overnight, try it on, and recut the hemline evenly if needed. Hem the skirt lower edge, easing in the fullness. Fold and press the edge under ½ in. Fold the edge under another 1 in. and pin the hem in place. Stitch in place along the first folded edge.

Mix It Up

⊕ Instead of cutting both skirts on the fold, add a ½-in. seam allowance to one of the center edges and install a zipper.

⊕ Create a waistband instead of a waistline facing.

PLACKET TRICK A-LINE SKIRT

Pattern Level 3 Sewing Level 2

By placing the center edge of the A-line skirt pattern on top of a large garment with a buttoned placket, you can easily create a button-up skirt without going through the whole fuss of creating a placket with buttons and buttonholes from scratch. I made my skirt from a floor-length gathered skirt, but you can recycle any large garment that has an existing placket. If your A-line pattern is a miniskirt, you might look to recycle an XL man's button-up shirt.

Special Gear

⊕ **A-LINE SKIRT** pattern from page 89

⊕ ¼ yd. light- to medium-weight interfacing

⊕ One button (same size as buttons on original placket)

DIY PATTERN

1 Measure the waistlines on the **A-LINE SKIRT Front** and **Back** patterns, do not include seam allowance. Add the measurements together and multiply by two. Then measure the placket width on the garment you are recycling and add this measurement to your earlier calculation. Draw a rectangle with this number as the width and 3 in. as the length. (If the garment you're recycling has a waistband that fits you, skip this step and go directly to the Cut Up, Sew Up instructions.)

2 Add ½-in. seam allowances to the entire pattern and draw a grainline parallel to the short side. Label with "Waistband" and "Cut 1."

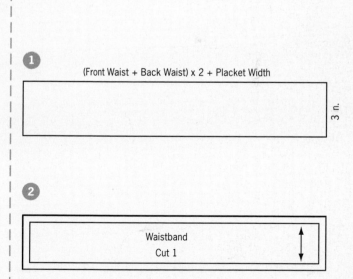

CUT UP, SEW UP

1 Remove any seams or darts in your garment that might keep it from lying flat on the table in a single layer. If the garment has a waistband, remove it and set aside. Place the A-line skirt front pattern face-up on top of the garment with the center front edge lined up along the center of the buttoned placket. The pattern upper edge should be at least 1 in. above the upper button. Pin the pattern in place and cut it out along the waist, side seam, and hem only. You should now have half of the skirt cut out. Remove the pattern and place it facedown on top of the placket to cut out the other side of the skirt front.

2 Cut one of the back skirt patterns on the fold. Cut one waistband.

3 Right sides together, pin and stitch the front skirt to the back skirt along the side seams. Press open and clean-finish the seam allowances.

4 Reattach the original waistband, if applicable, and skip to step **11**. If you made your own waistband, follow steps **5** to **10** below.

5 Wrong sides together, fold and press the waistband with the fold parallel to the long edges. Unfold the waistband and apply a 1½-in.-wide interfacing strip to the wrong side of the waistband piece along one side of the foldline, making sure the interfacing doesn't cross over into the seam allowances.

6 Clean-finish the long edge of the interfaced side of the waistband. Fold and press 1 in. of the clean-finished edge under ½ in. on both ends.

7 Right sides together, fold the waistband in half with the fold parallel to the long edges. Keep the interfaced edges folded under at the sides and stitch the short ends closed. Trim the seams to ¼ in., turn the waistband right-side out and press flat.

8 Unbutton the placket. Right sides together, pin the skirt edge to the non-interfaced side of the waistband. Stitch the waistband in place and press the seams toward the waistband inside.

9 From the right side of the skirt, topstitch on top of the seam that connects the skirt to the waistband, catching the long edge of the waistband underneath.

10 Stitch a button and buttonhole on the waistband in line with the rest of the placket.

11 Hem the skirt lower edge. Fold and press the edge under ½ in. Fold the edge under another 1 in. and pin the hem in place. Hand stitch in place along the first folded edge.

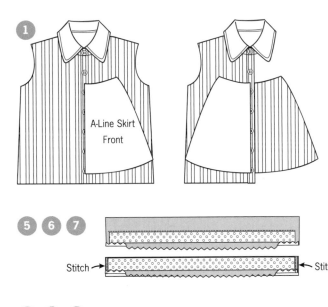

A-Line Skirt Front

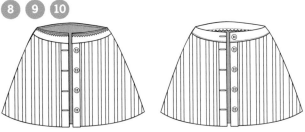

Stitch →   ← Stitch

TIERED SKIRT

Pattern Level 3 Sewing Level 3

I adore all things cute and feminine like ruffled skirts and dresses, especially when mixed into outfits with a bit of an edge or a hint of the casual. The multiple girly ruffles on this skirt makes adjusting the number, size, fullness, and location of each tier an opportunity for creativity and personalization. Since the ruffles are gathered, it's best to avoid bulky, heavyweight fabrics that don't gather well. Look for large woven items to redesign or piece together smaller items to get enough fabric for the tier widths needed. The underskirt can be made from the same fabric as the tiers or from something similar.

Special Gear

- ⊕ **A-LINE SKIRT** pattern from page 89 (no seam or hem allowances)
- ⊕ ¼ yd. light- to medium-weight interfacing
- ⊕ Invisible zipper (see page 26 in Chapter 1 for more about determining length)
- ⊕ ½ in. button

DIY PATTERN

1 Trace the **A-LINE SKIRT Front** and **Back** patterns onto a large piece of paper, connecting the sides to create one pattern piece. Label center front and center back edges. Clean up the waistline and hem, if necessary, creating smooth curves. Mark a double notch along the center back line at hip level.

2 Divide the center front line into three equal sections and mark with dots. Repeat for the center back and side lines. Hint: Center front and center back might not be equal in length. Connect the corresponding dots with smooth curves. Label the resulting sections "Underskirt 1," "Underskirt 2," and "Underskirt 3." Write "Cut 1 on Fold" on each section. Cut the sections apart.

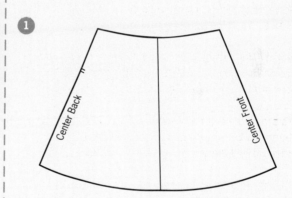

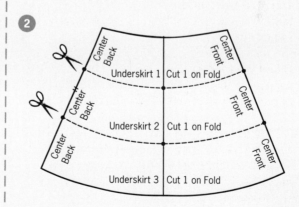

3 Measure the upper edge of Underskirt 1 and multiply by two. Draw a rectangle with this calculation as the width. The length of the rectangle is 2 in. longer than Underskirt 1. Label with "Tier 1."

4 Measure the upper edge of Underskirt 2 and multiply by two. Draw a rectangle with this calculation as the width. The length of the rectangle is 1½ times the length of Tier 1. Label with "Tier 2."

5 Measure the upper edge of Underskirt 3 and multiply by two. Draw a rectangle with this calculation as the width. The length of the rectangle is the same as Tier 2. Label with "Tier 3." Label one edge of each tier center front and write "Cut 1 on Fold."

6 Measure the upper edge of Underskirt 1, multiply it by two, and add 1 in. Draw a rectangle with this calculation as the width and 3 in. as the length. Draw a grainline parallel to the side edge and write "Waistband" and "Cut 1."

7 Add ½-in. seam allowances to the edges of all pattern pieces, except along center front.

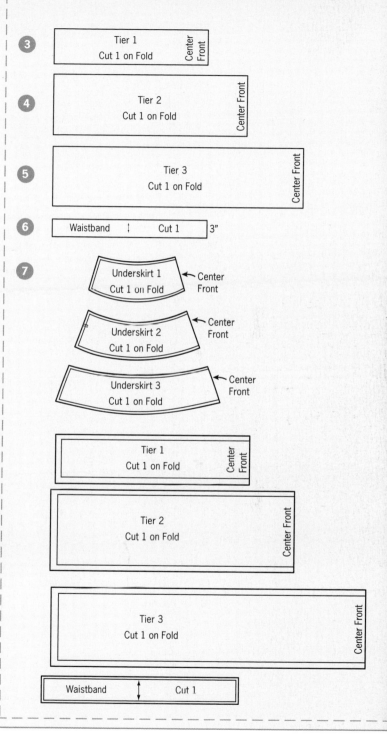

CUT UP, SEW UP

1 Cut one waistband pattern. Cut one of each of the remaining patterns on the fold. If you don't have enough fabric to cut the tiers on the fold, cut them in sections and seam together, or piece together several rectangles of fabric until you have enough width. Clip notches. Clip additional notches at center front on the upper and lower edges of each pattern piece.

2 Narrowly roll hem the lower and side edges of each tier.

3 Gather the upper edge of Tier 1 to match the upper edge of Underskirt 1. With the right side of the underskirt facing the wrong side of the tier, pin and stitch them together along the upper edge using a 3/8-in. seam allowance. Match the center front notches and make sure the gathered tier doesn't extend into the seam allowance at center back. Repeat for the other two tier sections.

4 Right sides together, pin and stitch the upper edge of Underskirt 2 and Tier 2 to the lower edge of Underskirt 1, matching notches. Clean-finish the seam allowances and press them downward.

5 Right sides together, pin and stitch the upper edge of Underskirt 3 and Tier 3 to the lower edge of Underskirt 2, matching notches. Clean-finish the seam allowances and press them downward. Clean-finish the lower edge of Underskirt 3.

6 Install a zipper along center back and sew up the remainder of the seam, being careful not to catch the ends of the tiers in the seam.

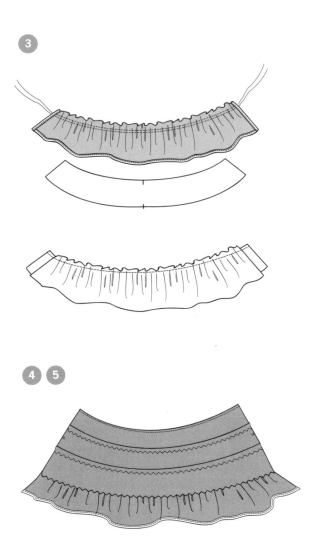

7 Wrong sides together, fold and press the waistband in half with the fold parallel to the long edges. Unfold the waistband and apply a 1½-in.-wide interfacing strip to the wrong side of the waistband along one side of the foldline, making sure the interfacing doesn't cross over into the seam allowances.

8 Clean-finish the long edge of the interfaced side of the waistband. Fold and press 1 in. of the clean-finished edge under ½ in. on both ends.

9 Right sides together, fold the waistband in half with the fold parallel to the long edges. Keep the interfaced edges folded under at the sides and stitch the short ends closed. Trim the seams to ¼ in.; turn the waistband right-side out and press flat.

10 Starting at center back, pin and stitch the skirt edge to the non-interfaced side of the waistband right sides together. One side of the back waistband should extend 1 in. Turn the waistband up and press the seams to the inside.

11 From the right side of the skirt, topstitch right on top of the seam that connects the skirt to the waistband, catching the finished edge of the waistband underneath.

12 Sew a button on the extended back waistband tab and a buttonhole on the other side.

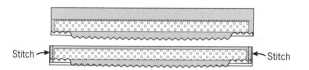

Stitch →   ← Stitch

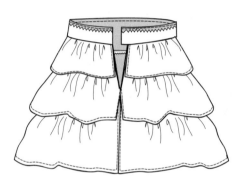

BUBBLE SKIRT

Pattern Level 3 Sewing Level 3

Sure, bubble skirts are cute and youthful, but they can also be figure flattering. In particular, I like how the waistband shows off the fitted high waist, while the gathered fullness just below the waist allows you to let your tummy relax just enough until the pegged hemline slims it back up again. The belt loops along the waistband let you wear a fun skinny belt, drawing the eye toward the waist even more. I like to wear mine layered over leotards and fitted blouses. To bubble-ize your wardrobe, salvage any medium-weight woven fabric in your favorite solid colors or an unusual print.

Special Gear

⊕ **TRUSTY PENCIL SKIRT Front and Back patterns** from page 85 (no seam or hem allowances)

⊕ **Invisible zipper** (see page 26 in Chapter 1 for more about determining length)

⊕ ½ in. button

⊕ ¼ yd. light- to medium-weight interfacing

⊕ Tube turner

DIY PATTERN

1 Trace the **TRUSTY PENCIL SKIRT Front** and **Back** patterns.

2 On the front pattern, draw a line from each of the dart points to the hem parallel to center front. Draw an additional line from the waist to the hem 1½ in. away from center front.

3 Starting at the upper edge, cut along each of the lines, stopping just short of the hem. Tape the pattern center front to a large, fresh piece of paper. Spread the sections apart 1½ in. at the waist and tape them in place. Trace around the new pattern shape with a sharp tracing wheel. Remove the cut up pattern and use rulers and a pencil to follow the tracing and create the final pattern shape. Label with "Bubble Skirt Front" and "Cut 1 on Fold."

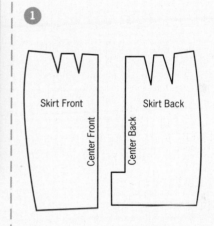

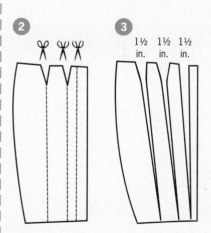

4 Repeat steps **2** to **3** for the back pattern, except spread the sections apart by only 1 in. Label with "Bubble Skirt Back" and "Cut 2."

5 Divide your **Full Waist** measurement in half and add ¼ in. Draw a 1½-in.-tall rectangle with the width equal to this calculation.

6 Cut the rectangle in half and label one side "Back Waistband" and the other "Front Waistband."

7 On the back waistband, label one side center back and extend it by 1 in. On the opposite side, mark a notch halfway down the side. Label with "Cut 4."

8 On the front waistband, label one edge center front. On the opposite side, mark a notch halfway down the side. Label with "Cut 2 on Fold."

9 Draw a 1-in. x 18-in. rectangle and label with "Belt Loops" and "Cut 1." Draw a grainline parallel to the short end.

10 Add ½-in. seam allowances to all pattern edges, except the belt loop pattern and the center front edges. Add an additional 1 in. to the lower edge of each skirt pattern for the hem. Since the skirt is tapered inward, the hem should taper outward slightly. Draw a grainline on the skirt back parallel to center back and on the back waistband parallel to the short sides. Mark a notch 5 in. below the waist along the sides of both skirts. Mark a double notch at hip level along center back.

11 Follow DIY pattern step **4** for the **DELUXE RECTANGLE SKIRT** on page 107 to create the pocket pattern.

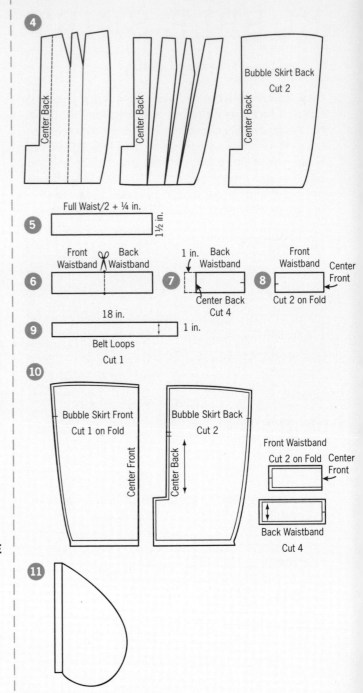

CUT UP, SEW UP

1 Cut one front skirt and two front waistbands on the fold, two back skirts, four back waistbands, and four pockets. Clip all notches. Clip an extra notch on the front skirt piece at the center front waist. Clip additional notches on both long edges of the front waistband pieces at center front. Cut one front waistband and two back waistbands from interfacing and trim ½ in. off each edge. Apply the interfacing to the wrong side of the matching pieces.

2 Right sides together, pin one pocket to each of the four sides of the skirt with the upper pocket edge lined up at the notch and the pocket bag pointing downward. Stitch the pockets to the skirt along the edges using a ⅜-in. seam allowance.

3 Flip the pockets outward and press the seam allowances toward the pockets.

4 Right sides together, pin the skirt backs to the front along the side seams, pinning the outer edges of the pockets together. Use a ½-in. seam allowance to stitch the sides together, pivoting around the pockets. Press open and clean-finish the seam allowances where possible.

5 Install a zipper along the center back seam and close up the remainder of the seam stopping ½ in. below the start of the kick pleat.

6 Right sides together, pin and stitch the long outer edge of the kick pleat together. Use a basting stitch to temporarily close the kick pleat along the center back. Press open the center back seam and the kick pleat, matching the center back seam with the kick pleat center seam. Tack the kick pleat in place along the upper edge and remove the basting stitches.

Mix It Up

⊕ Experiment with the fullness by increasing the amount of spread at the waist.

⊕ Cut and spread any number of lines at an angle instead of parallel to center front.

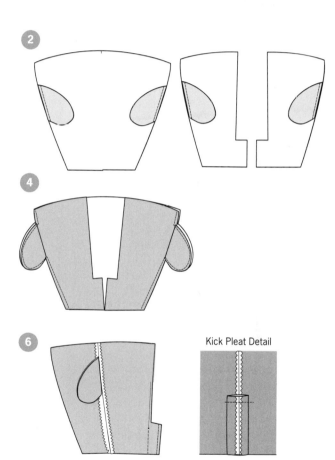

Kick Pleat Detail

7 Right sides together, pin and stitch the interfaced waistband pieces together along the short notched edges. Press seams open and repeat for the other waistband pieces.

8 Right sides together, fold the belt loop piece in half with the fold parallel to the long edges. Pin and stitch the long raw edges together using a ¼-in. seam allowance. Turn the loop strip right-side out using a tube turner. Press it flat with the seam down the center of one side. Cut the belt loop into 6 pieces, each 3 in. long.

9 Pin and stitch the belt loops to the non-interfaced waistband along the long edges, making sure the belt loop wrong side is facing the waistband right side. Place loops at the side seams and then space evenly along the waistband finished length. Baste the belt loops in place within the seamline at both edges.

10 Right sides together, pin and stitch the interfaced waistband to the non-interfaced waistband along one long edge, matching side seams. Note: The belt loops will be sandwiched between the layers. Trim the seam to ¼ in. Clean-finish the unstitched, long edge of the interfaced waistband.

11 Fold and press 2 in. of the clean-finished edge under ½ in. on both ends. Keep the interfaced edges folded under at the sides and stitch the short ends closed. Stitch one side with a ½-in. seam allowance and the other side with a 1½-in. seam allowance. Trim the seams to ¼ in. Turn the waistband right-side out and press flat.

12 Gather the upper skirt edge to fit the waistband.

13 Right sides together, pin the gathered skirt edge to the non-interfaced side of the waistband, matching raw edges, side seams, and center front notches. Adjust the gathers to fit. One side of the back waistband should be wider than the skirt by 1 in. Stitch the skirt to the waistband, turn the waistband upward, and press the seams toward the inside.

14 From the right side of the skirt, topstitch on top of the seam that connects the skirt to the waistband, catching the finished edge of the waistband underneath.

15 Sew a button on the extended back waistband tab and a buttonhole on the side with no extension.

16 Hem the lower skirt edge. Fold and press the edge under ½ in. Fold the edge under another 1 in. and pin the hem in place. Stitch in place along the first folded edge.

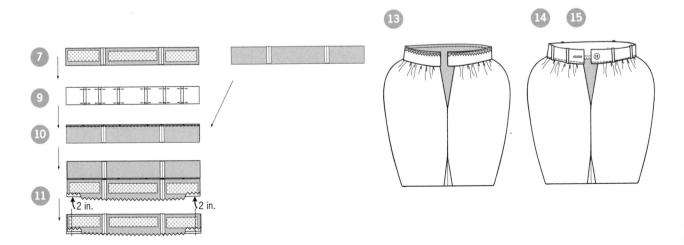

DELUXE RECTANGLE SKIRT

Pattern Level 3 Sewing Level 3

I adore drawstring and elastic waists, but occasionally I like to step it up a notch and go for a more put-together waistband for my gathered rectangle skirts. Here, a basic rectangle skirt gets dolled up with pockets and is gathered into one of two types of waistbands: a skinny waistband with belt loops or a wide midriff waistband. Recycle anything with enough space to cut out all your rectangles, and keep in mind that light- to medium-weight woven fabrics work best with gathers.

Special Gear

- ⊕ ULTRA MINISKIRT pattern, page 75 (no seam or hem allowance)

- ⊕ ¼ yd. interfacing

- ⊕ Invisible zipper (see page 26 in Chapter 1 for more about determining length)

- ⊕ ½ in. button (for skinny waistband option)

DIY PATTERN

1 Trace the **ULTRA MINISKIRT Front** and **Back** patterns onto new pieces of paper, include notches. Extend the length and width as desired. Remember, more width equals more gathers.

2 On the back pattern, measure ¼ in. down from the upper edge along center back and mark with a dot. Use your curved ruler to taper and trim the upper edge of the pattern to meet the dot, making sure it meets center back at a square angle.

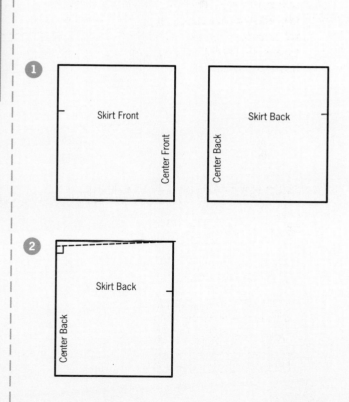

3 Add ½- in. seam allowances to the edges of both patterns, except along center front. Add an additional 1 in. to the lower edges for the hem. Draw a grainline on the back pattern parallel to center back. Mark a double notch along center back at hip level.

4 To draw a side seam pocket pattern, measure from your wrist to your longest fingertip and add 1 in. Draw a ½-in.-wide rectangle with this measurement. Measure the width of your hand and add 3 in. Draw a bubble at this width radiating out from the rectangle upper edge and dipping down slightly below the rectangle and traveling back up to meet it at the lower edge, as shown.

5 For the skinny waistband, follow DIY pattern steps **5** to **10** for the **BUBBLE SKIRT** on page 102. For the wide waistband, follow the DIY pattern directions for the **NIP-WAIST DRESS** on page 173.

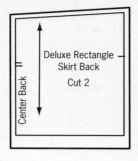

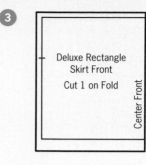

CUT UP, SEW UP

1 For the skirt with the skinny waistband, follow Cut Up, Sew Up steps **1** to **16** for the **BUBBLE SKIRT** on page 103, ignoring the kick pleat instructions.

2 For the skirt with the wide waistband, follow Cut Up, Sew Up steps **1** to **5** for the **BUBBLE SKIRT** on page 103, ignoring the kick pleat reference, and then follow the instructions below. When cutting out the front waistband, fold the fabric along the bias.

3 Right sides together, pin and stitch the interfaced waistband pieces together along the short notched edges. Press open the seams. Repeat for the other waistband pieces.

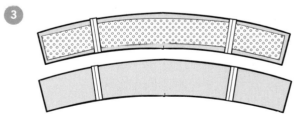

4 Right sides together, pin and stitch the interfaced waistband to the non-interfaced waistband along the upper edge, matching side seams. Trim the seam to ¼ in., turn right-side out, and press. Wrong sides facing, baste the remaining edges of the waistband together ⅜ in. from the edge.

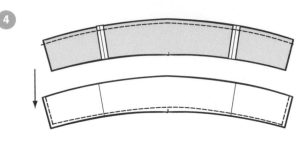

5 Gather the upper skirt edge to fit the waistband.

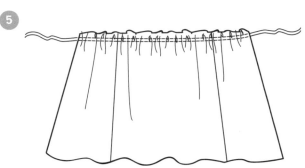

6 Right sides together, pin and stitch the gathered skirt edge to the waistband, matching side seams and center front notches. Clean-finish the seam allowances and press them toward the skirt.

7 Install a zipper along center back, positioning the upper zipper stop at the waistband upper edge. Close up the remainder of the seam.

8 Hem the skirt's lower edge. Fold and press the edge under ½ in. Fold the edge under another 1 in. and pin the hem in place. Stitch in place along the first folded edge.

Mix It Up

⊕ Cut off the lower edge of a vintage dress and gather it into a waistband made out of the bodice fabric.

⊕ Make a gathered skirt from a circle instead of a rectangle or mess around with various angles on a paneled trapezoid.

⊕ Change the shape and size of the midriff waistband.

SWOOSH SKIRT

Pattern Level 3 Sewing Level 4

Color-blocking is one of my favorite methods of designing something from old clothes. There is an art to color-blocking, though. Piece together the right fabrics—colors and prints as well as textures and weights that complement each other—or you'll end up with a garment that looks weird. To make this swoosh skirt, start with one or more inspiration garments, cut off little swatches, and head to the thrift store to find matching fabrics. I had four different colors in my skirt, but you could have more or less as you see fit.

Measure Up!

Full Waist ❸

(Check out page 34 for specific measuring instructions.)

Special Gear

⊕ **"YOU" DRESS SKIRT Front and Back** patterns from page 44 or a ready-made basic skirt pattern (no seam or hem allowance)

⊕ Invisible zipper (see page 26 in Chapter 1 for more about determining length)

⊕ ½ in. button

⊕ ¼ yard light- to medium-weight interfacing

DIY PATTERN

1 Trace the **"YOU" DRESS SKIRT Front** and **Back** patterns. Shorten both patterns to the desired length plus 1 in.

2 On the front pattern, mark a dot ½ in. below the waistline at the side seam. Mark another dot 1½ in. below the first. Draw a line from the bottom of the outer dart to the lower dot.

3 Starting from the outer edge of the side seam, cut along the line, stopping just short of the dart point. Shift the loose section to close the dart and create a new one at the side. Tape in place.

4 Repeat step **3** to move the remaining waist dart to the upper dot along the side seam.

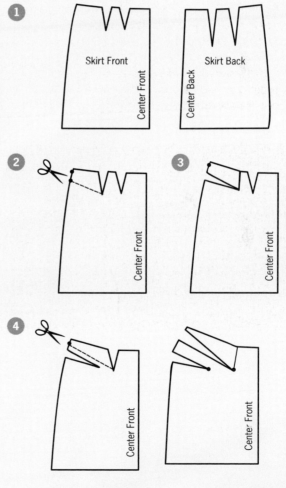

5 Fold a large piece of paper in half; secure the skirt front pattern on top of it with center front on top of the fold. Trace the new pattern with a sharp tracing wheel. Remove the cut up pattern and unfold the paper. Use rulers and a pencil to follow the tracing and create a full front pattern piece, smoothing out the angles along the waistline. Include the center front line to use as a grainline. On the left side, mark two dots 1½ in. apart and below the lower dart.

6 Draw four cutting lines on the skirt, as shown. The top two lines start from the left dart points; the bottom two start from the left side dots. Mark a single notch on the first line, a double notch on the second line, a triple notch on the third line, and a quadruple notch on the fourth line. Label each piece "1" through "5" and then cut them apart.

7 Draw a rectangle with the width equal to your **Full Waist** measurement plus 2 in. and the length 3 in. Label with "Waistband" and "Cut 1."

8 True the darts on front skirt section 1 as well as the back skirt pattern. Add ½-in. seam allowances to all pattern edges. Draw a grainline on the skirt back parallel to center back, on the waistband parallel to the short sides, and on the skirt front section 5 perpendicular to the lower edge. Mark a double notch along center back at hip level. Write "Cut 1" on each front skirt section.

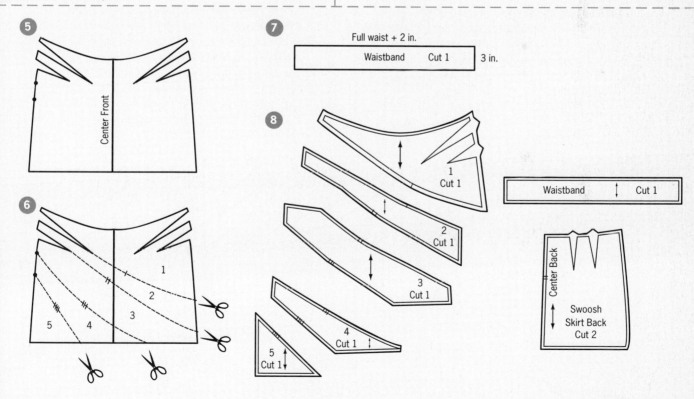

CUT UP, SEW UP

1 Cut one of each front skirt section in various colors. Since the design is asymmetrical, be sure to cut the pieces on the right side of all the fabrics. Cut two skirt backs and one waistband. Clip notches. Trace the darts on the wrong side of the skirt pieces with tracing paper and a tracing wheel.

2 Stitch the back skirt darts and press them toward the center. Stitch the darts on section 1 of the front skirt and press them downward.

3 For the decorative flat piping, cut several 1½-in.-wide bias strips (in skirt base fabric or any other you prefer) and fold them in half lengthwise with wrong sides facing. Pin the folded bias strip to the lower edge of skirt front section 1, matching raw edges. Right sides together, pin and stitch front skirt section 1 to skirt front section 2, matching notches, with the bias strip sandwiched between the two layers. Trim the seam to ¼ in. Clean-finish the seam allowances and press them downward. Repeat until all sections of the skirt front are sewn together.

4 Right sides together, pin and stitch the back skirt pieces to the skirt front along the side seams. Press open and clean-finish the seam allowances.

5 Install a zipper along the center back seam and close up the remainder of the seam.

6 Wrong sides together, fold and press the waistband in half with the fold parallel to the long edges. Unfold the waistband and apply a 1½-in.-wide strip of interfacing to the wrong side of the waistband piece along one side of the foldline, making sure the interfacing does not cross over into the seam allowances.

7 Clean-finish the long edge of the interfaced side of the waistband. Fold and press 1 in. of the clean-finished edge under ½ in. on both ends.

8 Right sides together, fold the waistband in half with the fold parallel to the long edges. Keep the interfaced edges folded under at the sides and stitch the short ends closed. Trim the seams to ¼ in., turn the waistband right-side out, and press flat.

3

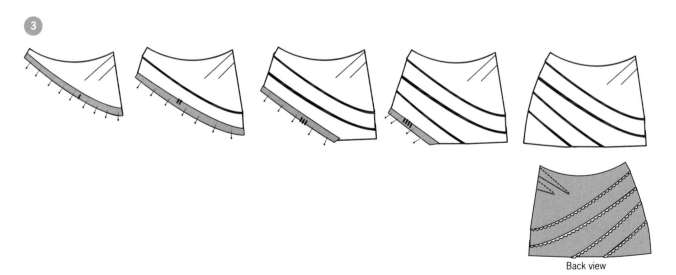

Back view

9 Right sides together and starting on the right side at center back, pin and stitch the skirt edge to the non-interfaced side of the waistband. One side of the back waistband should extend 1 in. Turn the waistband upward and press the seams toward the inside.

10 From the right side of the skirt, topstitch on top of the seam that connects the skirt to the waistband, catching the finished edge of the waistband underneath.

11 Sew a button on the extended back waistband tab and a buttonhole on the other side.

12 Hem the skirt's lower edge. Fold and press the edge under ½ in. Fold the edge under another 1 in. and pin the hem in place. Stitch in place along the first folded edge.

Mix It Up

⊕ Create your own color-block design.

⊕ Experiment with different dart placements.

6 7 8

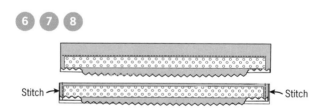

Stitch →   ← Stitch

9

10 11

Chapter 5
DRESSES

The dresses in this chapter offer a fab mix of color variations, techniques, and design ideas to add to your repertoire, including skills like adding volume, shaping new style lines, open-work, plackets, and more. Princess seams and frilly-to-the-max ruffles dominate the design work, too.

A handful of much loved indie designers also bring their best designs to this chapter. Chia Guillory reinvents drab silk garments to make a vivid **Ribbon-Striped Skirt Dress** on page 137. Mother-and-daughter team Fredda and Jennifer Perkins turn old into new with the **Bib Dress** on page 147.

Jesse Kelly-Landes demonstrates how easy it is to recycle with her **Sheer Tunic** on page 143. A dated vintage dress gets a new date for the prom from wonder girl, Amy Sperber, with her inspired **Maxi to Minidress** on page 185, while Elizabeth Dye shows you how to perform some major magic on a vintage wedding dress to create the **Bride's Dress, Revisited** on page 217.

AMBIGUOUS T DRESS

Pattern Level 1   Sewing Level 2

Why get bound up, when a carefree style like this one can be just as alluring? Slip it on over a tank or tube top and let it fall off your shoulder as you run out the door. To make this T-shape dress, rummage for oversize garments such as caftans or muumuus, or cut up interesting linens. I made mine from an experimental length of lightweight woven fabric I found at a garage sale, but feel free to test out other weights and types of fabric for your version. New seamsters should stick with medium-weight woven fabrics.

Measure Up!

Full Hip ④
(Check out page 34 for specific measuring instructions.)

Special Gear

⊕ **RECTANGLE TIE SHRUG Back pattern from page 53** (no seam allowances)

DIY PATTERN

1 Trace the **RECTANGLE TIE SHRUG Back** pattern and label the right edge "Center." Adjust the width of the rectangle from the opposite side to increase or decrease the sleeve length as desired; keep in mind that you will add 4 in. sleeve bands.

2 Measure from your center front neck to where you want the finished dress length. Subtract 4 in. from this number. Extend the center line on the pattern to this measurement.

3 Divide your **Full Hip** measurement by four and add 2 in. Square a line this distance from the lower center line to the left.

4 Use a straight ruler to connect the lower line with the double notch to create the side of the dress.

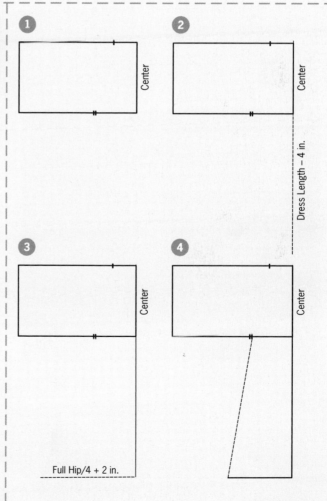

5 Transform the hard corner at the underarm into a soft curve with a curved ruler. Label with "Ambiguous T Dress" and "Cut 2 on Fold."

6 Divide your **Full Hip** measurement by four and add 2 in. Draw an 8-in.-long rectangle with this calculation as the width. Label the right side "Center." On the opposite edge, mark a notch midway down. Label the pattern "Lower Band" and "Cut 2 on Fold."

7 Draw another 8-in.-long rectangle with the width equal to the measurement of the lower sleeve edge. On both lengthwise edges, mark a notch midway down. Draw a grainline parallel to the sides. Label as "Sleeve Band" and "Cut 4."

8 Add ½-in. seam allowance to all pattern edges, except along the centers.

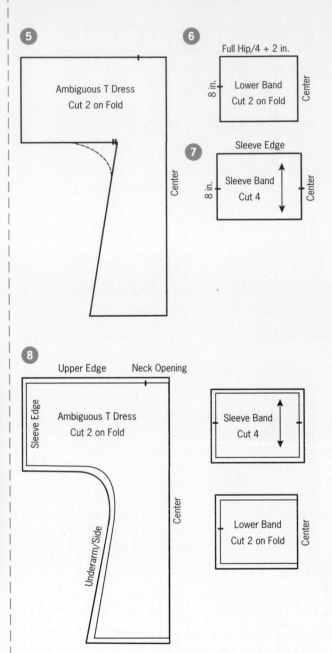

Mix It Up

⊕ Create more fullness at the hemline of the dress pattern and gather it into the band.

⊕ Make the dress in a stable heavyweight fabric and use faux fur or an ornate trim along the bands and neckline.

⊕ Use a contrasting fabric color for the bands and fuse interfacing on the wrong sides before attaching to give them extra body.

⊕ Experiment with the placement and width of the neckline for asymmetrical drama.

CUT UP, SEW UP

1 Cut two dress patterns and two lower bands on the fold. Cut four sleeve bands. Clip notches.

2 Right sides together, place the two dress pieces on top of one another. Pin and stitch the upper edge together, leaving the neck space open between the notches. (Don't forget to back stitch!) Press the seam allowances.

3 Narrowly roll hem the neck openings. Where the rolled hem meets a seam, roll slightly into the seam allowance. Clean-finish the seam allowances along the upper edge.

4 Right sides together, pin and stitch the underarm/side seams. Reinforce the underarm area with another stitching line. Press open and clean-finish the seam allowances. Clip along the underarm curve to release tension.

5 Right sides together, pin and stitch the two lower band pieces together along the short edges, matching notches. Press open the seam allowances.

6 Wrong sides together, fold the band in half with the fold parallel to the long edge. Slip the folded band over the dress lower edge, matching the raw edges and side seams. Pin and stitch all the way around the band. Clean-finish the raw edges and press them toward the band. On the outside of the dress, topstitch close to the seam on the band side, catching the seam allowances underneath.

7 Right sides together, pin and stitch two sleeve bands together along the notched edges. Press open the seam allowances. Repeat for the other two sleeve bands.

8 Repeat step **6** to attach the sleeve bands.

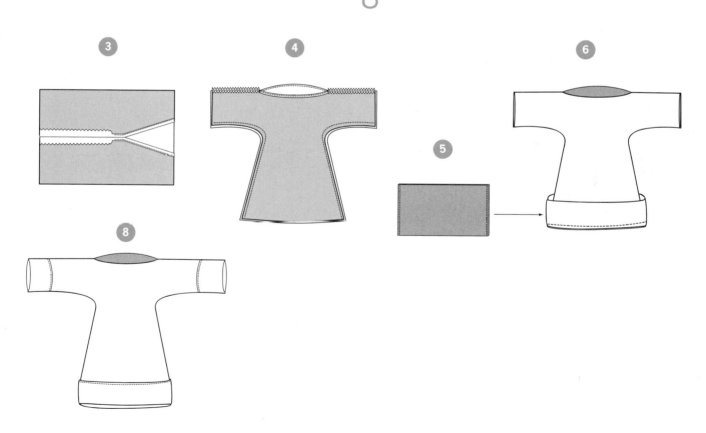

BODY TUBE

Pattern Level 1 Sewing Level 2

The body tube is like the T-shirt of the dress world. It has a comfortable and laid-back feel, but can go wild beyond the basic tube. For bold personalities, the design is great as-is with the addition of select accessories. For those of us who are a bit more timid, the body tube can be used to layer underneath a host of other garments. Try rocking it with the **Peek-A-Boo Jumper Dress** on page 177 or the **Vest**

Dress on page 165.
The pattern starts with a few main body measurements and can be tightened or loosened easily to fit like a glove in an average stretch knit. As always, use a very narrow zigzag stitch and a stretch needle for sewing knits.

Measure Up!

Full High Bust ②   **Full Hip** ④
Full Waist ③   **Side Hip Length** 29

(Check out page 34 for specific measuring instructions.)

DIY PATTERN

1   Measure from your **Full High Bust** to the desired finished length. Jot this measurement down as "Length." Divide your **Full Hip** measurement by four and jot this calculation down as "Width." Draw a rectangle using these measurements. Label the right edge "Center."

2   Measure from your **Full High Bust** to your **Full Waist**. On the pattern, measure this distance from the upper rectangle edge and draw a parallel line across the rectangle. Label the line "Waistline."

3   Measure down from the waistline your **Side Hip Length** and draw a parallel line across the rectangle. Label the line "Hipline."

4   Divide your **Full High Bust** measurement by four and measure over this distance from the center line along the upper edge; mark with a dot. Divide your **Full Waist** measurement by four and measure over this distance from the center line along the waistline; mark with a dot. Mark the left edge of the hipline with a dot. Measure inward from the left 1 in. along the lower line and mark with a dot. Connect the dots with smooth curves to create the silhouette of your body, and then cut along this line. Label the pattern "Body Tube" and "Cut 2 on Fold."

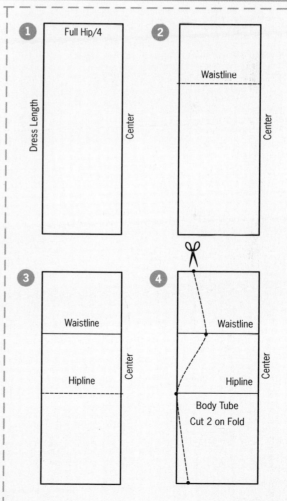

5 Subtract 1 in. from your **Full High Bust** measurement and then divide it by four. Draw a 3-in.-tall rectangle with this calculation as the width. Label "Upper Band" and "Cut 2 on Fold." Label the right edge "Center."

6 Divide your **Full Hip** measurement by four and then subtract 1¼ in. Draw a 3-in.-tall rectangle with this calculation as the width. Label "Lower Band" and "Cut 2 on Fold." Label the right edge "Center."

7 Add ⅜-in. seam allowance to all pattern pieces, except along the centers.

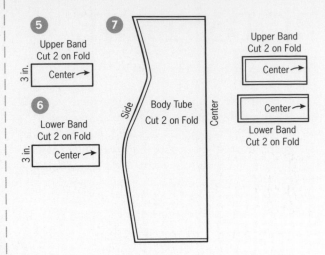

Mix It Up

⊕ Create a separate skirt or a tube top.

⊕ Create a dress that's loose on the top and fitted on the bottom. Keep the silhouette rectangle at the top and gather the top into the fitted top band.

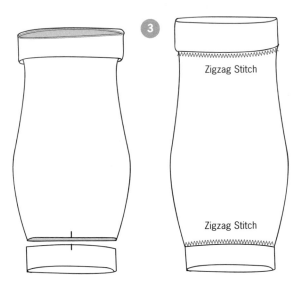

Zigzag Stitch

Zigzag Stitch

CUT UP, SEW UP

1 Cut two of each pattern on the fold. Clip center notches along the upper and lower edges of each piece.

2 Right sides together, pin and stitch the dress pieces together along the side seams. Press open the seams. Note: Clean-finishing isn't needed on most knit fabrics.

3 Right sides together, pin and stitch the upper bands together along the short ends to create a circle. Press open the seams. Wrong sides together, fold the band in half with the fold parallel to the long edge matching the raw edges. Right sides together, slip the band over the dress upper edge. Pin and stitch the band to the dress, matching side seams and notches, stretching the band slightly to fit. Press the seam toward the dress and topstitch it in place with a slightly wider zigzag stitch. Repeat for the lower band.

CAP SLEEVE CUTIE DRESS

Pattern Level 2 Sewing Level 2

If I was forced to choose one type of dress to make and wear for the rest of my life, the **Cap Sleeve Cutie Dress** would be near the top of my list. Sure, it's easy and comfortable, but it also scores major points for its classic silhouette and impressive versatility when it comes to customization. Whether you wear it loose or cinch it with a belt, introduce this core

element into your wardrobe in a variety of ways. Choose a knit fabric with light- to medium-stretch to make a slim version with a straight hem or choose a light- to medium-weight woven fabric to create a loose version with an A-line flare (shown on page 124). Either way, you'll need at least two yards of fabric from large salvaged items.

Measure Up!

Full Hip ④
(Check out page 34 for specific measuring instructions.)

Special Gear

⊕ SUCH A SQUARE BLOUSE pattern from page 61 (no seam allowance)

⊕ ½ yd. interfacing in a weight appropriate for your fabric

DIY PATTERN

1 Trace the **SUCH A SQUARE BLOUSE Front** pattern (including the underarm notch) onto a large piece of paper.

2 Measure from your shoulder at your neck down to the desired finished length (must be above knee). Draw a line this length, parallel to center front, starting at the high shoulder point.

3 Draw a perpendicular line at the end of the dress length line, representing the hemline. Don't worry about the width of this line, just draw it across the whole paper. Extend the center front line downward to meet the new hemline.

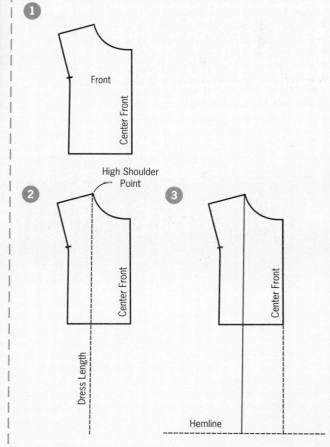

4 From this point you can go in one of two directions:

a To create a dress with a straight hem, extend the side straight down to meet the hemline. For this option to work, the dress must be wide enough to cover your hips. Measure the width of the pattern near the lower edge and multiply it by four. This number must be at least as big as your **Full Hip** measurement if using a knit fabric or larger if using a woven fabric. If it isn't, either start over with a wider Square Blouse or try option b.

b To create a dress with flare at the hem, draw another line 1 in. above the hemline and label it "Line A." Divide your **Full Hip** measurement by four and add 1½ in. (add more if you want a more dramatic A-line flare). Starting at center front, measure over this distance along Line A and mark with a dot. Draw a new side starting from the armhole notch meeting the dot on Line A. Use a curved ruler to draw a curved hemline starting at the dot and meeting center front at the hemline. Make sure the hem meets the side and center front lines at square angles.

5 Repeat steps **1** to **4** using the **SUCH A SQUARE BLOUSE Back** pattern to create the dress back. Test and correct the curved hemline on both the front and back dress patterns by placing the side seams together. Make sure the hem is a smooth shallow curve from center front to center back.

6 Add ½-in. seam allowance on all edges except the centers. Add an additional 1 in. to the lower edges for the hem. Label the patterns and write "Cut 1 on Fold." The front and back neck facings will not change from the blouse.

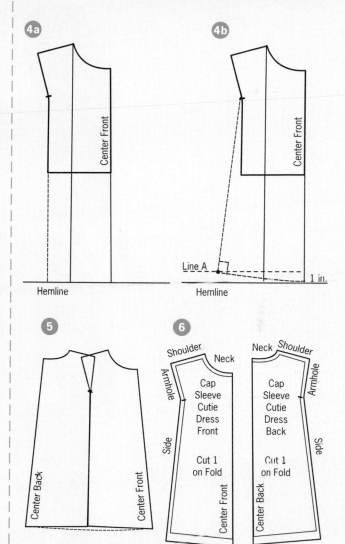

CUT UP, SEW UP

1 Cut and sew the dress in exactly the same manner as the **SUCH A SQUARE BLOUSE** (page 61), except for the hem.

2 For a straight hem, fold and press the raw edge under ½ in., fold and pin under another 1 in. to hide the raw edge, then stitch the hem in place along the first folded edge. For a flared hem, fold and press the raw edge under ¼ in., fold and pin under another 1 in. to hide the raw edge, then hand stitch the hem along first folded edge. If you're using knit fabric, only one hem fold is needed.

PIXEL DRESS

Pattern Level 2 Sewing Level 2

The Pixel Dress is essentially the straight hem, slim knit version of the **Cap Sleeve Cutie Dress** on page 123, but it's a good example of how you can cut up any pattern to color-block and use multiple fabrics in one design. I started with a vintage dress that had multiple colors already. You can use as many fabrics (and colors) as you want, but make sure they have similar amounts of stretch (light to average works best). If the stretch varies too much, you'll end up with a distorted garment—which could be cool in a trippy sort of way, or just strange.

DIY PATTERN

1 Trace a copy of the **CAP SLEEVE CUTIE DRESS Front** pattern (including notches) onto a new piece of paper. Draw a line parallel to and 14 in. above the hem and cut along the line to separate the pattern into two pieces. Label with "Upper Front" and "Lower Front."

2 Double the width of the Lower Front pattern. Measure the width of the rectangle and if it does not equal a whole even number, round it up until it does.

3 Divide the Lower Front pattern into 2-in. x 2-in. squares.

4 Measure the lower edge of the Upper Front pattern and use this measurement to draw a rectangle 2 in. high. Label the pattern with "Hem Facing" and "Cut 2 on Fold." Label the right edge "Center."

5 Add ½-in. seam allowance to the Upper Front pattern and the hem facing pattern everywhere except the centers.

6 The **CAP SLEEVE CUTIE DRESS Back** pattern, front neck facing, and back neck facing patterns remain the same.

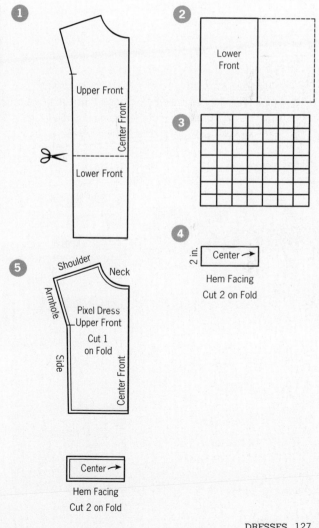

CUT UP, SEW UP

1 Cut one Upper Front dress, one **CAP SLEEVE CUTIE DRESS Back**, one front neck facing, one back neck facing, and two hem facings, all on the fold. Clip the armhole notches on the dress patterns. Cut a set of neck facings from interfacing and apply them to the facing wrong sides.

2 Count the number of squares on the Lower Front pattern and cut out that number of **3**-in. squares in various colors, making sure to align the grain of the fabric with the square edges.

3 Arrange the colored squares in a pleasing manner to match the Lower Front pattern. Starting with the upper row, pin and stitch the squares' right sides together using a ½-in. seam allowance, making sure the stretchiest fabric grain is positioned horizontally. Press open the seams as you go. Repeat for the remaining rows, and then sew the rows together, matching seamlines, to create one big rectangle.

4 Right sides together, pin and stitch the upper edge of the pixel rectangle to the lower edge of the Upper Front. Press open the seam. If the rectangle is wider than the dress front, center it and trim the edges to match.

5 Follow sewing instructions **2** to **6** on page 63 for the **SUCH A SQUARE BLOUSE**.

6 Right sides together, pin and stitch the hem facings together along the short ends to create a circle. Press open the seams. Fold and press one of the long edges of the hem facing under ½ in.

7 Right sides together, slip the hem facing over the lower dress edge, matching the raw edge of the dress with the unfolded edge of the hem facing. Pin and stitch the hem facing to the dress, matching side seams. Trim the seams to ¼ in., press the seam allowances toward the facing, and understitch. Fold the hem facing to the inside and hand stitch in place.

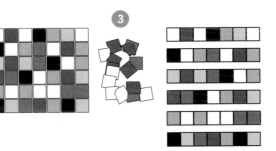 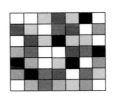 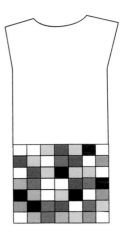

Mix It Up

⊕ Pixelize the whole dress.

⊕ Make the individual squares bigger or smaller.

⊕ Use this same process to add charm to any ready-made pattern.

DEEP V MINI DRESS

Pattern Level 2 Sewing Level 2

The simple structure of this dress works especially nicely in a medium- to heavyweight woven fabric or a knit fabric with light stretch. I started with a heavyweight woven, floor-length, bias-cut skirt, so I had lots of working space.

Measure Up!

Neck 23
(Check out page 34 for specific measuring instructions.)

Special Gear

⊕ CAP SLEEVE CUTIE DRESS pattern from page 123 (no seam or hem allowance)

DIY PATTERN

1 Trace the **CAP SLEEVE CUTIE DRESS Front**, except for the curved neckline but including the notch, making sure to leave space around the neck area for some alterations.

2 Extend the shoulder line upward to an undetermined point. Divide your **Neck** measurement by five and draw a perpendicular line from the center front neck inward that distance.

3 From this new line, draw another perpendicular line upward to meet the extended shoulder line. The point at which the two meet is your high shoulder point and this is where your new neckline will begin.

4 Determine how deep you want your V neck to be and mark that point with a dot on the center front line. Connect the high shoulder point and the V neck point with a slight curve to create the new V neck shape. It's okay if the neck shape passes over your previous lines, just make sure the V neck is deep enough to get your head through.

5 Trace the **CAP SLEEVE CUTIE DRESS Back** (including the notch), except for the curved neckline.

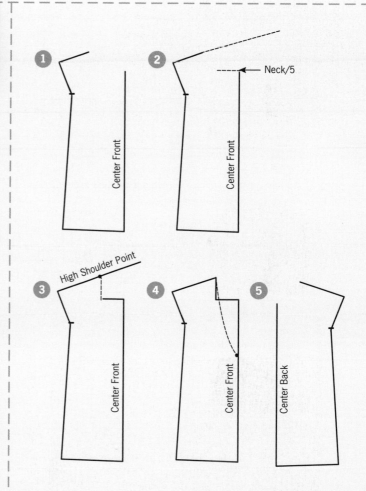

6 Measure the length of the shoulder line on the new front pattern and extend the shoulder line on the back pattern upward to match this length.

7 Draw a curved neckline connecting the new high shoulder point and the center back.

8 Shorten the front and back dress patterns to the desired length. Draw a line perpendicular to center front/center back about 8 in. above the hem and label it "Line A." Decide how much length you want to remove from the dress and draw another line this distance above line A and label it "Line B." Cut along Line A and tape it to Line B, matching up the center front lines. Draw a new side seam connecting the underarm point to the hem, taping some paper underneath the side area to redraw the shape.

9 Create neckline facing patterns for both the front and back patterns. For each of the patterns, place a piece of paper underneath the pattern and trace the neckline shape including 2 in. of the center front/center back lines and 2 in. of the shoulder lines. Finish the facing patterns by drawing a line consistently 2 in. from the neckline, closing up the pattern. When you close up the front pattern, taper the curve so that it meets the V-neck point.

10 Add ½-in. seam allowance to all pattern edges, except along the centers. Add an extra 1 in. to the lower edge of both dress patterns for the hem. Write "Cut 1 on Fold" on each pattern.

11 The high shoulder point on the front pattern may or may not need a little fix-up due to the angle at which the front and back necklines meet. Place the back pattern on top of the front pattern, matching up the shoulder lines and shoulder points. If the back neckline curve extends a bit at the point, tape a small section of paper behind the front pattern at the high shoulder point area and use your tracing wheel to trace ½ in. of the curved back neckline onto the paper. Remove the back pattern. Use a pencil to add this extension to the front pattern and taper it to meet the front neckline curve. Repeat for the facing patterns.

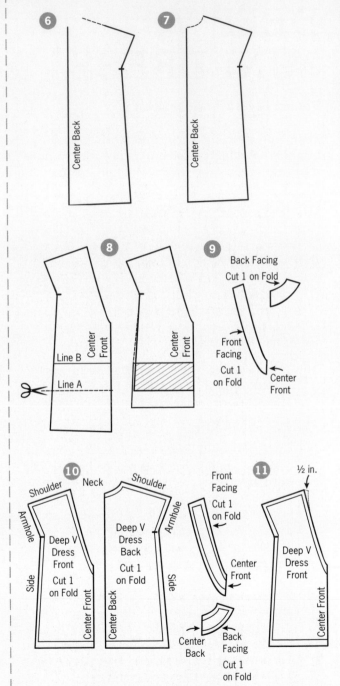

CUT UP, SEW UP

1 Cut one front dress, one back dress, one front facing, and one back facing, all on the fold. Clip the armhole notches.

2 Right sides together, pin and stitch the dress front to the dress back along the shoulder edges. Press open and clean-finish the seam allowances.

3 Right sides together, pin and stitch the front facing to the back facing along the shoulder edges. Press open the seam allowances and clean-finish the facing raw edges.

4 Lay the dress flat and face-up on the table and pin the neckline facing right sides together, matching shoulder seams; stitch, pivoting at the point of the V. Reinforce the point of the V by stitching again over the first stitching. Trim the seam allowances to ¼ in. and clip into the V to, but not through, the seamline. Press the seam allowance layers toward the facing. Understitch the facing; turn it to the inside and press. Hand stitch the facing to the inside of the dress along the outer edges of the facing.

5 Narrowly roll hem the armhole edges to just past the notches.

6 Right sides together, pin and stitch the side seams starting from the armhole notches. Press open and clean-finish the seam allowances.

7 Hem the dress lower edge. Fold and press the raw edge under ½ in. Fold again 1 in. to hide the raw edge and pin in place. Hand stitch the folded edge to the dress.

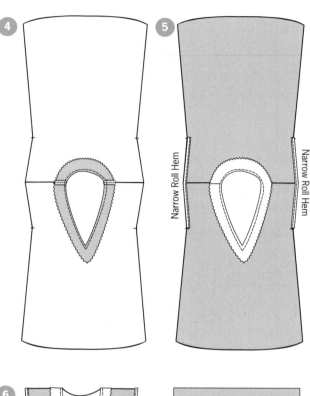

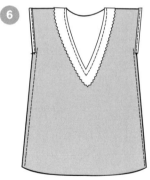

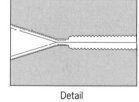

Detail

Mix It Up

⊕ Make a deep V in the back of the dress instead of the front.

⊕ Experiment with an asymmetrical neckline. Work with a whole front pattern for detailing.

DRAWSTRING MANIA DRESS

Pattern Level 2 Sewing Level 2

Tighten up, gather, and cinch loose and long areas of any dress with a drawstring; you can put one anywhere and everywhere that looks flattering! Here, sew up a loose dress and place drawstrings along the shoulders and waist. Side-seam pockets add to the relaxed and personal feel. I made mine from a long, medium-weight linen frock. At your next clothes swap, look for a light- to medium-weight garment with lots of fabric to cut up, or find extra garments to make the drawstrings a different color or print.

DIY PATTERN

1 Trace the **DEEP V MINI DRESS Front** pattern (including the notch), omitting the neckline. Adjust the length, if desired. Extend the center front line upward to draw a new shallow V neck. Make sure you leave enough room to get your head through!

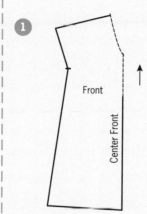

2 If you feel like your pattern already has enough fullness, feel free to skip this step. If you'd like to have more fullness, draw a line from mid-shoulder to the hem, parallel to center front. Mark a large dot somewhere along this line and then cut along the line to separate the two sides of the pattern. On a large piece of paper, draw two parallel lines the length of the dress, 2 in. apart. By adding 2 in. of fullness on the half pattern, the dress will get 8 in. of total fullness around the entire body. Feel free to adjust the amount as desired. Tape the front pattern pieces to the paper along the lines, making sure the large dot is lined up. Use a ruler to true up the shoulder and hemline spaces created by the insert.

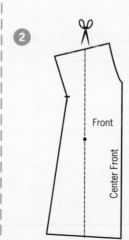

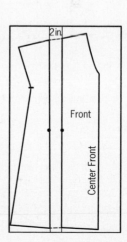

3 Trace the **DEEP V MINI DRESS Back** pattern, adjust the length to match the front and repeat step **2** to insert fullness.

4 Create a new neckline facing pattern for the front dress. Place a piece of paper underneath the pattern and trace the neckline shape including 2 in. of the center front and 2 in. of the shoulder line. Finish the facing pattern by drawing a line consistently 2 in. from the neckline, closing up the pattern. Taper the curve so that it matches the V-neck point. The back neck facing pattern remains the same as for the **DEEP V MINI DRESS**.

5 Label patterns "Drawstring Mania Dress Front" and "Drawstring Mania Dress Back." On both patterns, measure down 12 in. from the armhole notches and mark another notch for pocket placement. Add ½-in. seam allowance to all edges except for the centers. Add an extra 1 in. to the lower edges for the hem. Write "Cut 1 on Fold" on each pattern. If necessary, clean up the high shoulder point like you did for the **DEEP V MINI DRESS** on page 130, step **11**.

6 Follow DIY PATTERN direction step **4** on page 107 for the **DELUXE RECTANGLE SKIRT** to create the pocket pattern.

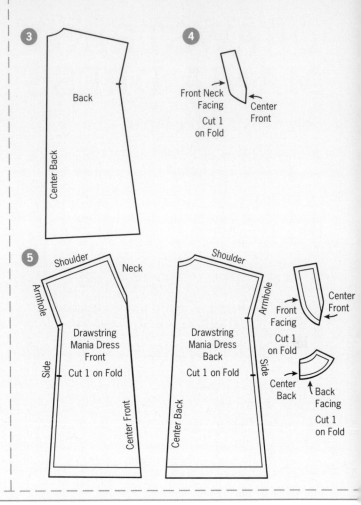

CUT UP, SEW UP

1 Follow steps **1** to **5** for cutting and sewing the **DEEP V MINI DRESS** on page 131. Reserve fabric to cut pockets, casings, and tube drawstrings.

2 Cut four pockets.

3 Right sides together, pin one pocket piece to each of the four sides of the dress with the top of the pocket lined up at the pocket notches, and the pocket bag pointing downward. Stitch the pockets to the dress along the raw edges using a ⅜-in. seam allowance.

4 Turn the pockets outward and press the seam allowances toward the pockets.

5 Right sides together, and starting at the armhole notch, pin the dress front to the dress back along the side seams, pinning the outer pocket together. Use a ½-in. seam allowance to stitch everything together, pivoting around the pocket corners. Press open and clean-finish the seam allowances where you can.

6 Hem the lower dress edge. Fold and press the raw edge under ½ in. Fold again 1 in. to hide the raw edge and pin in place. Hand stitch the folded edge to the dress.

7 Measure the finished shoulder length between the rolled hem and the facing and cut two 1-in.-wide bias strips of fabric this length to use for the shoulder casings.

8 On each bias strip, press the short edges toward the wrong side ¼ in. and stitch them in place. Press the long edges under ¼ in.

9 On the inside of the dress, pin and stitch a casing next to each of the shoulder seams on the dress front. Stitch along the long folded edges and leave the short edges open.

10 With the dress still inside out, try it on and mark your waistline with chalk at the side seams, center front, and center back. Take the dress off and complete the line freehand or using a curved ruler.

11 Measure the finished width of the dress at the waistline and cut a 1-in.-wide bias strip of fabric this length. Repeat step **8** for folding and pressing the bias strip, or substitute premade bias.

12 Starting at a side seam, pin the casing along the chalk line with the two short ends meeting up at the side seam. Before stitching in place along the long folded edges, stitch a buttonhole at the side seam where the open casing ends meet.

13 Create five tube drawstrings. You'll need one for the waistline casing (waist measurement plus 20 in.) and four for the shoulder casings (dress shoulder measurement plus 10 in.). You can also use ribbon, cording, or thin rope for the drawstrings.

14 Use a safety pin to thread the long drawstring through the waistline casing and pull both ends out through the buttonhole.

15 Thread one shoulder drawstring through a shoulder casing and stitch it in place near the neckline side of the casing. On the same shoulder, stitch another drawstring near the shoulder tip on the inside of the dress. Pull the threaded drawstring to gather the shoulder along the casing and tie it to the outer drawstring. Repeat for the other shoulder casing.

16 Tie knots at the end of each drawstring and trim ends.

Mix It Up

⊕ Use a loose-fitting vintage dress and add drawstrings to tie up.

⊕ Go overboard and insert more fullness at the top of the dress only. Your lines will not be placed parallel when you separate along the cutting line.

⊕ Place a drawstring along one of the side seams to bring up your hem at an asymmetrical angle.

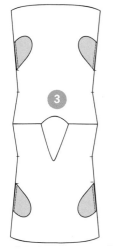
(3)

(5)

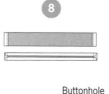
(8)

(12)

Buttonhole

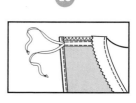
(16)

RIBBON-STRIPED SKIRT DRESS

By Chia Guillory

Pattern Level 1 Sewing Level 2

It's such a shame to see beautiful silk go to waste on unremarkable garments just sitting on the rack at the thrift store. Happily, designer Chia came up with a colorful way to recycle these duds to make an eye-catching garment that can be worn as either a skirt or a dress. To get started on your own pinwheel-like dazzler, hunt around for three to five 100% silk items (shirts, skirts, pants, etc.) in a selection of matching colors.

Measure Up!

Full Hip ④
(Check out page 34 for specific measuring instructions.)

Special Gear

- Pinking shears (or pinking rotary cutter and mat)
- Scrap of woven cotton fabric or interfacing

CUT UP, SEW UP

1 Deconstruct your garments by cutting off the sleeves, collars, cuffs, etc., and cut open the seams.

2 Use a ruler and fabric pencil to mark 2½-in.-wide strips in various lengths on the fabric sections following the grain. Be sure to incorporate any pockets and top-stitched details for added texture and interest. Cut out all the strips with pinking shears.

3 Decide the finished dress length, keeping in mind that it can double as a skirt, and add 1 in. to that measurement for the hem and 2 in. for the waistline. For each color, stitch the strips' right sides together end-to-end to create long dress-length sections. Press the seam allowances open after stitching.

Chia Guillory

Many people told Chia Guillory that she would grow up to be a fashion designer and she would indignantly say, "No, I am going to be an artist!" Well, they were right. Chia makes art in the form of fashion: everything from faux fur hats and couture pieces to costumes and dancewear. This eco-friendly designer uses the best fabrics from decades past to ensure that each one-of-a-kind piece is kind to the environment. For more information, visit www.chiahats.com.

4 Decide a color pattern and create stacks of strips in that order. Right sides together, sew the strip long edges together, pressing the seams flat as you go. Repeat the pattern once you have sewn one of each color.

5 Sew as many strips as needed to increase the width of the dress, reserving two to three strips for the drawstring. Right sides together, sew the sides to create a tube. Since the dress gathers with a drawstring, make it as full or narrow as you want. If the skirt hits below the knee, you'll need some fullness to comfortably move and walk. A good rule of thumb is to make it at least as wide as your **Full Hip** measurement plus some ease.

6 Cut a ¾-in. x 2-in. piece of cotton scrap to use as a stabilizer for the buttonholes. Pin and stitch the scrap to the inside of the dress, 1 in. below the upper edge at any spot around the circumference. On the outside of the dress, stitch two ¾-in. horizontal buttonholes ¼ in. apart.

7 Fold the waistline edge under 1 in. and press it flat. Pin and stitch it in place near the edge.

8 Sew the short ends of the drawstring strips together face-to-face to make one long drawstring and press the seams flat. Fold and press the long edges under ⅛ in. on both sides. Fold the drawstring in half lengthwise, wrong sides together, and press flat. Topstitch the perimeter.

9 Thread the drawstring through the buttonholes and casing. Tie knots at each end of the drawstring.

10 Hem the dress lower edge. Fold and press the raw edge under ½ in. Fold again ½ in. to hide the raw edge and pin in place. Hand stitch the folded edge to the dress.

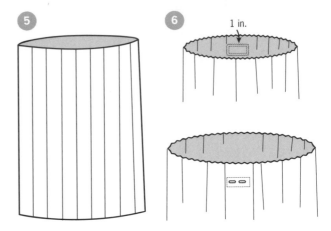

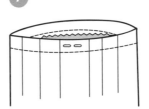

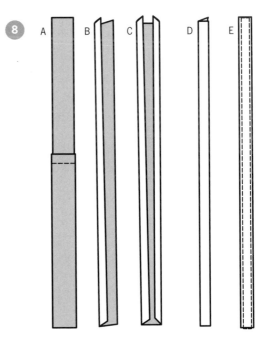

FRILLY CHOP-TOP SHIRTDRESS

Measure Up!

Full Hip 4

(Check out page 34 for specific measuring instructions.)

Pattern Level 1 Sewing Level 2

Chop up and rearrange a tired button-front shirt-dress to create something more frilly and feminine. This off-the-shoulder look can be crafted by simply removing the top of the dress and using fabric from the skirt to create a ruffle for the upper edge. If you have enough fabric, the remaining skirt section can also be gathered into a ruffled lower band. To cut up your own, find a long shirtdress with a full gathered skirt, front placket, and long sleeves. Look for one that fits you well or is slightly loose.

CUT UP, SEW UP

1. Lay the dress flat on the table, and with chalk or fabric pencil, draw a free-form cutting line 2 in. below the shoulder line across the front and back bodice and the sleeves, making sure it connects at the same point on the sleeves. Cut along the line and staystitch the upper edge ¼ in. from the raw edge all the way around.

2. On the skirt portion of the dress, measure down 13 in. from the waistline and draw a cutting line all the way around the skirt staying a consistent length from the waistline. Cut along the line and set aside the extra fabric to make all the ruffles and bands. If you don't have enough fabric to make the lower ruffle, just cut the skirt to a comfortable length.

3. Measure around the upper dress edge and multiply the measurement by two. Cut or piece together a 3½-in.-long rectangle of fabric this width for the ruffle.

4. Narrowly roll hem both ruffle short edges and one long rectangle edge.

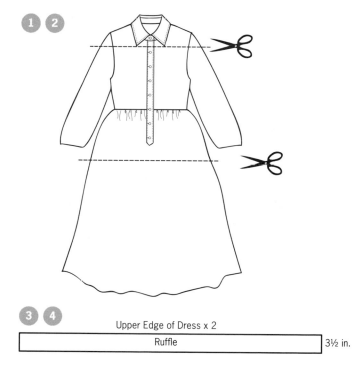

Upper Edge of Dress x 2

Ruffle	3½ in.

5 Gather the upper ruffle edge to match the dress opening. Unbutton the placket and, starting at the buttonhole side, pin and stitch the ruffle to the upper dress edge with the wrong side of the ruffle facing the right side of the dress. The ruffle should stop just short of the button side of the placket.

6 Measure around the upper dress edge and add ½ in. Cut a bias rectangle of fabric with the width equal to this calculation and 2 in. tall. This will be used to bind the ruffle edge and create a drawstring casing.

7 Fold, press, and stitch the short edges of the binding under ¼ in. Fold and press the binding in half with the fold parallel to the long edge and wrong sides together, then unfold and press one of the long edges under ½ in.

8 Right sides together, pin and stitch the unfolded edge of the binding to the upper dress edge, with the ruffle sandwiched between the two. Trim the seam to ¼ in., press all layers of the seam allowances toward the binding, and topstitch the binding folded edge to the dress wrong side, creating a casing.

9 Create a ⅜-in.-wide tube drawstring with the length equal to the upper edge of the dress plus 20 in. and thread it through the casing.

10 If you're skipping the lower ruffle, hem the dress and you're done! If you're adding a lower ruffle, continue with steps **11** to **16** below.

11 Cut or piece together one 3½-in.-tall rectangle with your **Full Hip** measurement times two as the width. Narrowly roll hem one long edge of the ruffle. Right sides together, stitch the two short ends together to create a circle. Press open the seam allowances. This creates the band ruffle.

12 Cut or piece together two rectangles the width of your **Full Hip** measurement plus 1 in. and 5 in. tall. Right sides together, stitch one of the rectangles together along the short ends to create a circle. Press open the seam allowances. Repeat for the other rectangle. These are the band circles.

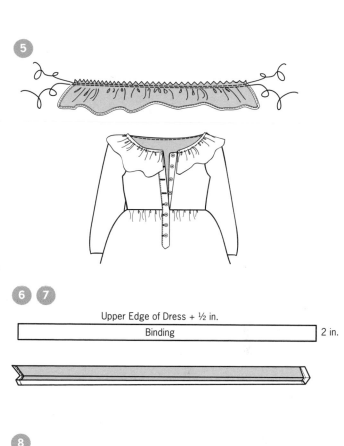

6 7

Upper Edge of Dress + ½ in.

Binding   2 in.

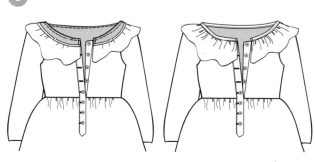

13 Gather the band ruffle and pin one of the band circle edges to the upper ruffle edge, matching raw edges and seams. The wrong side of the ruffle should face the right side of the band. Stitch the ruffle to the band.

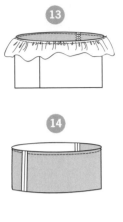

14 Right sides together, pin and stitch the two band circles together along the ruffled edge, matching seams. The ruffled circle will be hidden. Trim the seam to ¼ in. Turn right-side out and press.

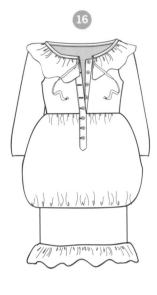

15 With wrong sides facing, pin and staystitch the two band circles together along the unruffled edge. You should now have a two-layer band circle with a ruffle at the bottom.

16 Gather the lower dress edge to fit the band loop. Slip the band over the lower dress edge matching raw edges and the seam at the back of the dress. Stitch all the way around. Clean-finish the seam allowances and press them toward the band.

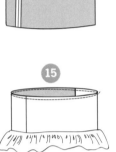

Mix It Up

⊕ **Chop the top off any garment!**

⊕ **Create a similar skirt from scratch by combining the DELUXE RECTANGLE SKIRT on page 105 with the ruffled banding process from this project.**

SHEER TUNIC

By Jesse Kelly-Landes

Pattern Level 1 Sewing Level 2

Inspired by a floor-length tunic spotted in a French *Vogue* from the early 1980s, Jesse used sheer curtains with pretty gold embroidery. She used a basic ready-made tunic pattern, but updated it with a few key details like sleeve cuffs and a waistline sash. Follow Jesse's pattern directions below to create the cuffs and sash and pair them with one of many available tunic patterns. Look for a set of sheer curtains at the thrift store to use for your dress, and, while you're there, pick up a slip if you don't already own one. Special trims save time on the hem.

Special Gear

⊕ **POSTER ART DRESS** pattern from page 153 and the **"YOU" DRESS** Sleeve pattern from page 42.

DIY PATTERN

1 To make the pattern for the sash, draw a rectangle approximately 9 in. x 36 in. On one short side, write "Cut 1 on Fold." Add ½-in. seam allowance to all edges except for the center.

2 To make the pattern for the sleeve cuff, draw a 4-in. tall upside-down trapezoid with one long edge measuring the sleeve edge width and the other long edge ½ in. longer than the first. Connect the short sides and on the longest side, write "Cut 2 on Fold." Add ½-in. seam allowance to all edges except the foldline.

3 If you want a challenge, you can skip the commercial pattern and create your own dress with a tunic-type neckline. Just trace a copy of the **POSTER ART DRESS Front** pattern from page 153 and draw a stitching line at the neck as shown. Do not cut along this line. Create a facing pattern to match the dress.

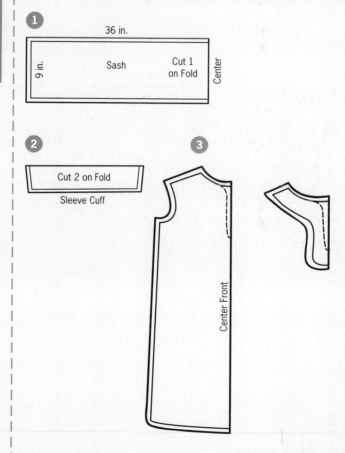

1

36 in.

9 in.

Sash

Cut 1 on Fold

Center

2

Cut 2 on Fold

Sleeve Cuff

3

Center Front

CUT UP, SEW UP

1 Cut and sew the tunic according to the pattern instructions, except the sleeve hem. If you altered the **POSTER ART DRESS**, cut and sew the dress like normal, except trace the neckline shape with tracing paper and then follow the new neckline when attaching the facing. Once it's stitched in place, trim close to the stitching to open up the neckline along center front. Match up the **POSTER ART DRESS** with the **"YOU" DRESS SLEEVE** pattern.

2 Cut two sleeve cuffs and one sash, each on the fold.

3 Right sides together, pin and stitch the short edges of one of the sleeve cuff pieces together, creating a circle. Press open the seams. Wrong sides together, fold the cuff in half with the fold parallel to the long edge. Pin and stitch the sleeve cuff to the wrong side of the sleeve edge with raw edges and seams matching. Trim the seam allowances to ¼ in. Turn the cuff outward and fold it up on the outside of the sleeve. Tack the cuff in place along the seam with a hand backstitch. Repeat the process for the other sleeve cuff.

4 Right sides together, fold and pin the sash in half lengthwise matching raw edges. Stitch all the edges, leaving 4 in. unstitched at the sash center for turning. Turn the sash right-side out through the opening and press. Fold the remaining raw edges in and hand stitch closed.

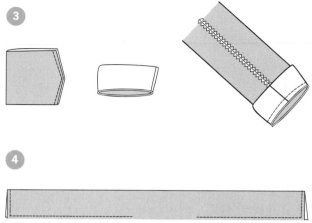

Leave Open

Mix It Up

⊕ Add a sash and cuffs to any pattern.

⊕ Use the sash as a headband.

⊕ Sew the short edges of the sash diagonally for a different look.

Jesse Kelly-Landes

Jesse's always had a penchant for cute dresses, even before she knew needle from thread. In addition to designing clothes for her business, Amet and Sasha, Jesse co-hosted the show *Stylelicious* on the DIY Network; co-produced *Stitch*, an Austin-based fashion and craft show; and is a founding member of the Austin Craft Mafia. Jesse's lifelong interest in recycling has led her in a new direction: local and sustainable foods. You can follow her adventures at her blog www.breadbaby.blogspot.com.

BIB DRESS

By Fredda and Jennifer Perkins

Sewing Level 2

Fellow Austin Craft mafiosa Jennifer Perkins came up with the design for this high-fashion dress using a jumper she already owned and a vintage Hawaiian shirt—and then got her mother Fredda Perkins to sew it for her. Use their idea to update a dress from your own closet or look for a dress at the thrift store with wide straps in a size that fits. Make sure the dress has a plain front to attach the cute bib. You'll also need a Hawaiian shirt or other woven fabric print for the band and buttons, and a matching scrap of solid-color woven fabric big enough to cut two 8-in. squares.

Special Gear

⊕ 1 yd. of thin cording (¼ in. wide or smaller)

⊕ Sixteen 1-in. buttons to cover

⊕ 7 in. sq. of interfacing

⊕ Fabric glue (optional)

Mix It Up

⊕ Sew jewels on the bib instead of buttons.

⊕ Experiment with changing the bib shape.

CUT UP, SEW UP

1 Trim the original hem from the dress and replace it with a band of fabric cut from the Hawaiian shirt. (See page 23 for instructions on banding.)

2 Cut 1½-in.-wide bias strips from the Hawaiian shirt to make the piping trim. Fold the bias strips wrong sides together over the thin cord, tucking the cord as close to the fold as possible. Use a zipper foot to stitch as close to the cord as you can. Make enough of the piping trim as needed to trim both sides of the dress straps and the 8-in.-square bib.

3 Cut two 8-in. squares from the scrap fabric to use for the bib. Apply interfacing to the wrong side of one of the squares.

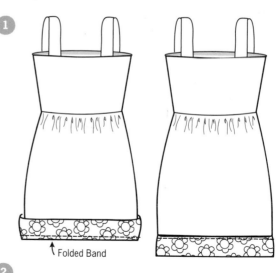

1

↑ Folded Band

2

4 Lay the interfaced square right-side up on the table and pin the piping trim to the edge of the square with the raw edges matching. For extra protection against slippage, lightly glue the trim lip in place. Right sides together, position the second square on top of the first and pin it in place. Stitch around the two squares using a zipper foot to get as close to the corded trim as possible. Leave a 2-in. gap unstitched. Trim the seam allowances and turn the fabric square through the gap. Press the square, tucking in the edges at the opening, and hand stitch closed.

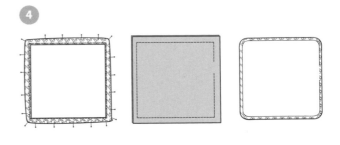

5 Center and pin the finished bib to the dress front and stitch the bib to the dress, stitching in the little ditch formed between the square and the cording.

6 Cover 16 buttons with scraps from the Hawaiian shirt.

7 Use chalk or a fabric pencil to measure and mark even button placement and sew them to the bib.

8 Remove the original straps from the dress, carefully take them apart with a seam ripper, and sew them back together adding the Hawaiian trim to the edges using the same technique used on the bib. Sew the straps back onto the dress.

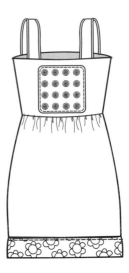

Fredda and Jennifer Perkins

Mother-daughter crafting duo Fredda and Jennifer Perkins are published authors, crafters, mothers, lovers of enchiladas, and native Texans. Jennifer is a founding member of the Austin Craft Mafia. Jennifer and Fredda's work has been featured in *Seventeen*, *The New York Times*, *Craft*, *Teen Vogue*, and *More*, among other publications. They have a synergistic relationship when it comes to crafting. Their motto is "two crafty Perkins heads are better than one." See their handiwork at www. naughtysecretaryclub.com.

OFFICE DANCING DRESS

Pattern Level 3 Sewing Level 2

Thrift stores are usually busting at the seams with ordinary office dresses. Many times these dresses are made with fabrics worth mentioning, but the styles are sometimes humdrum and easy to pass over. Electrify those dull dresses by restyling the skirt with cheerful tiers. Look for an office dress with a gathered or elasticized waistline made in either a woven or a knit fabric. Make sure to choose a dress that has a bodice that fits you like a blouse, and, since you won't change the bodice, be sure it's a style you like. While you're at the thrift store, look for something to recycle to use for the underskirt, preferably in a fabric that coordinates with the dress weight and color.

Special Gear

⊕ ³⁄₈-in.-wide elastic, the width of your full waist

CUT UP, SEW UP

1 Use a seam ripper or scissors to separate the skirt from the bodice by cutting along the waistline, removing any elastic or other waistline details and the center back skirt seam.

2 Clean up the lower bodice edge, if necessary—you can even trim it off to make an empire waist. Measure the entire lower bodice edge and divide this measurement in half. Jot this down as "Bodice Waist Width."

3 Follow DIY PATTERN step **1** on page 95 for the **TIERED SKIRT**, and then adjust the skirt pattern so that the upper edge of the pattern is equal to the Bodice Waist Width. Add space equally to the center front and center back edges through the entire pattern length.

4 Follow DIY PATTERN steps **2** to **5** and **7** on pages 95 and 97 for the **TIERED SKIRT** using the adjusted skirt pattern. Feel free to experiment with the number and length of each ruffled tier.

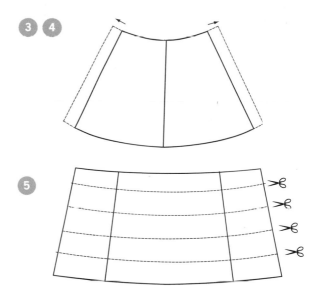

5 Follow CUT UP, SEW UP steps **1** to **5** on page 98 for the **TIERED SKIRT** to sew the skirt together, ignoring any reference to a waistband. Use the skirt fabric to cut out the tier patterns and the extra matching fabric to cut out the underskirt patterns. Piece together fabric, if necessary, to make the tiers long enough, and go with the flow, depending on the fabric you have.

6 Right sides together, pin and stitch the center back seam together. Press open and clean-finish the seam allowances.

7 Right sides together, place the bodice and skirt together at the waistline, matching the raw edges and center front. Pin and stitch all the way around the waistline. Trim the skirt side of the seam allowance to ¼ in. (don't trim the bodice side of the seam allowance). Clean-finish the bodice seam allowance and press it toward the skirt. Stitch the seam allowance to the skirt along the finished edge to create a casing, leaving a 1 in. opening to insert elastic into the casing.

8 Cut a piece of elastic equal to your **Full Waist** measurement. Attach a safety pin to both ends of the elastic and thread it through the casing opening. Once it's pulled all the way through the casing, overlap the ends of the elastic ½ in. and stitch them together, making sure it's not twisted. Stitch the casing opening closed.

Mix It Up

⊕ Create your own blouse design using the "YOU" DRESS BODICE or a ready-made basic bodice as a starting point. Combine the bodice with the tiered skirt to create a dress.

POSTER ART DRESS

Pattern Level 3 Sewing Level 3

Back in the swinging '60s, fashion-forward ladies once wore disposable paper dresses as perhaps a comment on the newly disposable times. The dresses were printed with artwork that you could hang on your wall after wearing. Beat poets and artists like Andy Warhol got in on the action, too. I love the idea of mixing fashion, art, and politics as a mode of expression. Structurally speaking, this dress has no darts and has a big working area, so it

doubles well as a blank canvas. To create your masterpiece, rescue large, white linens in medium-weight woven fabrics and get arty.

Special Gear

⊕ ¼ yd. light- to medium-weight interfacing

⊕ 7 in. invisible zipper

⊕ Any fabric-art medium such as fabric dye, paint, marker, crayon, etc.

DIY PATTERN

1 Follow directions **1** to **5** on page 38 for the **"YOU" DRESS BODICE Front**. Mark a notch at the center front waistline.

2 Measure from your shoulder at your neck down to the desired dress length. Starting at the high shoulder point on the pattern, draw a line parallel to center front this length. This is the "Length Line."

3 Draw a perpendicular line across the paper at the end of the Length Line, label it line "B." Draw another line 1 in. above this line and label it line "A." Extend center front downward to meet line B.

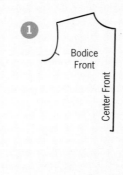

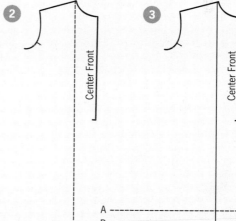

4 Divide your **Full Hip** measurement by four, and then add 4 in. Starting at center front, measure out this distance along line A and mark with a dot. Connect the underarm point to this dot with a straight line. If your bust measurement is bigger than your hip measurement, use your bust measurement for this step instead of your hip.

5 Use a curved ruler to draw the hem, connecting the side at line A to center front at line B. Make sure the hem meets the side and center front lines at square angles.

6 Follow steps **1** to **7** on page 40 for the **"YOU" DRESS BODICE Back**. Omit the side and waistlines. Mark a notch at the center back waistline.

7 Place the dress front pattern on top of the back bodice with the underarm points right on top of each other. Adjust the front dress pattern to make sure the center front line is parallel to the center back line on the bodice. Secure the pattern with tape and trace the side seam.

8 Extend center back downward to an undetermined point. Draw a perpendicular line from center back that meets the end of the side seam and label it line "A." Draw another line 1 in. below line A and label it line "B."

9 Use a curved ruler to draw the hem, connecting the side at line A to center back at line B. Make sure the hem meets the side and center back lines at square angles.

10 Test and adjust the curved hemline, if needed, on both the front and back dress patterns by placing the side seams together. Make sure the hem is a smooth, shallow curve from center front to center back.

11 Create facings: one each for the front neck, back neck, front armhole, and back armhole. To do this, trace the outside edge of each curve, trace 2 in. along both of the connecting edges (Shoulder, Center Front, Center Back, Side), and then draw the final line on each of the patterns parallel to the original curves.

12 Add ½-in. seam allowance to all the pattern pieces except along the center front edges. Add an additional 1 in. to the dress front and back lower edges for the hem. Draw grainlines parallel to center back and write "Cut 2" on all back pieces. Mark a double notch 7 in. from the finished neck edge along center back. Label the front pieces with "Cut 1 on Fold."

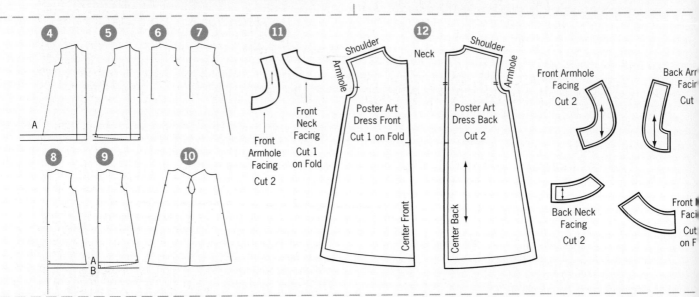

CUT UP, SEW UP

1 Cut one each of the dress front and front neck facing on the fold. Cut two each of the dress back, back neck facing, front armhole facing, and back armhole facing. Cut each of the facing patterns from interfacing and apply to the wrong side of the corresponding fabric pieces. Clip notches, except for the waist notches. After you have your pieces cut, this is a convenient time to paint or create a masterpiece on your fabric, let it dry, and then continue to sew it up. Keep any embellishment out of the seamlines.

2 Right sides together, pin and stitch the dress front to the dress back at the shoulders. Press open and clean-finish the seam allowances.

3 Right sides together, pin and stitch each of the front and back facings at the shoulders. Press open and clean-finish the seam allowances. Clean-finish the facing outer curved edges.

4 Right sides together, pin and stitch the facings to the dress along the neckline and armhole edges. Trim the seams to ¼ in. and press them toward the facings. Understitch, turn the facings to the inside of the dress, and press.

5 Right sides together, open the armhole facings outward along the side seams and pin and stitch the dress front to the dress back along the side seams, including the facing side seams. Start at the edge of the facing and end at the dress hem. Press open and clean-finish the seam allowances.

6 With wrong sides together, pin and staystitch the center back facing edges to the center back dress edges with a ⅜-in. seam. Install a zipper at center back with the upper stop aligned with the finished neckline edge. Close up the remainder of the seam. Press open and clean-finish the seam allowances.

7 Hem the dress lower edge. Fold and press the raw edge under ½ in., fold and pin under another 1 in., and hand stitch in place. Hand stitch the facing to the inside of the dress along the shoulder and underarm seams.

Mix It Up

⊕ Stitch on various strips and bits of fabric all over to create a collage dress or embroider a story or scene.

⊕ Create a V-neck on the back pattern big enough to get your head through and skip the zipper! Stitch the center back seam just like the side seams.

⊕ For a less voluminous dress with a slightly more fitted waist, decrease the amount of ease added to the hip measurement in step 4 of the DIY pattern instructions and draw shallow inward curves at the waist notches that taper out smoothly to the original seamlines.

⊕ Skip the facing and cut another set of dress patterns to make a fully lined dress and add pockets to the side seams.

EGG DRESS

Pattern Level 3 Sewing Level 2

Humpty Dumpty sat on a wall, but he never looked this cute! The extra fullness and gathers along the neck and the hemline band give this egg-shaped dress a bit of boyish flapper appeal. Pair it with a headband, bangs, and a poised attitude to complete the look. I used fabric from a large ethnic print tunic to stitch my dress together. Look for comparably

Measure Up!

Full Hip 4

(Check out page 34 for specific measuring instructions.)

large or extra-large woven garments that have lots of flat usable space (check the thrift store's plus-size and linen departments for likely candidates). Light-to medium-weight fabrics gather nicely.

Special Gear

⊕ POSTER ART DRESS Front and Back patterns from page 153 (no seam or hem allowances)

⊕ Scrap of interfacing

DIY PATTERN

1 Trace the **POSTER ART DRESS Front** and shorten it to about hip length.

2 Measure 2½ in. from the high shoulder point along the shoulder line and mark with a dot. Draw a slanted line connecting the underarm curve to the dot. Cut along this line and discard the small section.

3 Draw two evenly spaced lines parallel to center front, connecting the neckline with the hem. Starting at the neckline, cut along these lines, stopping just short of the hemline.

4 Tape the pattern to a large piece of paper along the center front. Spread each of the sections 1½ in. along the neckline and tape them in place. Trace around the pattern and use a curved ruler to true the new neckline.

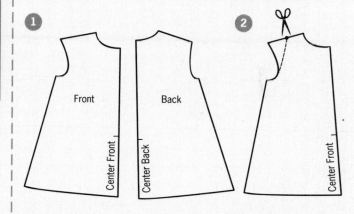

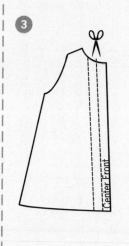

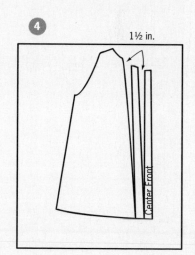

5 To create a front armhole facing, trace the outside edge of the armhole curve, 2 in. of the shoulder and 2 in. of the side, and close up the pattern with a curved line parallel to the original curve. Trace a grainline parallel to center front.

6 Repeat steps **1** to **5** for the dress back.

7 Divide your **Full Hip** measurement in half and add 1 in. Draw a 12-in. long rectangle with this calculation as the width. Label with "Lower Band" and "Cut 2." Draw a grainline parallel to the short sides and mark notches halfway down each of the sides.

8 Measure the front and back neck pattern edges, add them together, and then multiply by two. Draw a 3-in.-tall rectangle with this calculation as the width. Label with "Neck Band" and "Cut 1." Draw a bias grainline at a 45° angle from one short end.

9 Add ½-in. seam allowance to all patterns, except along the centers.

Mix It Up

⊕ Design a deeper, more dramatic neck band and use a contrasting fabric for both the neck and lower bands.

⊕ Gather the neck edge into a smaller neckline facing and close up the dress with a zipper along the center back. Add a ½-in. seam allowance to the center back edge and cut two separate pieces.

⊕ Add pockets to the side seams.

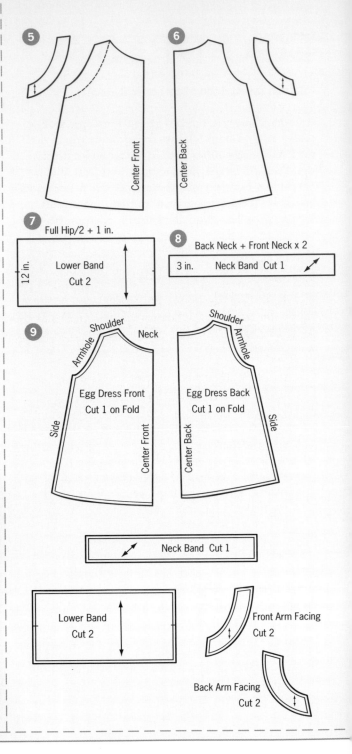

CUT UP, SEW UP

1 Cut one each of the dress front and back on the fold. Cut two each of the front and back armhole facings, and lower band. Cut one of the neck band. Clip notches. Clip an additional notch along the neckline at center back.

2 Right sides together, pin and stitch the dress front to the back at the shoulder seams. Press open and clean-finish the seam allowances.

3 Right sides together, pin and stitch the front armhole facings to the back armhole facings at the shoulder seams. Press open and clean-finish the seam allowances. Clean-finish the outer raw edge of the armhole facings.

4 Right sides together, pin and stitch the armhole facings to the dress along the armholes. Trim the seams to ¼ in.; press the seam allowances toward the facing and understitch.

5 Right sides together and with the armhole facing turned out, pin the side edges of the facing together. Continue pinning through the intersection of the facing and the dress to pin the side edges of the dress together. Sew together in one continuous stitch from the facing to the lower dress edge. Press open and clean-finish the seam allowances. Repeat for the other side of the dress.

6 Apply the interfacing scrap to the dress wrong side ½ in. below the center back neckline raw edge. On the right side, stitch a ½-in. horizontal buttonhole on top of the interfaced area.

7 Right sides together, stitch the two short edges of the neck band together to create a circle. Press open the seam allowances then fold the neck band in half with the fold parallel to the long edge and wrong sides together. Press. Slip the band over the neck edge of the dress with raw edges matching. Pin and stitch the neck band to the dress, matching the neck band seam with the dress center back. Clean-finish the raw edges, and press the seam allowance toward the inside of the dress. Stitch the seam allowance to the dress along the finished edges to create a casing.

8 Create a narrow tube drawstring the length of the neck edge plus 20 in. or use ribbon to thread into the neckline casing through the buttonhole.

9 Right sides together, pin and stitch the two lower band pieces together along the short edges, matching notches, to create a circle. Press open the seam allowances and then fold the band in half with the fold parallel to the long edge, wrong sides and raw edges together.

10 Gather the bottom edge of the dress to match the lower band size. Pin and stitch the band in place, matching side seams. Clean-finish the raw edges and press the seam allowances toward the band. Topstitch.

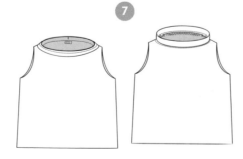

OUTER-SPACE DRESS

Pattern Level 3 Sewing Level 4

You might think this fascinating dress looks out-of-this-world complicated, but the openwork design isn't that hard to put together. The newspaper backing technique utilized makes it trouble-free. When I designed this dress, I just chopped directly into an already made tunic and kept the original hem. If you have an adventurous spirit, try doing the same thing; for those of you that want a flawless structure, keep to the pattern instructions below. In either case, working with a light- to medium-weight woven fabric is recommended.

Special Gear

- POSTER ART DRESS Front and Back patterns from page 153 (no seam allowance)
- 1 in. button
- 2 in. elastic cord (or an elastic hair tie)
- Extra recycled fabric for the dress lining (one large garment with about a yard of space)
- Tube turner
- Newspaper, tissue, or tear-away stabilizer

DIY PATTERN

1 Trace the **POSTER ART DRESS Front** pattern including the waistline notch. Mark a dot 4 in. below the neckline along the center front line. Draw a perpendicular line inward from the dot, connecting the center front to the armhole. Mark a dot along this line 5 in. from center front, another dot on the side seam 6 in. to 8 in. below the waistline, and a dot at the end of the shoulder. Use a curved ruler to connect the dots as shown. Cut along the lines to separate all the pattern pieces. Discard the side sections.

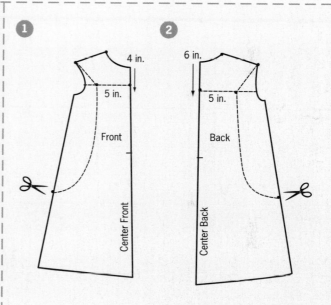

2 Repeat for the back pattern, except mark your first dot 6 in. below the neckline along center back. Make sure the dot along the side seam is exactly where you placed it on the front pattern.

3 Measure the front and back neck edges on the upper patterns. Add these measurements together and multiply by two. Draw a 3-in.-tall rectangle with this calculation as the width. Label with "Neck Band" and "Cut 1."

4 Measure the shoulder length on the upper front pattern, multiply this measurement by two. Draw a 1-in.-tall rectangle with this calculation as the width. Label with "Shoulder Strap" and "Cut 4."

5 Add ½-in. seam allowance around all the pattern pieces except along centers. Add an additional 1 in. to the dress back and front lower edges for the hem. On the neck band, draw a grainline 45° from the sides. On the shoulder strap, draw a grainline parallel to the short sides.

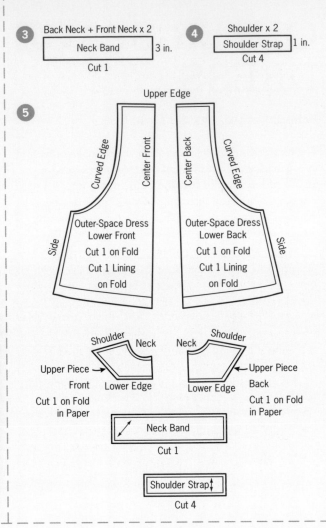

Mix It Up

⊕ Use this same concept to create openwork on any portion of any pattern.

⊕ String beads on the openwork tubes or weave the tubes together.

⊕ Braid or twist several strips of raw fabric instead of making tubes.

CUT UP, SEW UP

1 Cut two each of the lower dress front and back on the fold: one each in a regular fabric and one each in a lining fabric. Cut one each of the upper front and back patterns on the fold from newspaper or stabilizer. Cut four shoulder straps and one neck band from fabric. Cut one neck band interfacing. Clip notches at center front and center back along the upper edge of the lower pieces and the lower edge of the upper pieces.

2 Create several ½-in.-wide tubes and press them flat with the seam along the back side. Pin the tubes to the newspaper upper front and upper back as shown, leaving ½ in. along the corners and at center back. Staystitch the tubes in place along the edges.

3 Right sides together, pin and staystitch the lower edge of the upper front piece to the upper edge of the lower front piece, matching center front notches.

4 Right sides together, pin and stitch the lower front to the lower front lining along the upper and curved edges. Trim the seams to ¼ in., press them toward the lining, understitch, and turn the lining to the inside. The upper front will be sandwiched between the two.

5 Repeat steps **3** to **4** for the back.

6 Right sides together, pin and stitch the front to the back at the shoulders (you will be stitching newspaper). Trim the seam allowance to ¼ in. and topstitch the seams in the open position.

7 Right sides together, pin and stitch two of the shoulder straps together along the long edges. Trim the seams to ¼ in. and use a tube turner to turn the straps right-side out. Press flat. Repeat for the remaining shoulder straps.

8 Wrap and pin the shoulder straps around the shoulder lines with the short raw edges meeting up at the neckline. Stitch the folded straps together along the long edges, catching the tubes.

9 Fold and press the neck band in half with the fold parallel to the long edges and wrong sides together. Unfold the neck band and apply a 1½-in.-wide strip of interfacing to the wrong side of the neck band along one side of the foldline, making sure the interfacing doesn't cross over into the seam allowances. Press the long edge of the interfaced side under ½ in. Right sides together, fold the neck band in half along the long edge. Pin and stitch the short ends closed, sandwiching the raw edges of an elastic loop inside the seam on one side. Trim the seams to ¼ in., turn the band right-side out, and press.

10 Right sides together, pin and stitch the unfolded edge of the neck band to the neckline. Press the seam toward the inside of the neck band and hand stitch the folded edge to the inside of the dress. Sew a button on the side opposite the elastic loop.

11 Tear away the tissue or newspaper.

12 Right sides together, pin and stitch the front dress to the back dress along the sides, stitching the lining to the lining and the dress to the dress. Open the lining outward along the sides; start pinning at the bottom edge of the lining, cross over the intersection of the lining and the dress. Press open the seam allowances. Repeat for the other side seam.

13 Hem the lower edges of the dress and lining separately, making the lining ½ in. shorter.

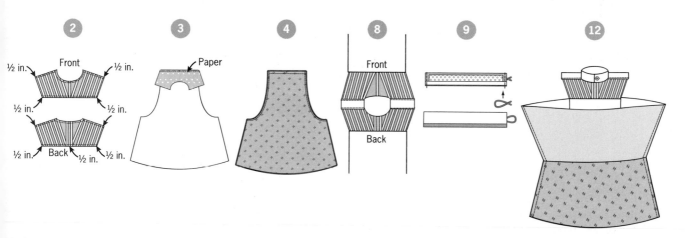

VEST DRESS

Pattern Level 3 Sewing Level 2

Masculine and feminine converge in this playful vest-shaped dress. Work it at the office with opaque tights and a billowy, ruffled blouse; or team it up with a fitted knit top and leggings to assert a uniquely casual style for everyday. I fussed with a length of salvaged, off-grain fabric to make my grid print dress. Make your vest work for you in a medium-weight woven fabric or a firm, light-stretch knit. Cover the buttons like those on the **Slouchy Vest** on page 65 or find some vintage buttons to spice things up.

Special Gear

- ⊕ POSTER ART DRESS Front and Back patterns from page 153 (no seam allowance)
- ⊕ ¼ yd. light- to medium-weight interfacing
- ⊕ Eight to twelve 1-in. buttons
- ⊕ Extra recycled fabric for the vest lining (one large garment like a long skirt)

DIY PATTERN

1 Trace the **POSTER ART DRESS Front** and **Back** patterns, including the waistline notches. Adjust the length if desired.

2 On the dress front, mark a dot 2 in. above the waistline center front. Extend outward from center front 2½ in. starting at this dot.

3 Mark a dot 3 in. from the neck along the shoulder line. Mark a dot 5 in. below the underarm point along the side seam. Use a curved ruler to connect the dots and create a new armhole shape, then connect the neck point with the extended center front to create the front neckline shape.

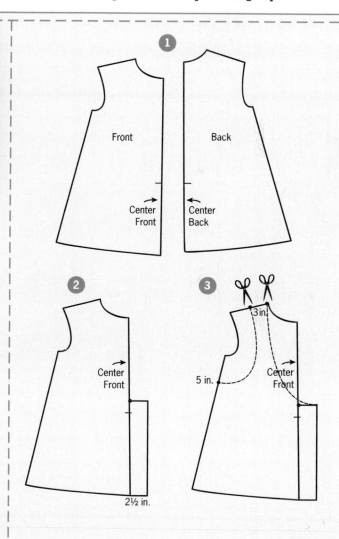

4 Measure 3 in. down and to the left from original center front at the hem and mark with a dot. Use a curved ruler to make connecting lines to this dot from the side seam and the extended center front.

5 On the dress back, mark a dot 3 in. from the neck along the shoulder line. Mark a dot 5 in. below the underarm point along the side seam. Use a curved ruler to connect the dots and create a deep racer-back armhole shape.

6 Add ½-in. seam allowance to both patterns, except along center back. On the front pattern, write "Vest Dress Front," "Cut 2," and "Cut 2 lining." The center front line acts as a grainline. On the back pattern, write "Vest Dress Back," "Cut 1 on Fold," and "Cut 1 lining on fold."

7 Measure the center front extension from the neckline to the hem. Draw a 5-in.-wide rectangle this length. Label with "Interfacing" and "Cut 2."

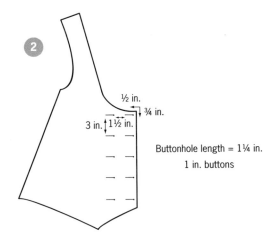

Mix It Up

⊕ **Use a tapered waist version of the poster dress to create a more fitted vest dress.**

⊕ **Create a collar and sandwich it between the dress and the lining before sewing together at the neckline.**

CUT UP, SEW UP

1 Follow sewing directions for steps **1** to **5** on page 66 to cut and sew the dress in exactly the same manner as the **SLOUCHY VEST**.

2 Use a ruler and fabric pencil to mark 1¼-in. buttonholes on the right front extension as shown. Stitch the buttonholes and hand stitch the buttons in place underneath.

Buttonhole length = 1¼ in.
1 in. buttons

BELL JAR DRESS COAT

Pattern Level 3 Sewing Level 2

Talk about a transformation! I turned a somewhat stinky blanket into this enchanting dress coat with wide bell sleeves and a Peter Pan collar. I found the beautiful and velvety corduroy blanket in a pile of vintage linens at a city-wide garage sale and immediately fell in love with it. It was in perfect condition aside from the dusty smell, but after a couple times through the washer, it was as good as new. Initially, I tried out some vintage plastic buttons along the placket, but quickly realized the coat needed something more special, so I made some Chinese knot buttons from scraps. Find a sizeable, heavyweight woven fabric to make yourself a charming fall coat.

Special Gear

- POSTER ART DRESS Front and Back patterns from page 153 (no seam allowance)
- "YOU" DRESS SLEEVE pattern from page 42
- ½ yd. medium-weight interfacing
- Extra recycled fabric for the lining like a lightweight blanket or table cloth
- 6 Chinese knot buttons (see page 25)

DIY PATTERN

1 Trace the **POSTER ART DRESS Front** and **Back** patterns including the armhole notches. On the front dress pattern, extend center front 1 in. to create the placket.

2 On a separate large piece of paper, place the dress back pattern on top of the front pattern at the shoulder, overlapping the shoulder at the armholes by ½ in. Trace the neck curve onto the paper from center front to center back (do not include the placket). Trace several inches of both the center front and center back lines. Mark a

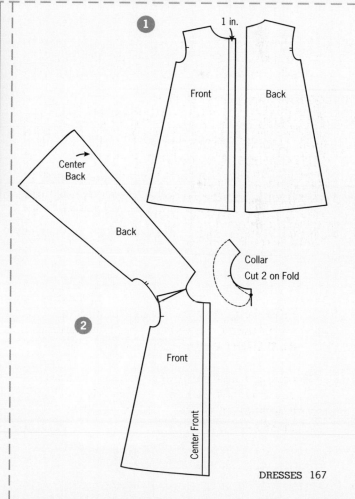

notch where the shoulders intersect. Mark a dot ½ in. down from the neckline at center front. Remove the patterns and use the tracing to draw the collar. Redraw the neckline at center front to meet the dot. From the dot, draw the outside edge of the collar, keeping 3 in. from the neck edge at all times after you round the corner. Label with "Collar" and "Cut 2 on Fold."

3 Trace the **"YOU" DRESS SLEEVE** pattern, including all markings, and shorten it by 3 in. Draw several evenly spaced lines parallel to the grainline, connecting the upper sleeve edge to the lower sleeve edge. Starting at the lower edge, cut along these lines, stopping just short of the upper edge.

4 Tape the pattern to a large piece of paper at the sleeve cap. Spread each of the sections by 1½ in. along the hemline and tape them in place (spread more or less depending on how much sleeve fullness you want). Trace around the new pattern and use a curved ruler to true everything up. Label with "Sleeve" and "Cut 2."

5 Measure the lower edge of the new sleeve. Draw an 8-in.-tall rectangle with this measurement as the width. Label with "Sleeve Band" and "Cut 2."

6 Add ½-in. seam allowance to all the pattern pieces except along the center back edges. Add an additional 1 in. to the front and back coat pattern lower edges for the hem. On the coat front pattern, mark a notch along the neckline at center front. On the sleeve band pattern, mark notches along the side edges at the midpoints and draw a grainline parallel to the short sides. On the sleeve, draw a grainline perpendicular to the bicep line.

Mix It Up

⊕ Experiment with other collar shapes.

⊕ Add extra fullness to the sleeve and gather it into the sleeve band.

⊕ Add pockets to the side seams or topstitch outside pockets in fun shapes.

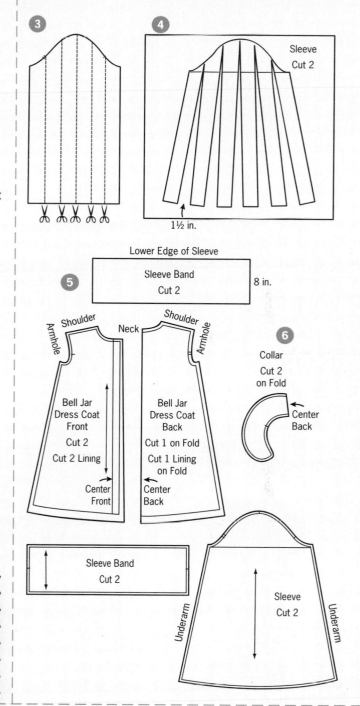

CUT UP, SEW UP

1 Cut four coat fronts: two from blanketing fabric and two from lining. Cut two coat backs on the fold: one from blanketing and one from lining. Cut two each of the sleeve and sleeve band from blanketing. Cut two sleeves from lining. Cut three collars on the fold: two from blanketing and one from interfacing. Cut two 2-in. x 20-in. strips of interfacing for the placket. Clip all notches.

2 Apply the placket interfacings to the wrong side of the coat front lining pieces along the center front extension, making sure the interfacing does not extend into the seam allowance. Trim the edges of the collar interfacing by ½ in. and apply to one collar wrong side.

3 Right sides together, pin and stitch the two collars together along the unnotched edge. Trim the seams to ¼ in., clip if needed, turn the collar right-side out, and press. Baste the raw edges of the collar together ⅜ in. from the edges.

4 Trim 1½ in. evenly from the lower edge of each lining piece and then narrowly hem each piece.

5 Right sides together, pin and stitch the coat front to the coat back at the shoulders. Press open the seam allowances. Repeat for the lining.

6 With the interfaced collar against the right side of the coat, pin the collar to the neckline, matching the notches on the collar to the coat shoulder seams. Line up the finished edges of the collar with the notches at coat center front (not the placket edge). Baste the collar in place ⅜ in. from the neckline edges.

7 Right sides together and the collar sandwiched in between, pin and stitch the lining to the coat along the neckline and front placket. Trim the seam allowances to ¼ in., press them toward the lining, and understitch where possible. Turn the lining to the inside of the coat and press along the seamlines. Note: Don't trim the unstitched seam allowance along the center near the hem area.

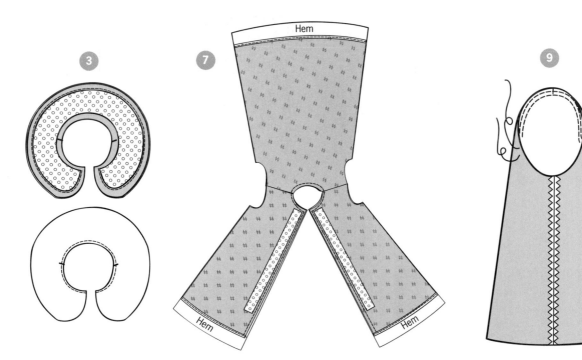

8 Right sides together, pin and stitch the coat side seams. Press open and clean-finish the seam allowances. Repeat for the lining.

9 Right sides together, pin and stitch the underarm sleeve seams together. Press open and clean-finish the seam allowances. Stitch two rows of basting stitches along the sleeve cap seam allowances between the notches. Repeat for the sleeve linings and then narrowly roll hem the sleeve lining lower edge.

10 Right sides together, pin and stitch each sleeve band together along the notched ends to create a circle. Press open the seam allowances. Wrong sides together, fold the band in half with the fold parallel to the long edges and press, matching raw edges. Slip the band over the sleeve lower edge. Pin and stitch the band to the sleeve, lining up the band seam with the sleeve underarm seam. Clean-finish the seam allowances and press them toward the band.

11 Right sides together, place the sleeve inside the coat and pin it to the armhole. Match the underarm seams, notches (single notch to single notch and double notch to double notch), and the shoulder seam on the coat to the top notch on the sleeve. Pull up the basting stitches to ease the sleeve cap to fit. Stitch in place and repeat for the other sleeve. Stitch the sleeve linings to the coat lining in the same manner. Slip the sleeve linings inside the coat sleeves and hand stitch them in place inside the sleeve near the lower edge.

12 Use a ruler and fabric pencil to mark the placement of the buttonholes, as shown. Stitch the buttonholes and hand stitch the buttons in place underneath.

13 Hem the coat lower edge. Fold and press the raw edge under ½ in., fold and pin under another 1 in. and hand stitch in place.

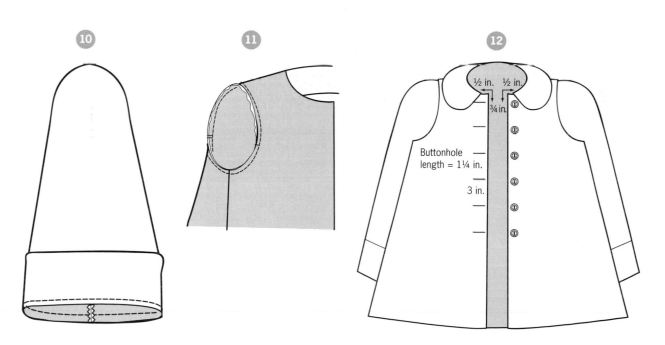

NIP-WAIST DRESS

Pattern Level 3 Sewing Level 3

Sometimes revamping an old garment to create something new is as easy as adding one pattern piece to the mix. Here you can take a dress with no shape and use a midriff pattern to bring in the waist and show off your girlish figure. Dig deep into your grandma's closet, or through the racks at the thrift

store to find a midi- or maxi-length loose dress with no darts or shaping. Try to uncover a dress with a fantastic print or unexpected bodice details like wild scallops, an asymmetrical neckline, or a surprising fold or burst of fullness at the shoulders.

Special Gear

⊕ "YOU" DRESS BODICE Front and Back patterns from page 38 or a ready-made basic bodice pattern (no seam allowance)

⊕ Invisible zipper (see page 26 in Chapter 1 for more about zipper measurement)

DIY PATTERN

1 Trace the **"YOU" DRESS BODICE Front** pattern. Draw a cutting line from the bust point to mid-shoulder.

2 Cut out the pattern and cut along the line, stopping just short of the *bust point*. Tape the original dart closed.

3 From the waistline, measure 4 in. upward along center front and the side and mark with dots. Connect the dots with a smooth shallow curve, making sure the curved line meets center front at a square angle. Cut the pattern apart along the new line. Trace a fresh copy of the pattern and clean up the waistline curve. Label with "Front Midriff" and "Cut 1 on Fold."

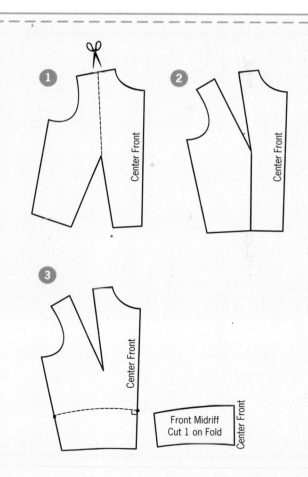

4 Repeat steps **1** to **3**, using the **"YOU" DRESS BODICE Back** pattern. Label with "Back Midriff" and "Cut 2."

5 Add ½-in. seam allowance to both midriff patterns, except along center front. Draw grainline arrows on both patterns 45° from center front/center back. Mark notches halfway down each side.

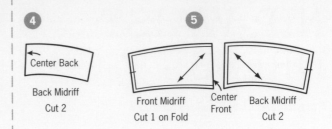

④

Center Back

Back Midriff

Cut 2

⑤

Front Midriff

Cut 1 on Fold

Center Front

Back Midriff

Cut 2

CUT UP, SEW UP

1 Try on the dress inside out. With a piece of chalk, draw a line at both side seams indicating the location of your waist. Take off the dress and lay it on the table inside out. Measure upward from the chalk marks 3½ in. Using these marks, draw a slightly curved waistline on both the front and back sides of the dress, as shown. Cut along this line and set the bodice (upper half) aside for now.

2 Decide the skirt length and measure up this distance from the lower edge along the sides and mark with chalk. Draw a slightly curved waistline on both the dress front and back as shown. Use extra fabric in the middle to cut one midriff front on the fold and two midriff backs. If you do not have enough space to cut the patterns on the bias, use the center front and center back as the grainline. Plan where the pattern pieces should go and cut the fabric section free from the rest of the skirt so you can lay it out flat and fold it along the appropriate grain. Clip the notches. Clip additional notches along the top and bottom edges of the front midriff at center front.

3 Right sides together, pin and stitch the front midriff to the back midriffs at the side edges, matching notches. Press open and clean-finish the seam allowances.

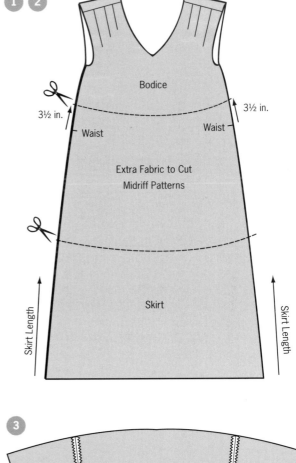

① ②

Bodice

3½ in.

Waist

3½ in.

Waist

Extra Fabric to Cut Midriff Patterns

Skirt

Skirt Length

Skirt Length

③

4 Cut open the bodice along center back and mark a notch along the waistline at center front. Gather the lower bodice edge to match the upper midriff edge; pin right sides together and stitch, matching side seams and notches. Clean-finish the seam allowances and press them toward the midriff.

5 Cut open the skirt along center back and mark a notch along the waistline at center front. Gather the upper skirt edge to match the lower midriff edge. Right sides together, pin and stitch the gathered skirt upper edge to the lower midriff, matching side seams and notches. Clean-finish the seam allowances and press them toward the skirt.

6 Install a zipper along the center back and close up the remainder of the seam. Hem the bottom edge, if necessary.

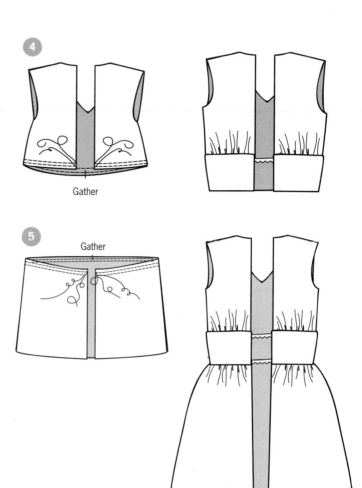

Gather

Gather

Mix It Up

⊕ **Cut the midriff from a contrasting fabric or separate the midriff into four pieces and use four different fabrics. Cut two front midriffs instead of cutting one on the fold.**

⊕ **Try creating a dress from scratch by combining the midriff pattern with the SUCH A SQUARE BLOUSE and DELUXE RECTANGLE SKIRT patterns.**

⊕ **Experiment with out-of-the-ordinary style lines when drawing the midriff pattern.**

PEEK-A-BOO JUMPER DRESS

Pattern Level 3 Sewing Level 3

Anyone obsessed with layering will love this little black dress. Truly a dress for all seasons, you can pop it on over a tube top or T-shirt for summertime frolicking or over a turtleneck or long-sleeve blouse for winter coffee dates. The dress opens up along the shoulders with a mini-placket and has a zipper along the side skirt. Once you get the pattern made, it sews up quickly. I like how structured the dress is in a medium- to heavyweight woven fabric, but it could also look pretty in a lightweight woven. You'll likely need to recycle more than one garment or item since the dress has a lining.

Special Gear

- ⊕ POSTER ART DRESS Front and Back patterns from page 153 (no seam or hem allowances)
- ⊕ A-LINE SKIRT Front and Back patterns from page 89 (no seam or hem allowances)
- ⊕ Invisible zipper (see page 26 in Chapter 1 for more about zipper measurement)
- ⊕ Four ½ in. buttons
- ⊕ ⅛ yd. light- to medium-weight interfacing
- ⊕ Extra recycled fabric for the dress lining (at least a yd. or so)

DIY PATTERN

1 Trace the **POSTER ART DRESS Front** and **Back** patterns on large pieces of paper; include the waistline notches, but omit the side seams and hemlines. Tape the **A-LINE SKIRT** patterns on top of the tracings with the center front/center back lines matching and the skirt waist matching up with the waistline notch. Trace the skirts.

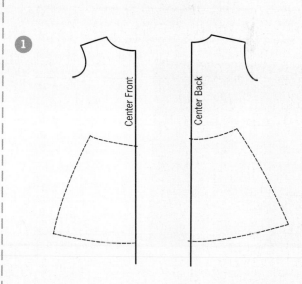

2 From the neckline, measure over 2 in. along each shoulder and mark with a dot. Use a curved ruler to draw new style lines connecting the dots along the shoulder to the side waist of the skirts.

3 On the back pattern, extend the shoulder line upward by 1 in. to create a placket.

4 Add ½-in. seam allowance on all edges of both patterns, except along the centers. Add an additional 1 in. to the lower edge for the hem. Label each of the patterns with "Peek-A-Boo Jumper," "Cut 1 on Fold," and "Cut 1 Lining on Fold."

Mix It Up

⊕ Add a collar to the neckline. Create one each for the front and back and have them meet in an interesting way at the shoulder lines.

⊕ Create a kangaroo pocket or play around with any type of topstitched outside pockets in various fun shapes.

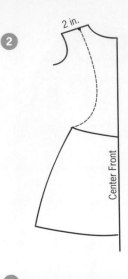

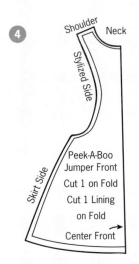

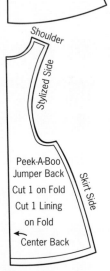

CUT UP, SEW UP

1 Cut two each of the dress front and back on the fold: one in a regular fabric and one in a lining fabric. Cut four 1-in. x 2-in. rectangles of interfacing. Apply the interfacing to the lining pieces at the shoulders, making sure to avoid the seam allowances.

2 Right sides together, pin and stitch the dress front to the dress front lining along the shoulder, neckline, and stylized side of the bodice. Don't stitch the side of the skirt together yet. Trim the seam to ¼ in. and press the seam allowances toward the lining. Turn the dress right-side out and press to neaten the edges. Repeat for the dress back/lining.

3 Place the front dress on the table, right-side up. Place the back dress on top of the front dress, right-side down. Pin and stitch the front dress to the back dress along the left skirt side seam, stitching the lining to the lining and the dress to the dress. Open the lining outward along the side seams, start at the lower lining edge and cross over the intersection of the lining and the dress; continue stitching to the dress lower edge. Press open and clean-finish the seam allowances.

4 Install an invisible zipper on the right skirt side seam and close up the remainder of the seam below the zipper. This can be a little tricky with the lining already attached, but open out the lining as if it were an extension of the seam and stitch the zipper in place with the upper zipper stop at the intersection of the dress and the lining. The excess zipper tape at the upper zipper gets stitched to the lining and flipped inside. Close up the remainder of the seam below the zipper and on the lining below the zipper area. Hand stitch the lining in place along the finished zipper.

5 Stitch two ⅝ in. vertical buttonholes on each of the back shoulder plackets, as shown. Stitch two buttons on each of the front shoulders under the buttonholes.

6 Hem the lower dress edge. Trim the dress lining lower edge ½ in. and hem separately.

Front

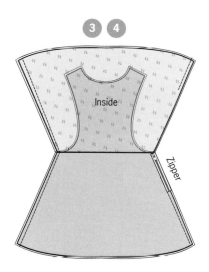

Inside

Zipper

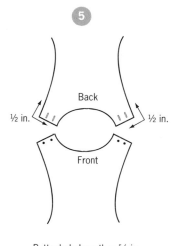

Back

½ in. ½ in.

Front

Buttonhole Length = ⅝ in.
½ in. buttons

CASHMERE HOODIE DRESS

Pattern Level 3 Sewing Level 4

Once upon a time, I discovered an XXXL black cashmere sweater on the men's rack at a thrift shop. With two more sweaters, I created this soft and fuzzy hoodie dress. The laced-up deep-front opening and generous hood give the dress a sexy, yet sporty, feel. I used two black sweaters to make the majority of

the dress and one poppy red sweater for the hood lining and trim details. Gather up as many large sweaters as needed to put yours together. Be prepared to do a combination of narrow zigzag stitching and hand stitching, since delicate sweater knits like to pucker under the machine needle.

Measure Up!

Full Hip 4
(Check out page 34 for specific measuring instructions.)

Special Gear

⊕ "YOU" DRESS SLEEVE pattern from page 42 (no seam allowance)

⊕ ⅛ yd. of lightweight tricot interfacing

DIY PATTERN

1 Follow DIY PATTERN steps **1** to **10** on page 153 to create a **POSTER ART DRESS Front** and **Back** pattern. Instead of making the length arbitrary in step **1**, make the dress end at your hip. Note: In step **4**, do not add 4 in. to your **Full Hip** calculation.

2 On the front pattern, mark a dot 4 to 5 in. below the neckline along center front. Draw a V neckline to this dot and cut along the line.

3 Measure down 4 to 5 in. from the lower point of the V-neck along center front and mark with a dot. Measure inward ½ in. from the dot and mark another dot. Draw an indent from the center front line to the V-neck, as shown. Cut it out.

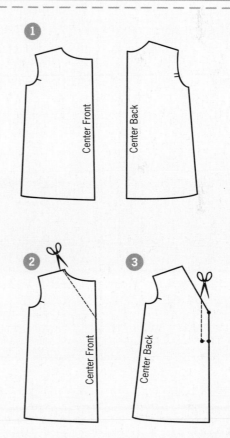

4 Draw a 10-in. x 12-in. rectangle. Label the left edge center back. Measure the front and back necklines and add them together (don't include the indentation at center front in this calculation). Using a curved ruler, draw a curved neckline this length starting at the lower left point of the rectangle, as shown.

5 Draw another curved line, connecting the lower neckline point with the right edge of the rectangle.

6 Draw a 2-in. square in the upper left corner of the rectangle and cut it out. Label the pattern with "Hood," "Cut 1 on Fold," and "Cut 1 Lining on Fold."

7 Divide your **Full Hip** measurement by four. Draw a 16-in.-long rectangle using this calculation as the width. Label with "Lower Band" and "Cut 2 on Fold." Label the right edge "Center."

8 Trace a copy of the **"YOU" DRESS SLEEVE** pattern and shorten it to just past the elbow. Label with "Sleeve" and "Cut 2." Draw a grainline arrow perpendicular to the bicep line.

9 Add ³⁄₈-in. seam allowance to all pattern pieces, except along the centers.

Mix It Up

⊕ Create a casing along the front edge of the hood and thread a drawstring through it to cinch it up.

⊕ Recycle sweatshirts and create a more traditional hoodie with a front zipper. Skip the V-neck and center front indentation, add a seam allowance to the center front edge, and make the lower band skinnier.

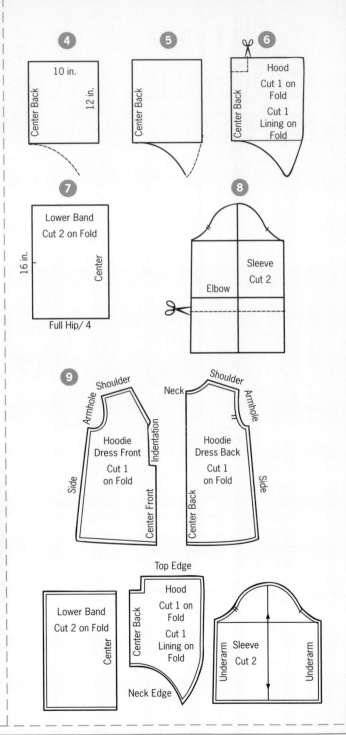

CUT UP, SEW UP

1 Cut one dress front, one dress back, and two lower bands, all on the fold. Cut two hoods on the fold: one from sweater fabric and one from lining. Cut two sleeves. Clip the notches. Clip an additional notch at the center back neckline of the dress and hood, and at the top of the sleeve at the grainline. Cut the ribbed arm, neck, and hem cuffs from the sweaters and set them aside for step **3** and step **9**. Try not to stretch any of the cut edges, as it might create runs in the fabric. Alternatively, you can stabilize the edges with a basting stitch.

2 Right sides together, pin and stitch the dress front to the dress back along the shoulders and the sides. Press open and clean-finish the seam allowances.

3 Measure the indentation along center front. Use some of the ribbing set aside in step **1** to cut a rectangle this length and 2 in. wide. Center and apply a 1¼-in. strip of interfacing to the wrong side of the ribbing. Fold the ribbing in half lengthwise wrong sides together. Pin and stitch the folded ribbing to the indentation along center front with a ⅜-in. seam allowance, matching raw edges. Clean-finish and hand stitch the seam allowance to the inside of the dress.

4 Right sides together, fold the hood along center back. Pin and stitch the upper hood edges together, pivoting around the corner. Repeat for the hood lining.

5 Right sides together, stitch the hood to the hood lining along the front edge. Turn right-side out, pin and staystitch the raw edges together along the neck ¼ in. from the edge.

6 Right sides together, pin and stitch the hood to the dress along the neckline, matching the hood seam to the center back dress notch. Clean-finish and hand stitch the seam allowances to the inside of the dress. Tuck the top raw edges of the ribbing inward and hand stitch to clean finish.

7 Right sides together, pin and stitch the underarm sleeve seams together. Press open and clean-finish the seams. Stitch two rows of basting stitches inside the seam allowance along the sleeve caps between the notches.

8 Right sides together, place the sleeve inside the dress and pin it to the armhole. Match the underarm seams, notches (single notch to single notch and double notch to double notch), and the shoulder seam on the dress to the top notch on the sleeve. Pull up along the basting stitches to ease the sleeve cap. Stitch in place.

9 Measure the widest part of your arm below the elbow. Use the ribbing set aside in step **1** to cut two pieces in contrasting colors this width plus 1 in. (length will vary depending on the original ribbing). Right sides together, pin and stitch the two pieces together along one long edge with a ¼-in. seam. Right sides together, pin and stitch the short ends of the ribbing together with a ¼-in. seam allowance to create a band. Stitch again to reinforce. Right sides together, slip the band over the sleeve edge matching raw edges. Pin and stitch the band to the sleeve with a ⅜-in. seam allowance, lining up the band seam with the underarm seam on the sleeve, stretching the band to fit the sleeve edge as you sew.

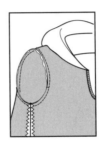

10 Right sides together, pin and stitch the lower bands together along the notched ends to create a circle. Press open the seams. Fold the band in half with the fold parallel to the long edges and wrong sides and raw edges together. Pin and stitch the band to the dress, aligning the side seams. Clean-finish the seam allowances and hand stitch them to the band.

11 Create six vertical buttonholes on the ribbing along the center front indentation and lace a 30-in. tube drawstring up the front of the hoodie.

MAXI TO MINIDRESS

By Amy Sperber

Sewing Level 4

When Amy found a brocade party dress at her local vintage shop, she channeled her inner Molly Ringwald, from the movie *Pretty in Pink*, to turn it into a flirty and fun minidress. To make a modern, prom-worthy minidress of your own, search the racks at your local vintage shop to find a maxi-length dress in a retro, ladylike fabric. Since they don't make fabrics in the types of prints and colors like they used to, yours will be one-of-a-kind, for sure.

Amy Sperber

Amy Sperber designs adorable accessories for her company, 31 Corn Lane, which she runs with her sisters in Brooklyn, NY. She also teaches at the Fashion Institute of Technology and is a freelance product designer. See her work at www.31cornlane.com.

Special Gear

⊕ **Dress form**

⊕ **1 yd. of ½-in-wide flat ribbon, any color**

CUT UP, SEW UP

1 Use a seam ripper to remove the zipper, open up the center back seam, and separate the bodice from the skirt. My dress didn't have sleeves, but if yours does, go ahead and remove those, plus any decorative elements like bows or sashes, and any lining.

2 Place the bodice inside out on a dress form matching the bust shaping darts to the bust apex on the form. If the bodice is much larger than your dress form, make a center front seam to remove some fullness and resize it at the side seams by pinching and pinning out as much as needed. Place the pins vertically along the seam and make sure to pin equally on both sides. Use chalk or a fabric pencil to mark the new side seamlines along the pins. Remove the bodice from the dress form, use a ruler to add ½-in. seam allowances, and then cut through all the layers. Right sides together, stitch the new side seams and press them open or toward the back of the bodice.

3 Pin ribbon to the front and back of the bodice to visually design the new strapless neckline shape. Use chalk or fabric pencil to trace along the outside edges of the ribbon. Remove the bodice from the dress form, use a ruler to add ½-in. seam allowances to the markings, and then cut through all layers. Set the bodice aside for now.

4 Place the skirt on the dress form, using a ribbon to hold it to the form. Choose a skirt length including a hem allowance, and measure down from the waistline this distance around the entire skirt. Mark the new length with chalk and cut along the line.

5 Remove the skirt from the dress form. Gather the upper edge to match the lower bodice edge. My dress had darts, so I just gathered between them at the side seams. Right sides together, pin and stitch the skirt to the bodice.

6 Cut a 2-in. fabric strip from the extra skirt fabric to use as a neckline facing on the bodice. My dress had hem tape sewn at the hem, so I kept it attached to have a clean-finished facing. If you have lots of extra fabric, consider cutting the strip on the bias so that it curves around the neckline easily. Right sides together, pin and stitch the facing to the neckline edge. Trim the seam allowances and press them toward the facing. Turn the facing under, press and hand-stitch it to the inside of the bodice.

7 Reinstall the zipper along center back, shortening it if necessary, and close up the remainder of the seam.

8 Hand-stitch three small horizontal tucks at the bodice upper edge center front to create a sweetheart neckline. Handstitch a bow or other decorative detail in place just below the tucks.

9 Hem the dress lower edge, if needed.

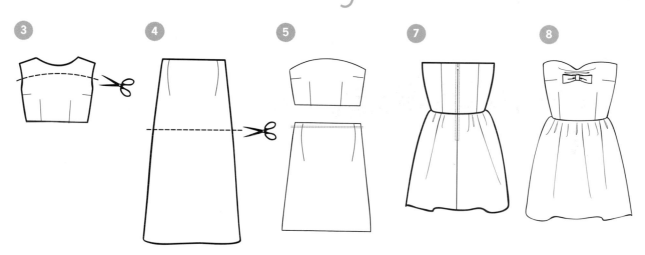

FAIRY RACER DRESS

Pattern Level 3 Sewing Level 4

Here, a racer-front bodice style is combined with a double-tier ruffle skirt to create a sleek, yet ethereal dress. I scored when I found this art-dyed silk fabric at a garage sale and originally used the yardage to make a sundress from a commercial pattern. A year later, I took the dress apart to use the fabric for this ruffled number. For added glamour, I hand stitched some beads and jewels from a broken necklace along the neckline. Make a weekend of it and search around at garage and estate sales for medium-weight woven fabric that you can use to make your own pixie of a dress. Use the same fabric for the bodice lining or pick up something separate in a compatible weight. Don't forget to keep your eyes open for matching jewels!

Measure Up!

Full Waist ③

(Check out page 34 for specific measuring instructions.)

Special Gear

- ⊕ **"YOU" DRESS BODICE** Front and Back patterns from page 38 or a ready-made basic bodice pattern (no seam allowance)
- ⊕ Invisible zipper (see page 26 in Chapter 1 for more about zipper measurement)
- ⊕ ½ in. button
- ⊕ ⅛ yd. interfacing
- ⊕ Extra recycled fabric for the bodice lining (approximately one yd.)

DIY PATTERN

1 Trace the **"YOU" DRESS BODICE Front** pattern. Draw a line from the *bust point* to mid shoulder. Cut along the line to separate the patterns.

2 On both pattern pieces, measure 3 in. above and below the bust point and mark notches. On the upper notches, measure inward ½ in. and mark dots. Connect the bust

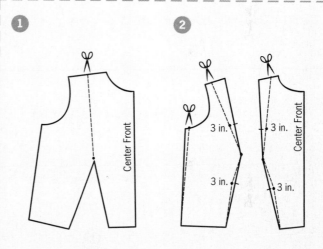

point to the shoulder through these dots. On the lower notches, measure inward ⅜ in. and mark dots. Connect the bust point to these dots, and then connect the dots to the original dart legs at the waist. Measure inward ½ in. along the side line at the underarm and mark with a dot. Draw a line from this dot that tapers to the waist. Cut along all the new lines.

3 Tape the patterns together temporarily at the top, matching bust points and dots. From the waistline, measure upward along the side line 6 in. and mark with a dot. From the neckline, measure out along the shoulder 1 in. and mark with a dot. Draw a new style line on the pattern, as shown, connecting these new dots with the upper dot above the bust point. Cut along the style line and separate the two pattern pieces.

4 Smooth the sharp angles along the bust edges. Draw a grainline arrow on the front side bodice perpendicular to the waistline. Mark notches in place of the dots, as shown.

5 Trace the **"YOU" DRESS BODICE Back** pattern, including the horizontal balance line (HBL). Mark a dot along the horizontal balance line directly above the dart point. Draw dart legs from the horizontal balance line point to the original dart legs at the waist. Measure inward ½ in. along the side line at the underarm and mark with a dot. Draw a line from this dot tapering to the waist. Cut along the horizontal balance line as well as the new lines.

6 Set the upper portion of the pattern aside for now. Tape the lower patterns together along the dart legs. From the waistline, measure upward along the side line 6 in. and along center back 4 in. Mark with dots. Connect the dots, making sure the line meets center back at a square angle. Cut along this line, discard the upper section, and label the lower portion with "Fairy Racer Dress Bodice Back," "Cut 2," and "Cut 2 Lining." Draw a grainline parallel to center back.

7 On the upper portion of the back pattern, measure down 1 in. along center back and 1 in. along the shoulder. Connect the dots with a curved line 1 in. from the neckline. Cut along the line and discard the lower section. Extend center back by 1 in. and label the pattern with "Back Neck Band," "Cut 2," and "Cut 2 Lining." Draw a grainline parallel to center back and notch the center back edge.

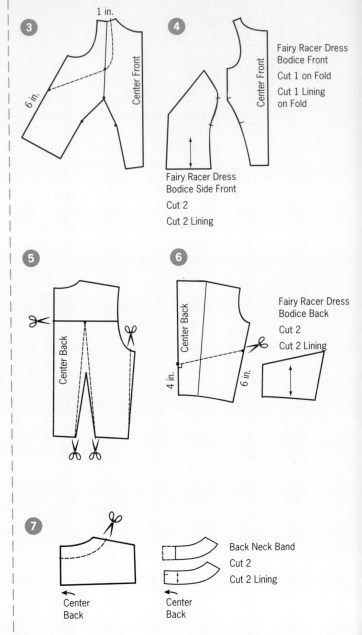

Fairy Racer Dress Bodice Front
Cut 1 on Fold
Cut 1 Lining on Fold

Fairy Racer Dress Bodice Side Front
Cut 2
Cut 2 Lining

Fairy Racer Dress Bodice Back
Cut 2
Cut 2 Lining

Back Neck Band
Cut 2
Cut 2 Lining

8 Draw a 13-in.-long rectangle with your **Full Waist** measurement as the width. Label the right edge "Center Front" and the left edge "Center Back." Measure down ¼ in. along center back and mark with a dot. Taper the upper edge of the rectangle down to meet this dot, making sure the line meets center back at a square angle. Label with "Fairy Racer Dress Tier 1 Skirt" and "Cut 1 on Center Front Fold."

9 Draw a 6-in.-long rectangle with your **Full Waist** measurement as the width. Label the right edge center. Label with "Fairy Racer Dress Tier 2 Skirt" and "Cut 2 on Fold."

10 Add ½-in. seam allowance to all pattern pieces, except along the centers. Mark a double notch along center back on the tier 1 skirt about midway down. Add an additional 1 in. to the lower edge of tier 2 skirt for the hem.

Mix It Up

⊕ Attach any skirt or shorts style to the bodice. I keep daydreaming of making a wedding gown with this bodice style!

⊕ Create a back bodice with more coverage by connecting the lower section to the back neck band in some creative way.

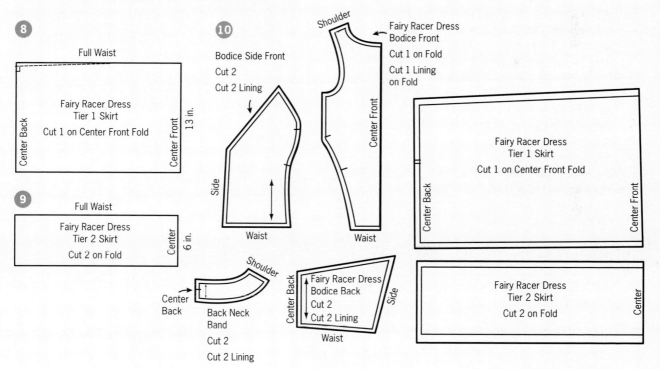

CUT UP, SEW UP

1. Cut two of the bodice front on the fold: one from regular fabric and one from lining. Cut four of the bodice side front, bodice back, and back neck band: two from regular fabric and two from lining. Cut one tier 1 skirt and two tier 2 skirts on the fold. If you don't have enough fabric to cut the tiers on the fold, cut them separately or piece together several rectangles of fabric until you have enough. Cut two back neck bands from interfacing, trim the seam allowances, and apply it to the wrong side of the neck band lining. Clip notches. Clip additional notches along the bodice front waistline center front and along both edges of the tier 1 skirt at center front.

2. Right sides together, pin and stitch the bodice front to the back neck band along the shoulders. Press open the seam allowances. Repeat for the lining.

3. Right sides together, pin and stitch the bodice front to the bodice side front pieces along the notched edges, matching notches and easing around the bust points. Press open the seam allowances and clip the curves. Repeat for the lining.

4. Right sides together, pin and stitch the bodice backs to the bodice side fronts along the sides. Press open the seam allowances. Repeat for the lining.

5. Right sides together, pin and stitch the bodice to the lining along all the edges, except center back and the waistline. Trim the seam to ¼ in. and press it toward the lining. Turn the bodice right-side out, understitch where possible, and press along the edges to neaten. Baste the bodice to the lining along the center back and waistline ⅜ in. from the edges.

6. Right sides together, pin and stitch the tier 2 skirt sections together along the short edge to create one big tier. Press open and clean-finish the seam allowances. Gather the upper edges of the tier 2 skirt to match the lower edge of tier 1. Right sides together, pin and stitch the upper edge of tier 2 to the lower edge of tier 1, matching the tier 2 seam with the tier 1 center front notch.

7. Gather the upper edge of the tier 1 skirt to match the lower bodice edge. Right sides together, pin and stitch the tier 1 skirt to the bodice, matching center front notches. Clean-finish the seam allowances and press them toward the skirt.

8. Install a zipper along center back and close up the remainder of the seam. Use the double notch as a guide.

9. Stitch a ⅝-in.-long buttonhole along the neck band edge and sew a button on the opposite side.

10. Hem the lower skirt edge. Fold and press the raw edge under ½ in., fold and pin under another 1 in. and stitch in place along the upper fold.

POWER SLOPE DRESS

Pattern Level 3   Sewing Level 4

Nothing says authority like powerful shoulders, nor mesmerizes like madcap stripes. Sculpted, all-in-one cap sleeves and a front bib are the main focus, but the bias-cut necktie is also a smart detail. I'm shocked that I had enough fabric to put this dress together since I used a three-paneled skirt I originally cut from a knee-length dress. I had to lay out the patterns in opposing directions, so the back bodice has horizontal stripes—a nice touch! Skip the stress and look for an oversized garment made from a medium-weight woven stripe to lay out your pattern.

Special Gear

- ⊕ "YOU" DRESS BODICE Front and Back patterns from page 38 or a ready-made basic bodice pattern (no seam allowances)
- ⊕ "YOU" DRESS SLEEVE pattern from page 42 or ready-made basic sleeve pattern (no seam allowances)
- ⊕ A-LINE SKIRT Front and Back patterns from page 89 (no seam or hem allowances)
- ⊕ Invisible zipper (see page 26 in Chapter 1 for more about zipper measurement)
- ⊕ ½ yard lightweight interfacing

DIY PATTERN

1 Trace the **BODICE FRONT** pattern, including the armhole notch. Find the mid-point along the side seam and mark with a dot. Draw a cutting line from the bust point to the dot.

2 Cut out the pattern and cut along the line, stopping just short of the bust point. Close the original dart halfway, opening up the side dart halfway. Tape in place. On both darts, create dart points 1 in. from the bust points and draw new dart legs to these points.

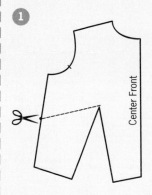

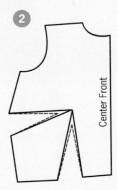

3 From the neckline, measure out 2 in. along the shoulder and mark with a dot. Measure down 6 in. along the center front line and mark with a dot. Connect the dots to create a bib-like style line, as shown. Make sure the style line meets center front at a square angle. Mark a notch along the line and then cut it out. Label the new pattern with "Bib" and "Cut 1 on Fold." Label the remaining section "Bodice Front" and "Cut 1 on Fold."

4 Trace the top portion of the **"YOU" DRESS SLEEVE**, including the bicep line, center line, and notches. Mark dots along the sleeve cap ½ in. above the notches. Connect the dots with a curved line, as shown. Cut along the curved line and the center line to separate the pattern. Discard the lower sections. Label the right pattern "Front" and the left pattern "Back." Label the center edge and mark the mid-point along the center edge with a notch.

5 On the bodice front, mark a dot ½ in. above the armhole notch. Place the front sleeve section on the dot, as shown. Trace the lower edge and the center edge up to the notch.

6 Free-form draw the upper sleeve curve, as shown. The upper edge should be about ¼ in. above the shoulder tip.

7 Trace the **"YOU" DRESS BODICE BACK** pattern, including the armhole notch. Repeat steps **5** and **6**, using the back patterns.

8 Create front and back armhole facings (see page 36), including the sleeve caps.

9 Measure the front neckline on the bib pattern and the back neckline on the bodice back. Add these measurements together, multiply by two and add 20 in. Draw a line using this calculation. Find the line mid-point and mark with a dot. Draw a perpendicular line 3 in. from the mid-point dot, and then connect the end of the mid-point line to the ends of the original line. Curve any sharp angles. Label the original line "Center" and draw a grainline 45° from the center. Label with "Necktie" and "Cut 1 on Fold."

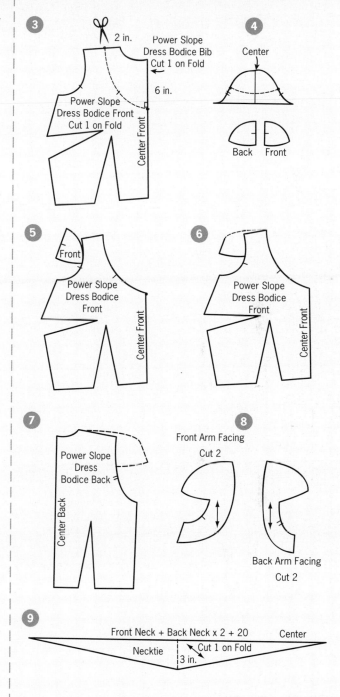

10 Trace the **A-LINE SKIRT Front** and **Back** patterns. Draw a grainline parallel to center back on the skirt back and mark a double notch along center back at hip level. True the darts on the bodice patterns. Add ½-in. seam allowance to all pattern edges, except along center front. Add an additional 1 in. to the skirt lower edges for the hem.

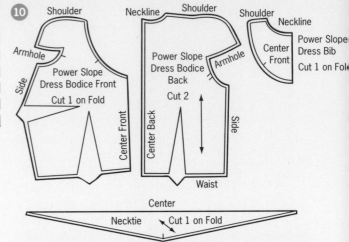

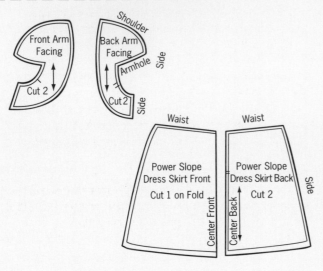

Mix It Up

⊕ **Insert shoulder pads between the facing and the dress to amp it up even more.**

⊕ **Add a dropped cap sleeve to a regular armhole on any pattern.**

⊕ **Create a square bib or experiment with other bib shapes**

CUT UP, SEW UP

1 Cut one front bodice, one bib, and one skirt front, each on the fold. Cut one necktie on a bias fold. Cut two back bodices, two front armhole facings, two back armhole facings, and two skirt backs. Cut two of each of the armhole facings and one necktie from interfacing. Trim the seam allowances from all the interfacing pieces and apply them to the wrong side of the corresponding fabric pieces. Clip notches. Clip additional notches along the upper and lower edges of the bib and bodice at center front. Clip an additional notch at the center front waistline skirt front. Trace the darts.

2 Right sides together, pin and stitch the bib to the bodice, matching notches. Stitch one side of the bib at a time, easing as you go. Press the seam allowances open and clean-finish. Clip the curves. Or, reinforce the stitching and trim the seam allowances to ¼ in.

3 Stitch the darts on the bodice front and backs. Press the waist darts toward center and the side darts toward the waist.

4 Right sides together, pin and stitch the bodice front to the bodice back pieces along the shoulders. Press open and clean-finish the seam allowances. Repeat for the armhole facings.

5 Right sides together, pin and stitch the armhole facings to the bodice along the armhole and the lower side of the cap sleeve, pivoting at the corners. Trim the seam to ¼ in., carefully clip inward at the corners, press the seam allowance toward the facing, and understitch where possible.

6 Right sides together, open the armhole facing outward along the side seams, pin and stitch the front bodice to the back bodice along the sides. Start at the edge of the facing and cross over the intersection of the facing and the bodice. Press open and clean-finish the seam allowances. Clean-finish the facing outer edge and hand stitch it to the inside of the bodice. Repeat for the other side.

7 Right sides together, pin and stitch the front skirt to the back skirt pieces along the side seams. Press open and clean-finish the seam allowances.

8 Right sides together, pin and stitch the skirt to the bodice along the waistline, matching side seams and center front notches. Press open and clean-finish the seam allowances, and then press them toward the skirt.

9 Install a zipper along center back and close up the remainder of the seam. Use the double notch as a guide.

10 Right sides together, fold the necktie in half lengthwise. Pin and stitch the raw edges closed, but start at one end and stitch only 10 in. Repeat on the other end, leaving a gap in the middle of the necktie. Trim the seams to ¼ in., turn the necktie right-side out, and press to neaten. Don't trim the unstitched edges along the gap.

11 Right sides together, pin and stitch one layer of the unstitched tie gap to the dress neckline, matching notches. Clip the curves and press the seam allowance to the inside of the necktie. Fold and press the unstitched edge of the necktie inside and hand stitch in place.

12 Hem the dress lower edge. Fold and press the raw edge under ½ in., fold and pin under another 1 in. and hand stitch in place along the upper fold.

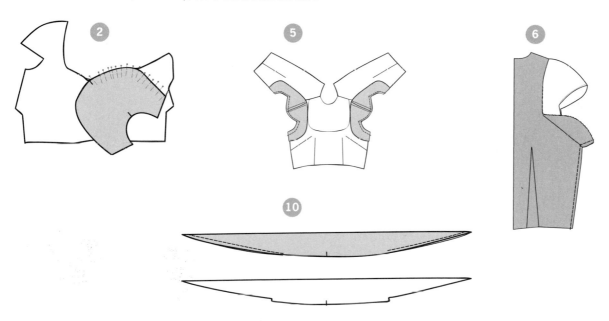

WEDDING CAKE DRESS

Pattern Level 3 Sewing Level 4

Whether you walk down the aisle or strut down the street, you'll most certainly feel like a treat in this delicious minidress. The white lace tiers on this strapless confection remind me of a yummy wedding cake, but you would never guess that the whole thing is made from two old tablecloths! When you're looking for fabric to make this dress, check out the linen department at your nearby thrift store for a large lace tablecloth, preferably with a pretty scalloped edge. You'll also need a medium-weight solid color woven to use for the lining and underlay (I used a white cotton table cloth).

Special Gear

⊕ **"YOU" DRESS BODICE Front and Back patterns from page 38 or a ready-made basic bodice pattern (no seam allowance)**

⊕ **Invisible zipper (see page 26 in Chapter 1 for more about zipper measurement)**

⊕ **Extra recycled fabric, like a large linen item, for the lining and skirt underlay**

DIY PATTERN

1 Follow DIY PATTERN steps **1** and **2** on page 189 for the **FAIRY RACER DRESS** and then tape the patterns together temporarily at the top, matching bust points and dots. From the armhole, measure down 1 in. or more along the side line and mark with a dot. Draw a strapless style line, as shown, connecting the dots to center front. Make sure the style line meets center front at a square angle. Cut along the style line and separate the two pattern pieces.

2 Smooth any sharp angles along the bust edges. Label the right pattern with "Wedding Cake Dress Bodice Front," "Cut 1 on Fold," and "Cut 1 Lining on Fold." Label the left piece with "Wedding Cake Dress Bodice

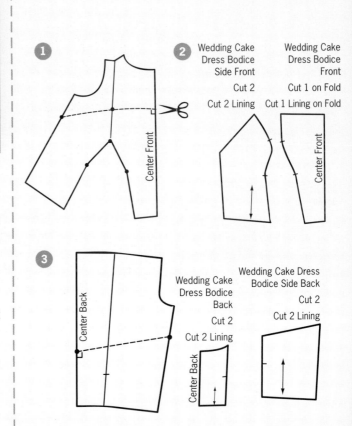

Side Front," "Cut 2," and "Cut 2 Lining." Draw a grainline on the bodice side front perpendicular to the waistline. Mark notches in place of the dots, as shown.

3 Follow DIY PATTERN step **5** on page 190 for the **FAIRY RACER DRESS**. Discard the upper portion of the pattern and temporarily tape the lower patterns together along the dart legs. From the armhole, measure down 1 in. or more (consistent with front pattern) along the side line and mark with a dot. From the waistline, measure upward 6 in. along center back and mark with a dot. Connect the dots, making sure the line meets center back at a square angle. Cut along this line and discard

the top section. Mark a notch along the dart legs and separate the two sides. Label the left pattern with "Wedding Cake Dress Bodice Back" and the right pattern with "Wedding Cake Dress Bodice Side Back." Label both patterns with "Cut 2" and "Cut 2 Lining" and draw grainlines parallel to center back.

4 Follow the DIY PATTERN instructions on page 95 for the **TIERED SKIRT** to create a tiered skirt pattern. Ignore any reference to a waistband and create four equal tiers instead of three unequal tiers. Add ½-in. seam allowance to all pattern pieces, except along center front.

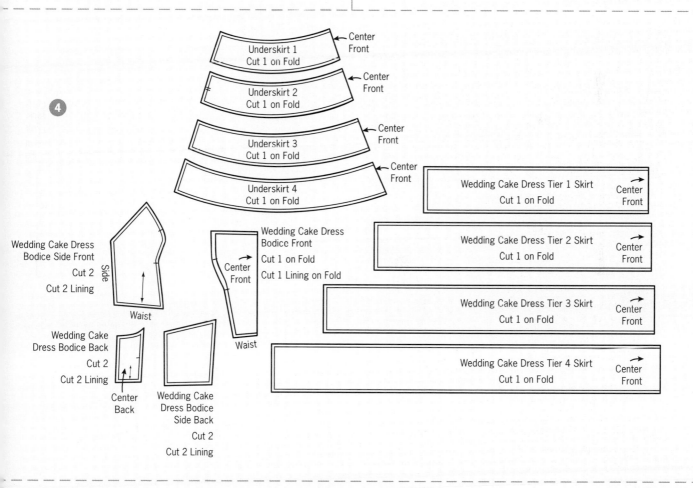

CUT UP, SEW UP

1 Cut two bodice fronts on the fold: one from lace fabric and one from lining. Cut four bodice side fronts, four bodice side backs, and four bodice backs: two each from lace fabric, and two from lining. Cut an additional set of all bodice pieces in an underlay fabric. Cut one of each underskirt and tier on the fold. If you don't have enough fabric to cut the tiers on the fold, cut them separately or piece together several rectangles of fabric until you have enough width. If you have a scalloped edge lace, try to cut the tiers with the scallops along the lower edge. Clip all notches. Clip additional notches at center front on the upper and lower edges of each pattern piece.

2 Right sides up, pin and stitch the lace bodice pieces to the underlay pieces ¼ in. from all edges.

3 Right sides together, pin and stitch the bodice front to the bodice side fronts along the notched edges, matching notches and easing around the bust. Press open the seams and clip the curves. Repeat for the lining.

4 Right sides together, pin and stitch the bodice back to the bodice side backs' matching notches. Press open the seams. Repeat for the lining.

5 Right sides together, pin and stitch the bodice front to the back along the sides. Press open the seams. Repeat for the lining.

6 Right sides together, pin and stitch the bodice to the lining along the upper edge, matching seams and notches. Trim the seam to ¼ in., press it toward the lining, and under-stitch. If you have a fuller bust, hand stitch strips of boning to the bust seams on the wrong side of the lining to help keep your top from falling down!

7 Turn the lining to the inside of the bodice and press to neaten. Wrong sides together, pin and staystitch the bodice to the lining along the back and waist edges with a ⅜-in. seam allowance.

8 Narrowly roll hem the lower and side edges of each skirt tier unless you have a scalloped lace edge, then leave them as is.

9 Gather the upper edge of tier 1 to match the upper edge of underskirt 1. With the right side of the underskirt facing the wrong side of the tier, pin and stitch them together along the upper edge using a ⅜-in. seam allowance. Match the center front notches and make sure the gathered tier does not extend into the seam allowance at center back. Repeat for the other three skirt sections.

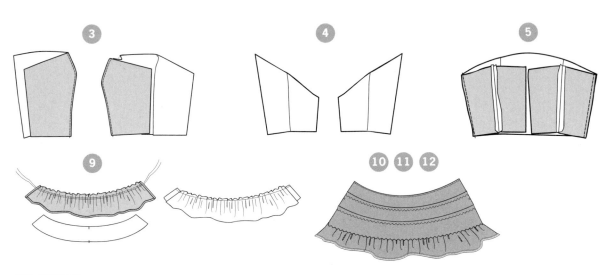

10 Right sides together, pin and stitch the upper edge of section 2 to the lower edge of underskirt 1, matching notches. Clean-finish the seam allowances and press them downward.

11 Right sides together, pin and stitch the upper edge of section 3 to the lower edge of underskirt 2, matching notches. Clean-finish the seam allowances and press them downward.

12 Right sides together, pin and stitch the upper edge of section 4 to the lower edge of underskirt 3, matching notches. Clean-finish the seam allowances and press them downward. Clean-finish the lower edge of underskirt 4.

13 Install a zipper along center back and sew up the remainder of the seam. Use the double notch as a guide.

Mix It Up

⊕ Add spaghetti straps to the bodice by sandwiching them between the layers at step 6.

⊕ Create a sweetheart neckline along the top of the bodice. You'll need to add seam allowance to the center front and cut the front bodice separately instead of on the fold.

BANANA DRESS

Pattern Level 3 Sewing Level 4

Can you see the three bananas on this dress? You get an extra star if you guessed the two ruffled inserts along the bodice and the necktie. Each of these pattern shapes resembles the shape of a banana, which makes them simple to fashion. The skirt has three attached tiers, each getting fuller as you move down the skirt. My dress was refashioned from a Hawaiian maxi-length dress and since it had several long skinny panels, I had to stitch together lots of small pieces of fabric to create the gathered tiers for the skirt. To make it easy on yourself, look for wide pieces of salvaged yardage in a medium-weight woven so you can cut the skirt tiers on the fold.

Measure Up!

Full Waist 3
(Check out page 34 for specific measuring instructions.)

Special Gear

- ⊕ **"YOU" DRESS BODICE Front and Back** patterns from page 38 or a ready-made basic bodice pattern (no seam allowance)
- ⊕ **Zipper** (see page 26 in Chapter 1 for more about zipper measurement)
- ⊕ **⅛ yd. lightweight interfacing**

DIY PATTERN

1 Trace the **"YOU" DRESS BODICE Front** pattern. Draw a cutting line from the *bust point* to mid-shoulder.

2 Cut out the pattern and cut along the drawn line, stopping just short of the bust point. Tape the original dart closed.

3 Evenly trim 2 in. from the pattern lower edge.

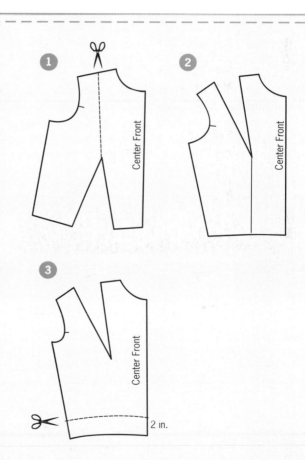

4 On the left side of the pattern, draw a grainline parallel to center front. From center front, measure 1½ in. inward along the new waistline and mark with a dot. Draw a cutting line from the dart point to the dot. Mark a notch at the dart point and cut along the line to separate the pattern into two pieces; smooth out the angles. Label the left pattern with "Banana Dress Bodice Side Front" and "Cut 2." Label the right pattern with "Banana Dress Bodice Front" and "Cut 1 on Fold."

5 Create a facing for the armhole (see page 36). Label with "Front Arm Facing" and "Cut 2."

6 Repeat steps 1 to 5 using the "YOU" DRESS BODICE Back pattern. Mark double notches at the dart point for step 4. Label the patterns "Banana Dress Bodice Side Back," "Banana Dress Bodice Back" and "Back Arm Facing." Label all the back patterns with "Cut 2." Draw a grainline arrow parallel to center back on the back bodice.

7 Measure the notched edges of the bodice side back and the bodice side front. Add these measurements together and multiply by two. Draw a line using this calculation. Find the midpoint and mark with a dot. Draw a perpendicular line 3 in. from the midpoint dot, and then connect the end of the midpoint line to the ends of the original line, creating a banana shape. Label the original line "Center." Mark a notch at the midpoint line and label the pattern with "Banana Dress Ruffle" and "Cut 2 on Fold."

8 Measure the front and back necklines. Add these measurements together, multiply by two, and add 20 in. Draw a line using this calculation. Find the midpoint and mark with a dot. Draw a perpendicular line 3 in. from the midpoint dot, and then connect the end of the midpoint line to the ends of the original line, creating a banana shape. Curve the sharp angle at the midpoint. Label the original line "Center" and draw a grainline 45° from the center. Label with "Necktie" and "Cut 1 on Fold."

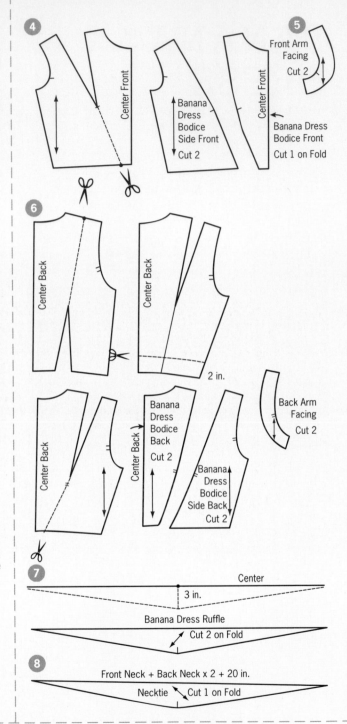

9 Draw a rectangle with your **Full Waist** measurement as the width and 7 in. long. Label the right edge "Center Front" and the left edge "Center Back." Measure down ¼ in. along center back and mark with a dot. Taper the top edge of the rectangle down to meet this dot, making sure the line meets center back at a square angle. Label with "Banana Dress Tier 1 Skirt" and "Cut 1 on Center Front Fold."

10 Draw a rectangle with your **Full Waist** measurement as the width and 7 in. long. Label the right edge "Center." Label with "Banana Dress Tier 2 Skirt" and "Cut 2 on Fold."

11 Draw a rectangle with your **Full Waist** measurement as the width and 7 in. long. Label the right edge "Center." Label with "Banana Dress Tier 3 Skirt" and "Cut 4 on Fold."

12 Add ½-in. seam allowance to all pattern pieces, except along the centers. Center Back receives seam allowance. Mark a double notch along center back on the tier 1 skirt about midway down. Add an additional 1 in. to the lower edge of the tier 3 skirt for the hem.

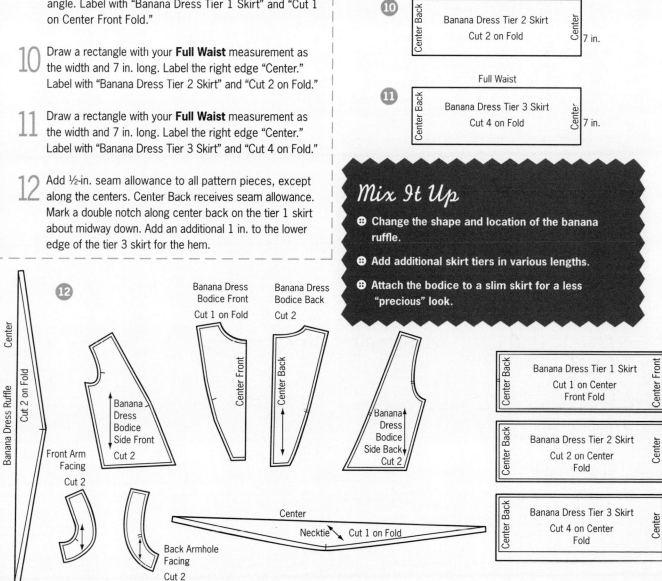

Full Waist

9 | Center Back | Banana Dress Tier 1 Skirt — Cut 1 on Center Front Fold | Center Front | 7 in.

Full Waist

10 | Center Back | Banana Dress Tier 2 Skirt — Cut 2 on Fold | Center | 7 in.

Full Waist

11 | Center Back | Banana Dress Tier 3 Skirt — Cut 4 on Fold | Center | 7 in.

Mix It Up

⊕ Change the shape and location of the banana ruffle.

⊕ Add additional skirt tiers in various lengths.

⊕ Attach the bodice to a slim skirt for a less "precious" look.

12

Banana Dress Ruffle — Center — Cut 2 on Fold

Banana Dress Bodice Side Front — Cut 2

Front Arm Facing — Cut 2

Back Armhole Facing — Cut 2

Banana Dress Bodice Front — Cut 1 on Fold — Center Front

Banana Dress Bodice Back — Cut 2 — Center Back

Banana Dress Bodice Side Back — Cut 2

Center — Necktie — Cut 1 on Fold

Center Back | Banana Dress Tier 1 Skirt — Cut 1 on Center Front Fold | Center Front

Center Back | Banana Dress Tier 2 Skirt — Cut 2 on Center Fold | Center

Center Back | Banana Dress Tier 3 Skirt — Cut 4 on Center Fold | Center

CUT UP, SEW UP

1 Cut one bodice front, one tier 1 skirt, two tier 2 skirts, four tier 3 skirts, and two banana ruffles, each on the fold. If you don't have enough fabric to cut the skirt tiers on the fold, cut them separately or stitch together several fabric rectangles until you have enough. Cut two each of the bodice side front, bodice back, bodice side back, front armhole facing, and back armhole facing. Cut one necktie on the bias fold. Cut the armhole facing and necktie patterns from interfacing and apply to the wrong side of the corresponding fabric pieces. Clip notches. Clip additional notches along the bodice front waistline and neckline at center front and along both edges of the tier 1 skirt at center front.

2 Right sides together, pin and stitch the bodice front to the bodice back along the shoulder seams. Press open and clean-finish the seam allowances. Repeat for the bodice side front and bodice side back pieces. Repeat for the armhole facings. Clean-finish the outer edges of the armhole facings.

3 Right sides together, pin and stitch the armhole facings to the bodice side sections along the armholes, matching shoulder seams. Trim the seams to ¼ in., press the seam allowances toward the facing, and understitch.

4 With the banana ruffle still in the folded position (wrong sides together), gather the raw edges to match the notched edge of the bodice section. Pin and stitch the gathered banana ruffle to the bodice section, matching the notch on the ruffle to the shoulder seam. Repeat for the other side.

5 Right sides together and the banana ruffle sandwiched in the middle, pin and stitch the bodice front and back section to the bodice side section, matching notches and shoulder seams. Clean-finish the seam and press toward the bodice side section. Repeat for the other side.

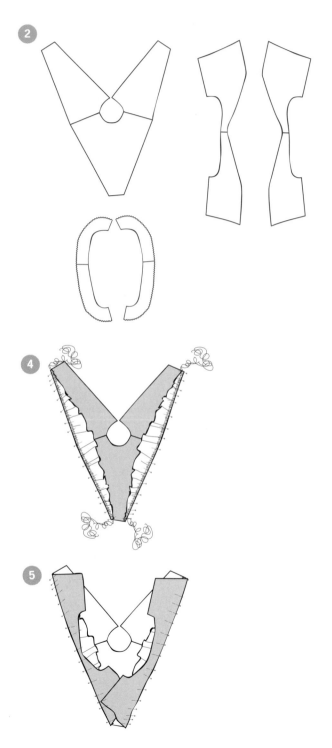

6 Right sides together, open the armhole facing outward along the side seams; pin and stitch the front side bodice to the back side bodice along the side seams. Start at the edge of the facing and cross over the intersection of the facing and the bodice. Press open and clean-finish the seam allowances. Hand stitch the armhole facing to the inside of the bodice. Repeat for the other side.

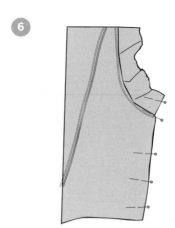

7 Right sides together, pin and stitch the tier 2 skirt sections together along the short edge to create one long tier. Press open and clean-finish the seam. Gather the upper edge of the tier 2 skirt to match the bottom edge of the tier 1 skirt. Right sides together, pin and stitch the upper edge of the tier 2 skirt to the lower edge of the tier 1 skirt, matching the tier 2 seam with the tier 1 notch at center front. Repeat process to stitch the tier 3 skirt to the tier 2 skirt.

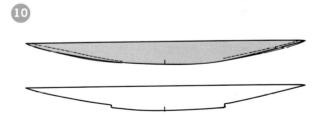

8 Gather the upper skirt edge to match the lower bodice edge. Right sides together, pin and stitch the skirt to the bodice, matching center front notches. Clean-finish the seam and press it toward the skirt.

9 Install a zipper along center back and close up the remainder of the seam. Use the double notch as a guide.

10 Right sides together, fold the necktie in half lengthwise. Pin and stitch the raw edges closed, but start at one end and stitch only 10 in. Repeat on the other end, leaving a gap in the middle of the necktie. Trim the seams to ¼ in., flip the necktie right-side out and press to neaten. Do **not** trim the unstitched edges along the gap.

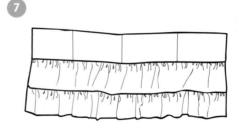

11 Right sides together, pin and stitch one layer of the unstitched gap to the neckline, matching notches. Clip the curves and press the seam allowance to the inside of the necktie. Fold and press the unstitched edge of the necktie inward and hand stitch in place.

12 Hem the dress lower edge.

CRISSCROSS JUMPER DRESS

Pattern Level 3 Sewing Level 4

Details like covered buttons, a looped placket, and crisscross straps give this jumper an innocent feel with sly styling. You can also create an outfit that screams sweet without looking like a little girl—just add boots and your favorite beat-up T-shirt.

I recycled a cotton duvet cover to make the peach version and a linen table cloth to make the black version. For each of these, I had enough fabric from the one recycled item for both the dress and the bodice lining. For your dress, use any medium-weight woven that happens to have bundles of space.

Special Gear

⊕ **NIP-WAIST DRESS** Front and Back Midriff patterns from page 173 (no seam allowances)

⊕ **"YOU" DRESS BODICE** Front and Back patterns from page 38 or a ready-made basic bodice pattern (no seam allowances)

⊕ **DELUXE RECTANGLE SKIRT** Front and Back patterns from page 105 (no seam or hem allowances)

⊕ ½ yd. light- to medium-weight interfacing

⊕ Extra recycled fabric for the bodice lining, approximately one yd.

⊕ Twelve ⅝-in. covered buttons

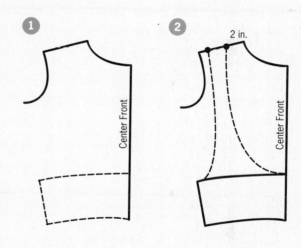

DIY PATTERN

1 Trace the **"YOU" DRESS BODICE Front** pattern; include the waistline notch, but omit the side and waist lines. Tape the **NIP-WAIST DRESS Front Midriff** pattern on top of the tracing with the center front lines matching and the lower midriff matching up with the waistline notch. Trace the midriff.

2 Measure over 2 in. from the neckline along the shoulder and mark with a dot. Measure over an additional 1½ in. and mark another dot. Draw the front strap style lines, as shown, meeting the dots along the shoulder.

3 Trace the **"YOU" DRESS BODICE Back** pattern; include the waistline notch, but omit the side and waist lines. Tape the **NIP-WAIST DRESS Back Midriff** pattern facedown on top of the tracing with the center back lines matching and the lower midriff matching up with the waistline notch. The midriff should be on the opposite side of the bodice pattern. Trace the midriff.

4 Measure 2 in. from the neckline along the shoulder and mark with a dot. Measure over an additional 1½ in. and mark another dot. Draw the back strap style lines, as shown, meeting the dots along the shoulder. Make sure to keep the strap consistently 1½ in. wide.

5 Trace the **DELUXE RECTANGLE SKIRT Front** and **Back** patterns, including the side notches. Label with "Crisscross Dress Skirt Back Cut 1 on Fold" on the back and "Crisscross Dress Skirt Back Cut 2" on the front.

6 Measure the center front skirt edge and add 5 in. Draw a 2-in.-wide rectangle with this calculation as the length. Label with "Placket Facing" and "Cut 2."

7 Add ½-in. seam allowance to all pattern pieces, except the center back skirt edge. Draw grainlines on all pieces parallel to center front/center back. On each of the bodice patterns, label with "Cut 2" and "Cut 2 Lining"; mark a single notch on each of the sides at the midpoint and a double notch along center back.

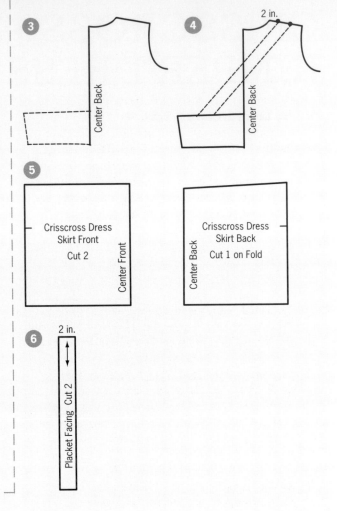

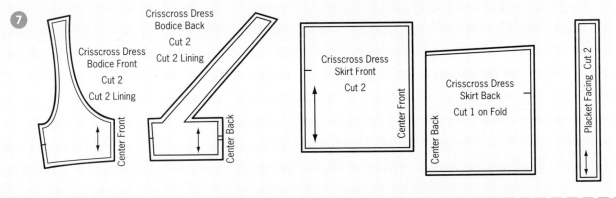

CUT UP, SEW UP

1   Cut four bodice front and bodice back patterns: two each in regular fabric and two in lining fabric. Cut two placket facings from fabric and two from interfacing. Cut two skirt fronts, and one skirt back on the fold. Clip notches. Clip an additional notch along the skirt back waistline center. Trim the seam allowance from the interfacing and apply it to the wrong side of the placket facings.

2   Lay both bodice front pieces right-side-up on the table with the center front edges together. Lay both bodice back pieces right-side-down on top of the front pieces with the center back edges together; the straps will crisscross. Right sides together, pin and stitch the bodice front to the bodice back shoulder seams. Press open the seam allowances. Repeat for the lining shoulders.

3   You should now have four sections each connected at the shoulders: two bodices and two linings. Right sides together, pin and stitch one bodice piece to one lining piece along the top and strap edges, pivoting at the back strap corners. Everything but the center front/center back, side, and waistline edges should be sewn at this point. Trim the seams to ¼ in., carefully clip inward at the sharp angles, and then use a tube turner to turn the bodice right-side out. Press to neaten. Repeat for the other side.

4   Right sides together and matching double notches, pin and stitch the center back seam together, stitching the bodice to the bodice and the lining to the lining. Open out the dress and the lining to create one big intersected seam. Press open the seam allowances.

5   Right sides together and matching single notches, pin and stitch the bodice side seams together. Use the same process as for the center back seam.

6   Right sides together, stitch the front skirt pieces to the back skirt piece along the sides. Press open and clean-finish the seam allowances.

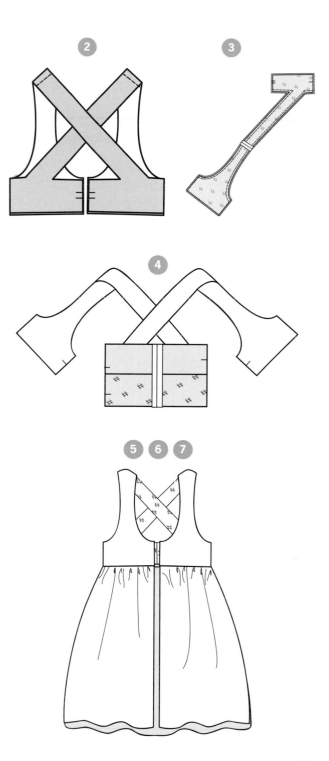

7 Gather the upper skirt edge to match the lower bodice edge. Right sides together, pin and stitch the skirt to the bodice, matching side seams and notches. Clean-finish the seam allowances and press them toward the skirt.

8 Create a ¼-in.-wide, 30-in.-long tube to use for the button loops. Cut the tube into twelve 2½-in. pieces.

9 Trace the placket facing pattern onto a piece of newspaper and cut it out. Fold and pin one of the button loops to the right edge of the paper at the very top. The two raw edges of the loop should be on the right edge and the button loop should take up 1 in. of space along the right edge. Measure ½ in. from the bottom of the first button loop and pin the next button loop in place. Continue pinning all the 12 button loops in this way. Use a basting stitch to temporarily stitch the loops to the newspaper with a ½-in. seam allowance.

10 With the dress face-up on the table, pin and stitch the button loop newspaper to the left center front edge. The loops should face-up with the raw edges aligned with the center front edges.

11 Fold and press one short edge of the placket facing under ½ in. Right sides together, pin and stitch the placket facing to the left center front edge, with the folded edge at the top and the button loops between. Tear the newspaper from the dress and press the seam allowances and the placket toward the inside of the dress. Fold and press the long unstitched edge of the placket facing under ½ in. and hand stitch it to the inside of the dress. Repeat for the other placket facing (no button loops).

12 Cover twelve ⅝-in. buttons and stitch them to the right side of the placket.

13 Hem the lower dress edge. Fold and press the raw edge under ½ in., fold and pin under another 1 in. and stitch in place along the upper fold.

Mix It Up

⊕ Add pockets to the side seams.

⊕ Stitch the bodice to another skirt style, such as the bubble skirt.

⊕ Install a zipper at center front instead of the buttons.

⊕ Experiment with other style lines along the front bodice.

DROPPED WAIST DAISY DRESS

Pattern Level 3 Sewing Level 4

You will certainly say yes to this party dress! Bubbly and confident tiers spring out at just the right moment to create a festive dropped-waist style dress that flatters your figure. The princess seams allow you to tailor the dress to body-hugging perfection and you can customize it even more by adjusting the number and length of the tiers. A '60s era bright, crazy print became my first go at this dress, but I'm excited to try it out in something a little less shocking, like black canvas or denim. Pick a silly print or your favorite solid color in a medium-weight woven fabric and keep in mind that the bodice will require a lining.

Measure Up!

Full Hip 4
Front Waist Width 15
Back Waist Width 16
Back Hip 18

Side Hip Length 29
Back Dart
Front Dart

(Check out page 34 for specific measuring instructions.)

Special Gear

⊕ **WEDDING CAKE DRESS BODICE** patterns from page 198 (no seam allowance)

⊕ **Zipper** (see page 26 in Chapter 1 for more about zipper measurements).

⊕ **Boning** (optional)

⊕ **Extra recycled fabric** for the bodice lining, approximately one yd.

DIY PATTERN

1 Trace the **WEDDING CAKE DRESS BODICE** patterns and set them aside.

2 Follow the **"YOU" DRESS SKIRT** steps **1** to **4** on page 44. Measure the waist edge of the bodice front pattern. On the skirt pattern, measure over this distance from center front along the waist and mark with a dot. From this dot, measure over your **Front Dart** measurement and mark another dot. Find the midpoint between the dots to draw a 3-in. dart. Measure the bodice back waist edge. On the skirt pattern,

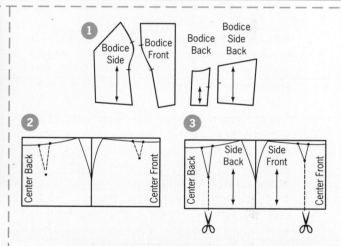

measure over this distance from center back along the waist and mark with a dot. From this dot, measure over your **Back Dart** measurement and mark another dot. Find the midpoint between the dots to draw a 5-in. dart.

3 Draw a line from each of the dart points on the skirt, parallel to center front/center back. Cut along these lines as well as the dart legs to separate the pattern pieces. Draw grainlines on the side pieces parallel to center front/center back.

4 Match up each of the skirt pieces with the corresponding bodice piece and tape them together along the waist. Since the waistlines curve in various directions, do some fudging. Make sure the pattern pieces match at the inner, notched seams and allow them to overlap or separate at the outer and center front/center back seams, keeping the grainlines parallel and the center front/center back edges in line.

5 Trace the patterns onto new pieces of paper and use rulers to clean up the patterns and smooth the sharp angles. Adjust the side seams as necessary to match in length. Transfer the notches and grainlines, as shown. Label the bodice front patterns "Cut 1 on Fold" and "Cut 1 Lining on Fold." Label the side patterns and the back bodice patterns "Cut 2" and "Cut 2 Lining." At this point, the bodice waist will be dropped to hip level. If you want the bodice shorter, trim evenly from the lower pattern edges. Measure the lower edges of all four pattern pieces and add them together. Jot this calculation down as "Drop Waist Width."

6 Follow DIY PATTERN step **1** on page 95 for the **TIERED SKIRT**, and adjust the skirt pattern so that the upper edge is equal to the Drop Waist Width calculation. Add space equally to the center front and center back edges through the entire length of the pattern.

7 Follow DIY PATTERN steps **2** to **5** on page 95 for the **TIERED SKIRT** using the adjusted skirt pattern. Feel free to experiment with the number and length of each ruffled tier. This dress has three even tiers.

8 Add ½-in. seam allowance to all pattern pieces, except along center front.

Note: Cut and sew this dress like the **WEDDING CAKE DRESS** on page 200.

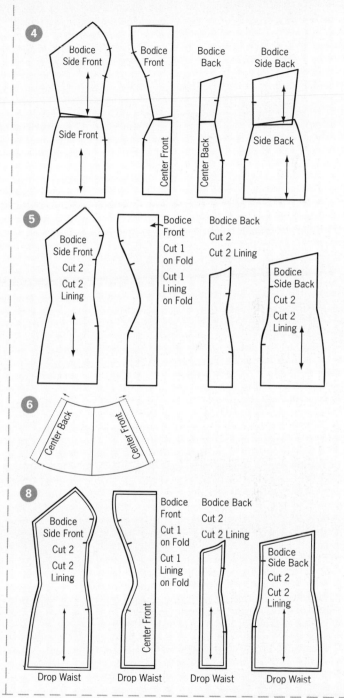

BRIDE'S DRESS, REVISITED

By Elizabeth Dye

Pattern Level 3 Sewing Level 4

In just a few magical steps, you can convert a fussy, dated wedding gown into a chic cocktail dress. The best wedding dresses are those long-sleeved, high-necked numbers from the '60s, which are often unlined and easily dismantled. The fabrics and lace are usually durable and can absorb dye well, but take stock of the fiber since dresses of this era were often made with a mix of natural and synthetic materials, which respond to dye and hot water differently. Make sure you select a dress reasonably close to your size or larger.

Elizabeth Dye

Elizabeth Dye is a Portland, Oregon-based clothing designer and owner of The English Dept., a dress shop specializing in alternative bridal and party dresses. She takes inspiration from the past, often using rare fabrics and one-of-a-kind details in her handmade pieces. Check out her designs at www.elizabethdye.com.

Special Gear

⊕ Dress form

⊕ Fabric dye

⊕ NIP-WAIST DRESS Front and Back Midriff patterns from page 173 (optional)

Mix It Up

⊕ Experiment with special dyeing methods like ombré. Put the entire dress into the dye bath for just a few minutes and then lift just the bodice out of the bath, leaving the skirt in the dye bath for a few more minutes. Continue lifting portions of the dress out of the bath to create a graduated color pattern.

CUT UP, SEW UP

1 Use a seam ripper to remove the sleeves and the zipper, if applicable.

2 Place the dress on the dress form and examine the neckline. Use a fabric pencil to draw a soft scoop neck, making sure to follow the lines of any lace overlay or other details, and carefully trim along the lines. Staystitch the neckline and armhole edges.

3 Shorten the dress to just below the knee. Measure and mark the hem with a fabric pencil or simply hold your scissors level as you cut sideways around the skirt circumference. You don't have to be perfectly precise, but start out conservatively—you can always shorten it more if needed. Hem the skirt lower edge.

4 If you like the silhouette of the dress as is, move on to step **9**. My dress had an empire waistline that rode a little too high, so I decided to add to the length of the bodice using fabric from the removed sleeves. To create an empire dress with a midriff like mine, follow steps **5** to **8** below.

5 Use a seam ripper to separate the bodice and the skirt along the waistline. If necessary, trim evenly from the bodice lower edge to create an empire waistline.

6 Use the **NIP-WAIST DRESS Front** and **Back Midriff** patterns from page 173 and the extra fabric from the sleeves to create a midriff to fit the lower bodice edge. If needed, adjust the pattern or the bodice to make sure they match up. Right sides together, pin and stitch the midriff together at the side seams. Press open and clean-finish the seam allowances.

7 Right sides together, pin and stitch the midriff to the lower bodice edge. Clean-finish the seam allowances and press them toward the midriff.

8 Before you reattach the skirt to the bodice, you may find you want to add a little oomph to the skirt. Use extra fabric from the bottom of the original skirt or bring in fabric from another source to create a gathered rectangle overlayer. Gather the upper overlayer edge with the original skirt, and with right sides together, stitch them to the lower midriff. Clean-finish the seam allowances and press them toward the skirt.

9 Reinstall the zipper along center back.

10 Dye the dress following the manufacturer's instructions. I have found that light to medium shades work best— dye is unpredictable, and going pale tends to produce a prettier and more uniform result. Since there are no do-overs with dyeing, dip some of your fabric scraps from the dress in the dye bath first to test out the color.

Sleeve opened up at seam. Cut midriff pieces from here.

Midriff

Finished Dress

Hem

Skirt Overlay

GO USA SWEATER DRESS

Pattern Level 2 Sewing Level 4

I was inspired to make this sweater dress after watching the episode of *Project Runway* where they had the designers make an outfit for the opening ceremony of the Olympic games. The sweaters are pieced together in a somewhat rock 'n' roll fashion, so leave your rule books at the door and have fun

with it. If you're not as into the USA spirit, just find three large, complementary sweaters with similar weights and textures; avoid super bulky sweaters with a loose weave. It took me a couple weeks to find the perfect sweaters for this project, so just be patient! Remember to use a narrow zigzag stitch and a stretch needle when sewing it up.

Measure Up!

Arm Length 24
(Check out page 34 for specific measuring instructions.)

Special Gear

⊕ **CAP SLEEVE CUTIE DRESS** Front pattern from page 123 (straight hem version with no seam or hem allowance)

DIY PATTERN

1 Trace the **CAP SLEEVE CUTIE DRESS Front** pattern (including the notch) onto a large piece of paper. Adjust the dress length to a few inches below the hip.

2 Subtract 6 in. from your **Arm Length** measurement and extend the shoulder line downward this distance. From the underarm notch, extend the underarm downward and parallel to the extended shoulder line. Connect the shoulder line and the underarm line at the end with a perpendicular line.

3 Transform the angle at the underarm into a soft curve.

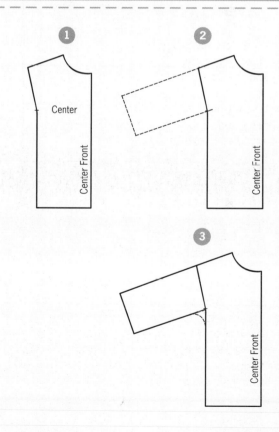

4 Fold a large piece of paper in half. Tape the front dress pattern to the folded paper, with the center front line on the fold. Trace the pattern with a sharp tracing wheel. Remove the pattern, unfold the paper, and follow the markings with a pencil and rulers to create a full-front pattern. The center front edge will now act as a grainline.

5 Draw a diagonal line across the pattern as shown. Cut along the diagonal line to separate the pattern into two sections. Label them "Left" and "Right."

6 You may need to cut the pattern sections into several smaller parts to piece together enough sweater fabric. Just how many will depend on the size of your pattern and the size of your sweaters. On my dress, I had to separate the sleeves from the main patterns. Start by doing the same, and if needed, separate even more. Label the sleeve patterns "Left Sleeve" and "Right Sleeve" and "Cut 2." Mark notches at the midpoints along all separating lines; keep grainlines parallel to the original ones.

7 Label pattern "Go USA Sweater Dress Left," "Go USA Sweater Dress Right," "Go USA Sweater Dress Left Sleeve," and "Go USA Sweater Dress Right Sleeve." Add ½-in. seam allowance to all edges, except the neckline.

Mix It Up

⊕ **Experiment with the design of the color-blocking.**

⊕ **Make this dress out of T-shirts instead of sweaters for a less bulky look.**

CUT UP, SEW UP

1 Cut the waistband and sleeve cuffs on all the sweaters, but keep the bands intact.

2 Keep one sweater neckline intact, so choose the sweater with the best neckline and lay it flat on the table. Smooth out any wrinkles and align the left pattern piece on top of the sweater. Make sure the center front grainline on the pattern is directly on top of the center front of the sweater. Push the pattern upward along the grainline until the shoulders on the pattern meet the sweater shoulders about ½ in. from the neckband. The pattern piece might be covering up the sweater's neckline. Place fabric weights on top of the pattern to keep it in place and trace around the pattern piece with chalk, ignoring the neckline.

3 Remove the pattern and pin the front and back of the sweater together in several spots so it doesn't move. Cut along the chalk lines through both the sweater front and the back. Don't cut through the sweater neck edge and leave at least ½ in. of stitched shoulder space near the neck edge. You should now have a front and back "left" piece connected by the neckline.

4 Use the remaining remnants of this sweater to cut out the left sleeve patterns. Right sides together, pin and stitch each of the sleeve sections to the left sweater section, matching notches.

5 Turn the left sweater section inside out. Right sides together, pin and stitch the upper sleeve edge together. Start at the sleeve opening and taper as you reach the neckline.

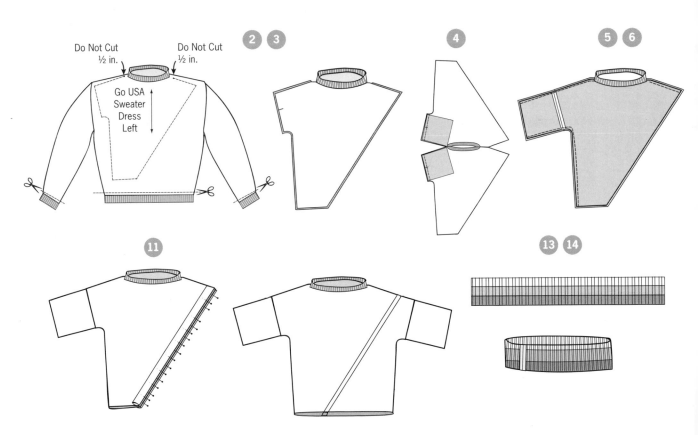

6 Pin and stitch the underarm and sides together. Set the left sweater section aside.

7 Decide which sweater you want to use for the "right" section. Place the pattern piece on top of the sweater, keeping the center front grainline parallel to the sweater's grainline. Secure the pattern with weights, trace around the entire pattern with chalk, remove the pattern, pin the front and back of the sweater together making sure the grainlines align, and then cut out the pattern piece through both sweater layers. If grainlines don't align, cut two separate pieces (flipping the pattern).

8 Use the remaining remnants of this sweater to cut out the right sleeve patterns. Right sides together, pin and stitch each of the sleeve sections to the right sweater section, matching notches.

9 Right sides together, pin and stitch the upper sleeve edges together.

10 Right sides together, pin and stitch the underarm and side seams together.

11 Measure the diagonal line on either the left or right pattern piece and add 1 in. Cut two 2-in.-wide fabric strips this length from the last sweater to use as a contrast trim along the diagonal. Right sides together, pin and stitch the two strips together along the short ends to create one long strip. Fold the strip in half lengthwise wrong sides facing and pin it to the front and back left diagonal section, matching the seam on the strip with the shoulder seam. Right sides together, pin the right sweater section to the left sweater section along the diagonals, sandwiching the contrast strip between. Stitch through all four layers of sweater to connect the sections.

12 Clean-finish all the seam allowances.

13 Open up all three sweater waistbands so they look like rectangles and stitch them together face-to-face along the long edges with a ¼-in. seam allowance to create one tri-colored rectangle hem band.

14 Measure the circumference of the dress lower edge and add 1 in. Trim the hem band so that it equals this number. Right sides together, stitch the short ends of the hem band together to create a circle.

15 Slip the band over the lower dress edge matching raw edges and side seams. Pin and stitch, and then topstitch each section of the hem band to reinforce and catch the seam allowances in one direction.

16 Gather the lower sleeve edge to fit your wrist and repeat the tri-color banding process to create cuffs.

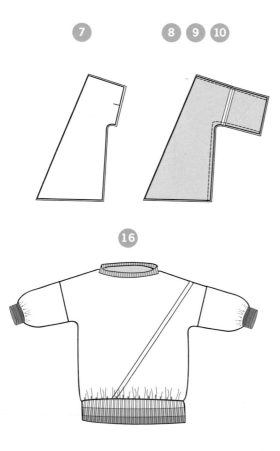

Chapter 6
BOTTOMS & ROMPERS

Like many other types of garments, the patterns for bottoms and rompers can start from a simple shape. For the breezy **Summer Shorts** on page 227, you'll start out with the basic rectangular shape of the **Ultra Miniskirt** then add a couple of rectangles to guide you in drawing your crotch curves.

The **Wild Child Romper** on page 231 is a variation on the **Summer Shorts** pattern, in which you extend the top of the shorts.

The **Vintage Romper** on page 243 and the **Culottes Romper** on page 245 both restyle boring dresses into poppy new pieces. The skirt portion of the dress is removed and turned into shorts and then the shorts are reattached to the original dress' bodice to create an all-in-one romper. Bottoms up to effortless and adorable!

SUMMER SHORTS

Pattern Level 2   Sewing Level 2

Loose, gathered mini-shorts are the perfect answer to an intensely hot summer day when nothing seems to feel right on your body. These all-around shorts can be thrown on over your swimsuit to cover up at the pool or can be matched with a T-shirt for a day working in the garden. Use a fancy fabric and conceal the drawstring waist with a swanky belt for

a more put-together look. I cut up a lightweight rayon skirt with a bright, bold print to make my shorts, but any light- to medium-weight woven or average- to lightweight stretch knit fabric will give you great results. You can also try using multiple small garments to make these shorts since you will cut out four separate sections to make the pattern.

Measure Up!

Front Hip 17
Back Hip 18
Crotch Depth 30
(Check out page 34 for specific measuring instructions.)

Special Gear

⊕ ULTRA MINISKIRT pattern from page 75 (no seam or hem allowance)

⊕ ¾-in. scrap of interfacing

DIY PATTERN

1. Trace the **ULTRA MINISKIRT Front** pattern on a new piece of paper, including the notch. Add 2½ in. to your **Crotch Depth** measurement, and measure down this distance from the upper edge along center front and mark with a dot.

2. Divide your **Front Hip** measurement by four and subtract 1 in. Starting at the dot on center front, draw a rectangle crotch extension using this calculation as the width.

3. Use a curved ruler to draw a crotch curve along center front. Start at the upper edge and connect the curve to the outer edge of the rectangle extension, making sure the curve is about 1½ in. away from the dot on center front.

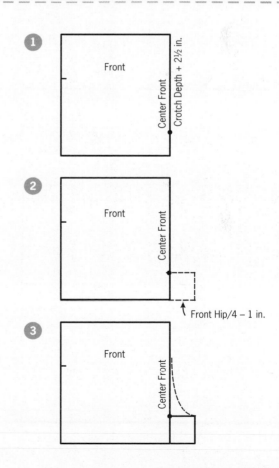

4 Trace the **ULTRA MINISKIRT Back** pattern on a new piece of paper, including the notch. Add 2½ in. to your **Crotch Depth** measurement, and measure down this distance from the upper edge along center back and mark with a dot.

5 Divide your **Back Hip** measurement by four and add 1 in. Starting at the dot on center back, draw a rectangle crotch extension using this calculation as the width.

6 Use a curved ruler to draw a crotch curve along center back. Start at the upper edge and connect the curve to the outer edge of the crotch extension, making sure the curve is about 2 in. away from the dot on center back.

7 On the back pattern, measure ¼ in. down from the upper edge along center back and mark with a dot. Taper and trim the top edge of the pattern to meet the dot, making sure it meets center back at a square angle.

8 Add ½-in. seam allowances to the front and back pattern edges. Add an additional 1 in. to the lower edges for hems. Draw grainlines parallel to the sides. Label "Summer Shorts Front" and "Summer Shorts Back" and write "Cut 2" on both patterns. Mark a single notch along center front and a double notch along center back.

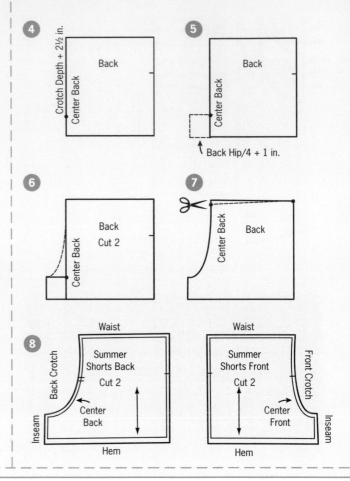

CUT UP, SEW UP

1 Cut two each of the front and back shorts patterns.

2 Right sides together, pin and stitch one front to one back along the inseams. Clean-finish and press open the seam allowances.

3 Working with the same front and back section, pin and stitch the side seams together, matching notches. Clean-finish and press open the seam allowances.

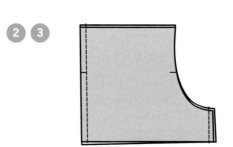

4 Repeat steps **2** and **3** for the other front and back pieces.

5 Right sides together, place one shorts section inside the other. Pin the sections together along the front and back crotch curves, matching notches. Stitch the two sections together starting at one waist edge, crossing over the inseams and ending at the other waist edge. Press open and clean-finish the seam allowances. Clip the curves.

6 Decide where you want your buttonhole along the waist edge (mine was near the side seam). Measure down 1¼ in. from the waist edge at your chosen spot and apply the scrap of interfacing to the wrong side of the fabric. On the outside of the shorts, stitch a ⅝-in. horizontal buttonhole at this spot.

7 Fold and press the waist edge under ½ in. Fold the edge under another ¾ in. and pin in place. Stitch the casing in place along the first folded edge.

8 Create a ⅝-in.wide tube drawstring the length of your waist measurement plus 20 in. or grab a piece of ribbon to use as a drawstring. Attach a safety pin to both ends of the drawstring and thread it through the buttonhole casing.

9 Hem the shorts legs. Fold and press the edges under ½ in. Fold the edges under another 1 in. and pin the hem in place. Stitch in place along the first folded edge.

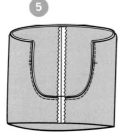

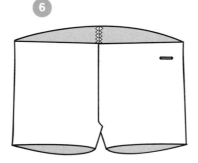

Mix It Up

⊕ Experiment with the amount of pattern fullness by increasing or decreasing the width at the side seams.

⊕ Instead of creating a drawstring waist, gather the upper edge of the shorts into a waistband and install a zipper in the side seam.

⊕ Run elastic through the casing, like the Ultra Miniskirt, instead of using a drawstring.

⊕ If you don't like to wear shorts at the high natural waist, trim evenly from the upper pattern edges to lower the waistline.

WILD CHILD ROMPER

Pattern Level 2 Sewing Level 2

Whenever I wear a romper, I get this frisky feeling that makes me want to do a cartwheel or a high kick. It could be due to the childlike styling, but it probably has more to do with feeling free. This particular romper has a loose waist meant to be cinched with a belt or sash in whatever position works for you. Since the front and back patterns are combined into one big piece and there's a ruffle and binding involved, this pattern tends to need large sections of fabric, so look for a muumuu or maxi-dress in an exotic print or find any other large woven item to recycle into a romper. Steer clear of heavyweight fabrics because of the gathered ruffle.

Measure Up!

Waist to High Bust 3 to 2

(Check out page 34 for specific measuring instructions.)

Special Gear

- ⊕ **SUMMER SHORTS** pattern from page 227 (no seam or hem allowance)
- ⊕ ⅜-in. wide elastic, the width of your high bust plus ½ in.

DIY PATTERN

1 Trace the **SUMMER SHORTS Front** and **Back** patterns on a large piece of paper connecting the sides to create one pattern piece. If desired, remove up to 1 in. from each of the sides before connecting them to reduce the fullness. Include the center front and center back notches.

2 Measure from your waist to your high bust. Subtract 1½ in. from this measurement and extend the front pattern upward this distance along center front. Subtract another 2 in. and extend the back pattern upward this distance along center back.

3 Connect center front and center back with a curved and slanted line, making sure the line meets center front and center back at square angles. Extend the side line upward to meet the slanted line. This side line will be used as a grainline for the pattern.

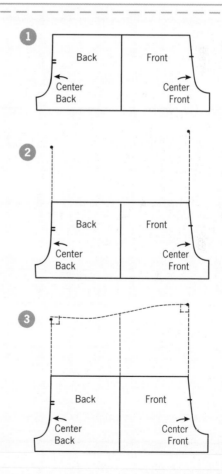

4 Measure the upper romper edge and multiply this measurement by two. Draw a 5-in.-tall rectangle using this calculation as the width. Label the pattern "Ruffle" and "Cut 2"; draw a grainline parallel to the short sides.

5 Measure the upper romper edge and multiply this measurement by two. Draw a 1-in.-tall rectangle using this calculation as the width. Label the pattern "Binding" and "Cut 1." Draw a grainline 45° from the rectangle short side.

6 Add ½-in. seam allowance to all the pattern edges. Add an additional 1 in. to the lower romper edge for the hem. Mark a single notch along the upper romper edge at the grainline. Label the pattern "Wild Child Romper" and "Cut 2."

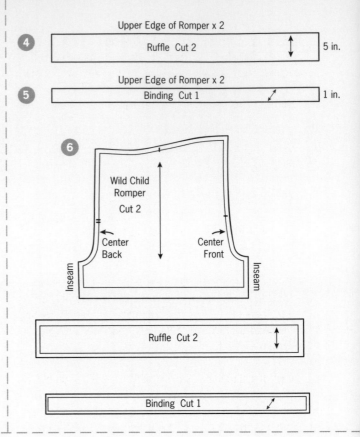

CUT UP, SEW UP

1 Cut two of the romper and ruffle, and one bias binding. Clip the notches.

2 Right sides together, fold one of the romper sections in half. Pin and stitch the inseams together. Press open and clean-finish the seam allowances. Repeat for the other romper section.

3 Rights sides together, pin the two sections together along the center front, center back, and crotch curves, matching the notches. Stitch the two sections together starting and ending at the upper edges. Press open and clean-finish the seam allowances. Clip the curves.

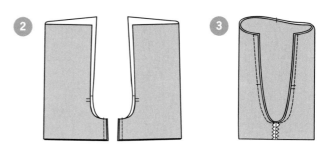

4 Right sides together, pin and stitch the two ruffles to each other along the short edges to create one big circle. Press open and clean-finish the seam allowances.

5 Narrowly roll hem the ruffle lower edge.

6 Gather the ruffle upper edge and adjust the gathers to fit the romper neckline.

7 Pin and stitch the gathered ruffle edge to the upper romper edge with the wrong side of the ruffle facing the right side of romper. Match the ruffle seams to the romper notches.

8 Right sides together, stitch the short ends of the binding together to create a circle. Wrong sides together, fold and press the binding in half with the fold parallel to the long edges, open it out, then fold and press one long edge under ½ in.

9 Right sides together, pin and stitch the unfolded edge of the binding to the upper romper edge with the ruffle sandwiched between. Trim the seam to ¼ in., press all seam allowances toward the binding, and topstitch the folded edge of the binding to the inside of the jumper, leaving a 1-in. opening to insert the elastic into the binding. Note: The binding will show on the garment outside.

10 Cut a piece of elastic equal to your high bust measurement. Attach a safety pin to both ends of the elastic and thread it through the binding opening. Once it's pulled all the way through the binding, overlap the ends 1 in. and stitch them together, making sure the elastic isn't twisted. Topstitch the binding opening closed.

11 Hem the romper legs. Fold and press the edges under ½ in. Fold the edges under another 1 in. and pin in place. Stitch the hem in place along the first folded edge.

12 Create a tube double your waist measurement to tie around your waist or simply use an already existing belt.

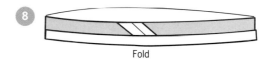

Fold

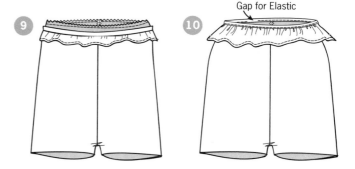

Gap for Elastic

Mix It Up

⊕ Extend the lower jumper edge to create a full pantsuit.

⊕ Create skinny tubes and stitch them to the top of the romper to use as spaghetti straps.

⊕ Create a separate casing along the inside edge of the waist and cinch up the waist with a drawstring or elastic.

DISCO SHORTS

Pattern Level 2 Sewing Level 2

Measure Up!

Full Hip 4
Back Hip 18
Crotch Depth 30
(Check out page 34 for specific measuring instructions.)

Like the best clothes in your closet, these teeny tiny shorts can have multiple personalities depending on your daily whims. Become a disco-dancing machine one day and get sporty the next. Wear them under your micro-miniskirts and dresses to avoid a Marilyn moment, or under sheer skirts and dresses for bold days. They sew up swell in most light- to medium-weight stretch knits, but avoid slinky and super-stretch knits. I made mine from an old stable knit wool dress, but you might also try making a pair out of reused sweatshirts, sweaters, or T-shirts. Use a narrow zigzag stitch and stretch needle for flexible seams.

Special Gear

⊕ Knit shorts/yoga pants that fit you well in the crotch (optional)

⊕ Interfacing scrap

DIY PATTERN

1 Divide your **Full Hip** measurement in half and add ½ in. Add 3½ in. to your **Crotch Depth** measurement. Draw a rectangle using the hip calculation as your width and the crotch depth calculation as your length.

2 Divide your **Back Hip** measurement in half and add ¼ in. Measure over from the left this distance and mark dots along the upper and lower rectangle edges. Connect the dots with a line. Label this line "Side Seam" (SS). Label the left side of the rectangle "Disco Shorts Back" and the right side of the rectangle "Disco Shorts Front." Label the left edge "Center Back" and the right edge "Center Front."

3 Measure the upper edge of the back shorts side. Divide this number in half and jot it down as "Back Crotch" (BC). Add a 3-in.-tall rectangle to the back side of the pattern with the back crotch extending outward. Measure the upper edge of the front pattern. Divide this number by four and jot it down as "Front Crotch" (FC). Add a 3-in.-tall rectangle to the front side of the pattern with the front crotch extending outward.

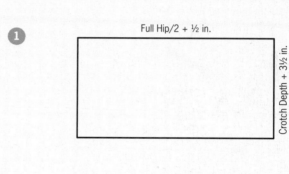

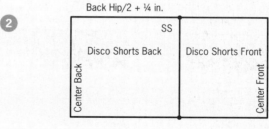

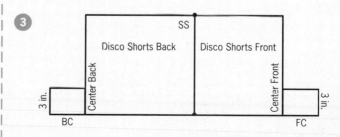

4 On the back side of the pattern, mark dots in the following locations:

⊕ 1 in. inward and ¼ in. upward from the center back upper edge

⊕ 2 in. diagonally from the intersection of the upper crotch rectangle and center back

⊕ Upper left point of the crotch rectangle

⊕ ¾ in. inward from the lower left point of the crotch rectangle

⊕ 1 in. inward and upward from the side seam at the hem

On the front side of the pattern, mark dots in the following locations:

⊕ ¼ in. inward and downward from the center front upper edge

⊕ 1½ in. diagonally from the intersection of the upper crotch rectangle and center front

⊕ Upper right point of the crotch rectangle

⊕ ¾ in. inward from the lower right point of the crotch rectangle

⊕ 1 in. inward and upward from the side seam at the hem

5 Use a curved ruler and start connecting the dots. Draw your crotch curves, create a stylized hem at the side seam and a slanted waistline. Note: An easy way to get your crotch curve right is to use a pair of knit shorts or yoga pants that you already own as a guide. Grab the ones that fit you best and stick one leg inside the other leg. Trace the front crotch curve on the right-hand side and the back crotch curve on the left-hand side closing up the patterns. Essentially, a crotch curve resembles a "J." Depending on your body shape, the J might be deep, shallow, or askew, and a deeper curve allows more room for the body.

6 Separate the front and back patterns. Extend each of the waistlines upward ½ in. for the casing and add ⅜-in. seam allowance to the remaining edges of the pattern. Label pattern "Disco Shorts Front" and "Disco Shorts Back" and write "Cut 2" on both patterns. Mark single notches along the side seam just above crotch level, double notches along center front, and triple notches along center back. Draw grainlines parallel to the upper portion of the side seam.

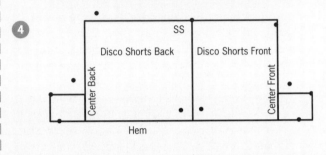

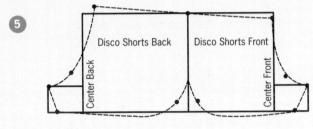

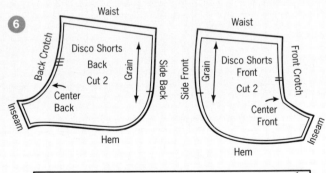

CUT UP, SEW UP

1 Cut two short fronts and two short backs, reserving fabric to create bindings (see step **3**). Clip notches.

2 Right sides together, pin and stitch one front to one back at the inseam. Press open and clean-finish the seam allowances, if necessary. Repeat with the other front and back pieces.

3 Lay one of the back/front pieces face-up on the table. Measure the outer edge of the shorts from the notch at side back all the way around to side front at the waist. Cut two 1½ -in.-wide bias strips of fabric this length.

4 Wrong sides together, fold one bias strip in half lengthwise and press. Pin the folded strip to the outer edge of one of the connected pieces, matching raw edges. Start pinning at the notch at side back all the way around to the side front at the waist and stitch through all three layers using a ⅜-in. seam allowance. Trim the seam to ¼ in. Clean-finish the seam allowances and all remaining raw edges on the shorts. Press the seam allowances toward the shorts. Repeat for the other side.

5 Lap and pin the front side seam over the back side seam, covering up any area of the back side seam that doesn't have a bound edge. The right side of the back will be facing the wrong side of the front and the front should overlap the back by ⅜ in. Make sure the seam allowances from the binding step are pressed toward the shorts. Starting at the waist, topstitch the front and back together at the side seam, making sure to stitch on the shorts side, catching all layers of the seam allowance. When you get to the lower side seam, keep topstitching all the way around the entire shorts section until you arrive back at the other side seam. Be careful not to stretch anything when you're rounding the corners, otherwise it will start to ripple. Topstitch along the binding at the side seam to tack the flap down. Repeat for the other side.

6 Right sides together, pin one shorts section inside the other, matching the crotch curves and notches. Stitch in place using one continuous stitching line from waist to waist. Press open the seam allowances and clip curves.

7 Apply the interfacing scrap to the wrong side of the shorts near center front ½ in. down from the waist edge. Create a ½-in. horizontal buttonhole in the same spot.

8 To create a casing, fold the edge under ½ in. and pin in place. Stitch the casing in place along the raw edge.

9 Create a ⅜-in.-wide tube drawstring double the width of your waist or use rope or ribbon as a drawstring. Attach a safety pin to both ends of the drawstring and thread it through the buttonhole casing.

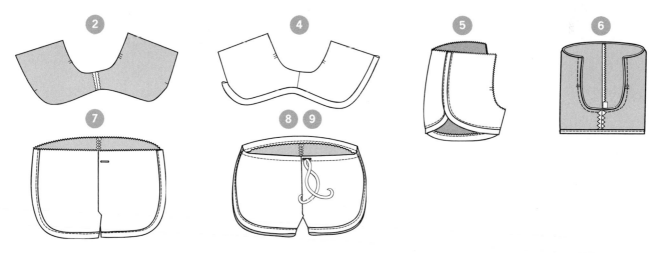

GENIUS LEGGINGS

Pattern Level 2 Sewing Level 2

Whoever invented no-side-seam leggings is a mad genius because they're a cinch to sew. After spotting a pair that a friend of mine designed, I was hooked on the idea of skipping the side seam and inspired to make my own version of the pattern. My pattern starts with your exact body measurements, which means they will be fitted in an average stretch knit. They might be a little looser if you make them from a super stretchy knit. When on the hunt for fabric, look for extra large slinky long knit dresses or make them out of knit sheets like I did. Another option is to get creative and try to piece together several stretchy T-shirts. Don't forget to use a really narrow zigzag stitch when sewing these together and make sure to use a stretch needle.

Measure Up!

Full Waist ③   **Crotch Depth** ㉚
Full Hip ④   **Outseam** ㉜
Front Hip ⑰   **Ankle** ㉝
Back Hip ⑱

(Check out page 34 for specific measuring instructions.)

Special Gear

⊕ A pair of knit shorts/yoga pants that fit you well in the crotch (optional)

⊕ ¾-in.-wide elastic, the length of your waist measurement

DIY PATTERN

1 Divide your **Full Hip** measurement in half and draw a rectangle with this calculation as the width and your **Crotch Depth** measurement as the length. Label the left side "Center Back," the right side "Center Front," and the lower edge "Crotch."

2 Divide your rectangle in half widthwise and starting from the rectangle upper edge, draw a line the length of your **Outseam**. This is the balance line. Center a perpendicular line at the bottom of the balance line the length of your **Ankle** measurement.

3 Divide your **Back Hip** measurement by four and jot it down as "Back Crotch" (BC). Extend the crotch line outward from center back the length of **Back Crotch**.

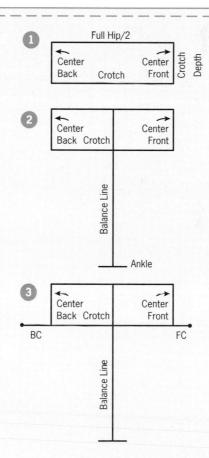

Divide your **Front Hip** measurement by eight and jot it down as "Front Crotch" (FC). Extend the crotch line outward from center front the length of **Front Crotch**.

4 Divide your **Full Waist** measurement by four and add 1 in. From the balance line along the upper pattern, measure out this distance in both directions and label "Waist" (W). Mark dots in the following locations:

⊕ ¼ in. upward from the waist on the left side of the pattern

⊕ ¼ in. downward from the waist on the right side of the pattern

⊕ 2 in. diagonally outward from the crotch line at center back

⊕ 1½ in. diagonally outward from the crotch line at center front

⊕ At both ends of the crotch line

Use a curved ruler to connect the dots and create your waistline and crotch curves. See DIY pattern step **5** for the **DISCO SHORTS** on page 236 for tips on drawing a crotch curve.

5 Using a curved ruler, draw inward curves to create inseams that connect the crotch line with the ankle. This part can be a little tricky because the inseams need to match exactly in length; however, the front and back sides of the pattern don't extend equally. This means the curves are going to be slightly different, but equal in length. The bulk of the difference should happen along the upper half of the inseam tapering to equal as you get closer to the ankle. A helpful trick is to fold the pattern in half along the balance line and match the crotch lines to compare the two inseam curves. At this point, you can also stack the curves on top of each other to measure the distance. Try not to make the inseam curve too sharp just below the crotch; otherwise you might end up with a weird tubular point at the intersection when you sew it. Be prepared to draw, erase, redraw, and test until you get it right.

6 Label pattern "Genius Leggings" and "Cut 2." Add ⅜-in. seam allowances to the inseams and crotch curves. Add 1 in. to the lower pattern edge for the hem and 1 in. to the waistline for the casing. Mark a single notch on the front crotch curve and a double notch on the back crotch curve. Measure down 7 in. along each of the inseams and mark a notch. The balance line becomes the grainline.

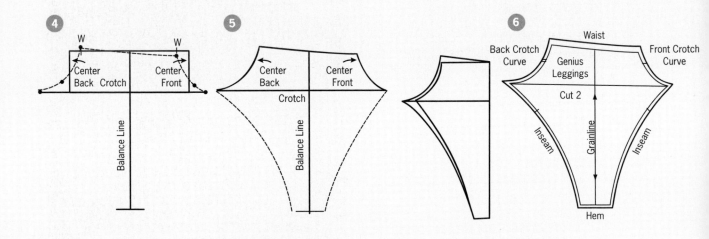

CUT UP, SEW UP

1 Cut two of the pattern. Clip notches.

2 Right sides together, fold one of the pattern pieces in half lengthwise. Pin and stitch the inseams together, matching the notches. Press open and clean-finish the seam allowances, if necessary. Repeat for the other pattern piece.

3 Rights sides together, pin the two sections together along the entire crotch, matching up the crotch curve notches and inseams. Stitch the crotch from front to back crossing the inseams. Stitch the whole seam again to reinforce it. Press open and clean-finish, if necessary.

4 To create a casing, fold the upper edge under 1 in. and pin it in place. Stitch the casing in place along the raw edge. Leave a 1-in. opening unstitched so you can insert elastic into the casing.

5 Cut a piece of elastic equal to your full waist measurement. Attach a safety pin to both ends and thread the elastic through the casing. Once it's pulled all the way through the casing, overlap the ends ½ in. and stitch them together, making sure the elastic isn't twisted. Stitch the casing opening closed.

6 Hem the legs. Fold the edge under 1 in. and pin it in place. Stitch the hem in place along the raw edge.

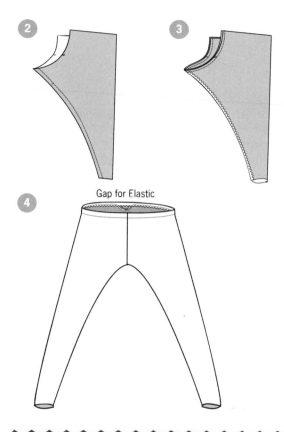

Gap for Elastic

Mix It Up

⊕ Extend the pattern at the ankle to get a gathered, pushed-up look, or trim them down to make cropped leggings or bike shorts. To adjust the length of the leggings, increase or decrease the length of the balance line in step 2 of the pattern instructions. Check out the cropped version on page 164.

⊕ Depending on your fabric choice, you might need to make the pattern bigger or smaller. Cut open the pattern along the balance line to add or subtract space.

⊕ Use white knit sheets to sew up the leggings and then tie-dye them for an artsy look (see page 56).

VINTAGE ROMPER

Pattern Level 2 Sewing Level 2

Vintage dresses always seem to turn me on with their fabrics and funky bodice styles. Many times though, the skirt portions of these dresses are too long and full in all the wrong ways. Creating a romper from a vintage dress is an easy and dynamite way to bring those dresses up-to-date quickly. Look for a vintage knit dress with a gathered or elasticized waistline and lots of skirt fullness. Try to avoid skirts with small panels and dresses with zipper closures that extend below the waistline. Make sure to choose a dress that has a bodice style that can open to or near the waist or has a neckline opening big enough to step into because we need to be able to get into the romper once all is said and done!

Special Gear

- ⊕ DISCO SHORTS Front and Back patterns from page 235
- ⊕ Scrap of interfacing

DIY PATTERN

1 Trace copies of the **DISCO SHORTS Front** and **Back** patterns. See page 37 to split open and add an even ½ in. of vertical fullness to each of the pattern pieces parallel to the grainline. This will give the shorts a total 2 in. of extra space.

Mix It Up

- ⊕ Adjust the Such a Square Blouse pattern on page 61 to create a wide neck opening and combine it with the Disco Shorts pattern to make a version of this romper from scratch.
- ⊕ Skip the drawstring casing altogether and just layer a belt or two or three at the waistline.

CUT UP, SEW UP

1   Use a seam ripper or scissors to separate the skirt from the bodice by cutting along the waistline, removing any elastic or other waistline detailing.

2   Cut the skirt apart at the side seams and use the sections of fabric to make the shorts. Follow steps **1** to **6** in the Cut Up, Sew Up section on page 237 for the **DISCO SHORTS**. If you don't have enough fabric in the skirt to make the shorts, find a complementary fabric and do some color-blocking.

3   Clean up and adjust the dress bodice. The lower bodice edge represents your waistline and should be shaped with a shallow curve that moves upward slightly toward the side seams. Make sure the distance around the lower bodice edge matches the distance around the upper shorts edge. Make adjustments by altering the side seams on the bodice. If the bodice is bigger, you can also gather it to match the shorts waist. Button the placket if it extends to the waist.

4   Right sides together, pin and stitch the shorts to the bodice, matching the raw edges and the side seams. Clean-finish the seam allowances.

5   Apply the interfacing to the wrong side of the shorts just below the center front waistline and stitch a ½-in.-long horizontal buttonhole.

6   Fold the waistline seam allowances down toward the shorts. Pin and stitch it in place along the finished seam allowance edges forming a casing.

7   Create a ⅜-in.-wide tube drawstring double your waist measurement or use rope or ribbon for a drawstring. Attach a safety pin to both ends and thread the drawstring through the buttonhole casing.

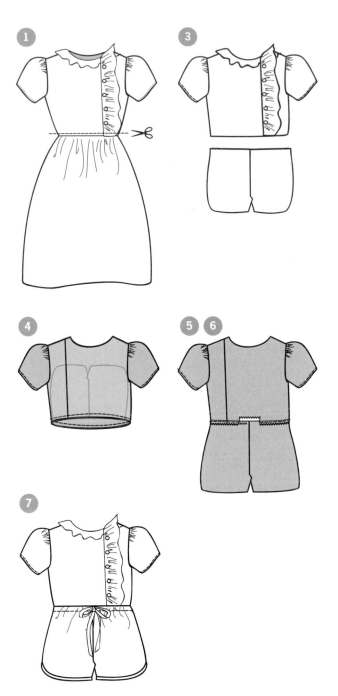

CULOTTES ROMPER

Pattern Level 2 Sewing Level 3

Hop on your scooter, straddle a broomstick, or ride your bike to the dance party around the block in a most ladylike fashion with this sneaky romper jumper that actually looks more like a dress. The roomy, gathered culottes pattern can attach to most any bodice, which makes it perfect for recycling old dresses. Like the **Vintage Romper** on page 243, you'll want to update any dress with a long, voluminous skirt and a bodice that you dig, but this time you can use woven dresses. Ideal candidates for this pattern are dresses that fit you well and have side seam pockets and a zippered back closure.

DIY PATTERN

1 Trace the **SUMMER SHORTS Front** and **Back** patterns onto a large piece of paper, connecting the sides to create one pattern piece. Include the center front and center back notches.

2 Trim the upper pattern edge 1½ in. Extend the lower pattern edge 4 in. or to the desired length.

3 Add ½-in. seam allowance to all the edges and an additional 1 in. to the lower edge for the hem. The original side line becomes the grainline. Mark a notch 2 in. down along each of the inseams. Label the pattern with "Culottes Romper" and "Cut 2."

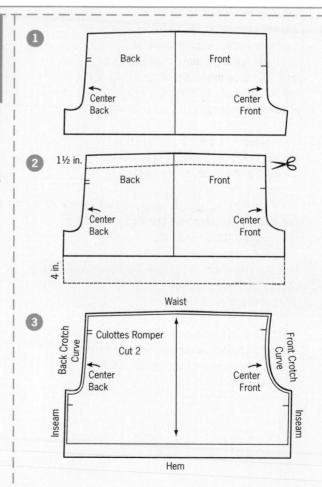

CUT UP, SEW UP

1 Use a seam ripper to remove the zipper from the dress, separate the skirt from the bodice, and remove the center back seam. Press the skirt to remove wrinkles from any previous gathering or pleating. Measure the front waistline and front hem on the skirt to find the exact center of the skirt front. Use a ruler and fabric chalk to draw a center front line on the skirt and then cut along the line. You should now have two skirt sections, each with a side seam.

2 Lay one of the skirt sections face-up on the table. If the front of the skirt is to your right, position your pattern face-up on top of the skirt. If the front of the skirt is to your left, position your pattern facedown on top of the skirt. Position the pattern so that the grainline aligns with the side seam and the front side of the pattern is on the front side of the skirt. Some side seams may not lie flat, so you might have to fudge a little. Pin the pattern in place and cut it out. Repeat for the other skirt section. If you do not have enough space to cut out the entire pattern, trim the skirt lower edge and sew it to the sides to increase the width of the sections.

3 Right sides together, fold each culotte in half. Pin and stitch the inseams together, matching notches. Press open and clean-finish the seam allowances.

4 Rights sides together, pin and stitch the front crotch seams together, matching notches and inseams. Continue stitching across the inseams onto the back crotch side 2 in.

5 Make adjustments to the bodice side seams, if desired. Clean up the lower bodice edge, if necessary.

6 Gather the upper culottes edge to match the lower bodice edge.

7 Right sides together, place the culottes inside the bodice, matching the raw edges and side seams. Pin and stitch around the waistline. Clean-finish the seam allowances and press them toward the culottes.

8 Install/reinstall the zipper along the center back of the jumper and stitch up the remaining area of the back crotch. Press open and clean-finish the seam allowances, and clip the notches along the front and back crotch curves.

9 Hem the leg edges. Fold and press the edges under ½ in. Fold the edges under another 1 in. and pin the hem in place. Stitch in place along the first folded edge.

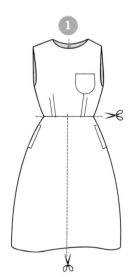

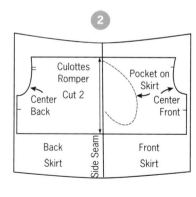

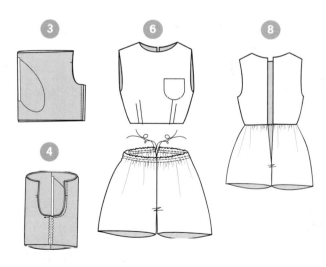

RESOURCES AND REFERENCES

BASIC FITTING PATTERNS ("YOU" DRESS)

McCalls M2718
mccallpattern.com

Vogue V1004
voguepatterns.com

Butterick B5746 or B6092
butterick.com

Customized Basic Patterns
pattern.stringcodes.com

PATTERNMAKING AND SEWING SUPPLIES

South Star Supply Company
southstarsupply.com

Sew True
sewtrue.com

Atlanta Thread
atlantathread.com

SEWING STUDIOS AND CLUBS

Home Ec
Los Angeles, CA
homeecshop.com

Sew L.A.
Los Angeles, CA
sew-la.com

Stitch Craft
Petaluma, CA
stitchcraftonline.com

The Urban Craft Center
Santa Monica, CA
theurbancraftcenter.com

The Sewing Studio
Pasadena, CA
4theloveofsewing.com

Craft Haven Collective
San Francisco, CA
crafthaven.org

Rock Paper Scissors
Collective
Oakland, CA
rpscollective.com

Fancy Tiger Crafts
Denver, CO
fancytiger.com

Sew Fresh Studio
Niwot, CO
sewfreshsewingclasses.com

Crafty Planet
(Minneapolis, MN)
craftyplanet.com

Make Workshop
New York, NY
makeworkshop.com

PURL
New York, NY
purlsoho.com

Flirt/Home Ec
Brooklyn, NY
flirt-brooklyn.com

Brooklyn General
Brooklyn, NY
brooklyngeneral.com

Wholly Craft
Columbus, OH
whollycraft.net

Bolt
Portland, OR
boltfabricboutique.com

Cut & Sew Studio
Pittsburg, PA
cutandsewstudio.com

Philadelphia Sewing
Collective
Philadelphia, PA
phillysewing.org

Make Shop & Studio
Dallas, TX
themakesite.com

Selvedge Sewing
Austin , TX
selvedgesewing.com

Sew Crafty Houston
Houston, TX
sewcraftyhouston.com

The Stitch Lab
Austin, TX
glitzkrieg.biz

WonderCraft Studio
(Austin, TX, and roving)
thewondercraft.com

Craft & Sew Studio
Virginia Beach, VA
craftandsewstudio.com

Double Knot Studio
(roving locations in
New York)
doubleknotstudio.com

BurdaStyle Sewing Clubs
(everywhere!)
burdastyle.com

GENERAL SEWING BOOKS

Threads Sewing Guide by
Editors of *Threads*

*Reader's Digest Complete
Guide to Sewing* by Editors
of *Reader's Digest*

*The New Vogue Sewing
Book* by Buttericks

INDEX

Note: **Bold** page numbers indicate a photo, and *italicized* page numbers indicate an illustration. (When only one number of a page range is **bold** or *italicized*, a photo or illustration appears on one or more of the pages.)